A Companion to the Muslim World

The Institute of Ismaili Studies

MUSLIM HERITAGE SERIES, 1

General Editor: Amyn B. Sajoo

This series will explore vital themes in the civilisations of Islam – including the nature of religious authority, ethics and law, social justice and civil society, the arts and sciences, and the interplay of spiritual and secular lifeworlds. In keeping with the Institute's mandate, the series will be informed by the plurality of communities and interpretations of Islam, as well as their locus in modernity and tradition.

A Companion to
the Muslim World

Edited by
AMYN B. SAJOO

I.B.Tauris *Publishers*
LONDON • NEW YORK
in association with
The Institute of Ismaili Studies
LONDON

Published in 2009 by I.B.Tauris & Co. Ltd
6 Salem Road, London W2 4BU
175 Fifth Avenue, New York, NY 10010
www.ibtauris.com

in association with The Institute of Ismaili Studies
210 Euston Road, London NW1 2DA
www.iis.ac.uk

Distributed in the United States and Canada Exclusively by Palgrave Macmillan,
175 Fifth Avenue, New York, NY 10010

ISBN: 978 1 84885 193 1

A full CIP record for this book is available from the British Library
A full CIP record for this book is available from the Library of Congress

Library of Congress catalog card: available

Typeset in Minion Tra for The Institute of Ismaili Studies
Printed and bound in Great Britain by CPI Antony Rowe, Chippenham, Wiltshire

FSC

Mixed Sources
Product group from well-managed
forests and other controlled sources

Cert no. SGS-COC-2953
www.fsc.org
© 1996 Forest Stewardship Council

The Institute of Ismaili Studies

The Institute of Ismaili Studies was established in 1977 with the object of promoting scholarship and learning on Islam, in the historical as well as contemporary contexts, and a better understanding of its relationship with other societies and faiths.

The Institute's programmes encourage a perspective which is not confined to the theological and religious heritage of Islam, but seeks to explore the relationship of religious ideas to broader dimensions of society and culture. The programmes thus encourage an interdisciplinary approach to the materials of Islamic history and thought. Particular attention is also given to issues of modernity that arise as Muslims seek to relate their heritage to the contemporary situation.

Within the Islamic tradition, the Institute's programmes promote research on those areas which have, to date, received relatively little attention from scholars. These include the intellectual and literary expressions of Shi'ism in general, and Ismailism in particular.

In the context of Islamic societies, the Institute's programmes are informed by the full range and diversity of cultures in which Islam is practised today, from the Middle East, South and Central Asia, and Africa to the industrialized societies of the West, thus taking into consideration the variety of contexts which shape the ideals, beliefs and practices of the faith.

These objectives are realised through concrete programmes and activities organized and implemented by various departments of the Institute. The Institute also collaborates periodically, on a programme-specific basis, with other institutions of learning in the United Kingdom and abroad.

The Institute's academic publications fall into a number of inter-related categories:

1. Occasional papers or essays addressing broad themes of the relationship between religion and society, with special reference to Islam.
2. Monographs exploring specific aspects of Islamic faith and culture, or the contributions of individual Muslim thinkers or writers.
3. Editions or translations of significant primary or secondary texts.
4. Translations of poetic or literary texts which illustrate the rich heritage of spiritual, devotional and symbolic expressions in Muslim history.
5. Works on Ismaili history and thought, and the relationship of the Ismailis to other traditions, communities and schools of thought in Islam.
6. Proceedings of conferences and seminars sponsored by the Institute.
7. Bibliographical works and catalogues which document manuscripts, printed texts and other source materials.

This book falls into category two listed above.

In facilitating these and other publications, the Institute's sole aim is to encourage original research and analysis of relevant issues. While every effort is made to ensure that the publications are of a high academic standard, there is naturally bound to be a diversity of views, ideas and interpretations. As such, the opinions expressed in these publications must be understood as belonging to their authors alone.

Contents

About the Contributors   xi
List of Illustrations   xvii

1. Introduction
   AMYN B. SAJOO   1

2. The Prophet's City
   REZA ASLAN   25

3. Reading the Quran
   ABDULLAH SAEED   55

4. Islam in the Plural
   AMIR HUSSAIN   87

5. Networks of Solidarity
   BRUCE LAWRENCE   107

6. Women and Social Change
   AZIZAH YAHIA AL-HIBRI   133

7. Inclusive Governance: A Fatimid Illustration
   SHAINOOL JIWA   157

8. The Art and Architecture of the Mosque
   HASAN-UDDIN KHAN   177

9. The Umma in the City
   AMIRA K. BENNISON   209

10. Cultures of Learning
   ANIL KHAMIS   237

11. A Conference of Bards: Rumi to Adonis
   RAFICQ ABDULLA   263

12. The Digital Umma
   GARY R. BUNT   291

Index   311

Did He not find you an orphan, and shelter you?
And did He not find you wandering, and guide you?
And did He not find you destitute and enrich you?

Quran, 93:6–8

What you have as heritage, take now as task;
for thus you will make it your own.

Goethe, *Faust*, Part 1

About the Contributors

Raficq Abdulla is a writer, barrister, public speaker and broadcaster. He was formerly the University Secretary and legal adviser to Kingston University, where he is a Visiting Fellow. His publications include *Words of Paradise: Selected Poems by Rumi* (London, 2000), and a fresh interpretation of *Conference of the Birds* (Northampton, MA, 2003), the allegorical poem by the medieval poet and mystic, Farid al-din Attar. Raficq Abdulla has written and presented numerous programmes on Islam for BBC World Service radio, and has authored screenplays for Channel 4 television, including the award-winning films *Blood of Hussein* and *Born of Fire*. He is a trustee of the UK's Poetry Society and the writers' organisation, PEN. Raficq Abdulla was awarded an MBE for his interfaith work in 1999.

Reza Aslan lectures at the University of California at Riverside. He is the author of the international bestseller, *No god but God: The Origins, Evolution, and Future of Islam* (London, 2005), which has been translated into 13 languages, and serves as the basis for his chapter in this volume. He was president of the Harvard University chapter of the World Conference on Religion and Peace, and serves on the advisory board of the Council on Foreign Relations in New York. Aslan is a regular contributor to the news media on both sides of the Atlantic, including the *Guardian*, the *Washington Post*, the *New York Times* and CBS News. His forthcoming book, *How to Win A Cosmic War: God, Globalization, and the End of the War on Terror*, will be published by Random House.

Amira K. Bennison is deputy-chair of the Faculty of Oriental Studies at the University of Cambridge, and senior lecturer there in Middle Eastern and Islamic Studies. Dr Bennison's interests include the early modern and medieval Maghreb, and the impact of European modernity and colonialism in the 19th century, which she is looking at through comparative religious internationalisms. Her books include *Jihad and its Interpretations in Pre-Colonial Morocco* (London, 2002), and the edited volume (with A.L. Gascoigne), *Cities in the Premodern Islamic World: The Urban Impact of Religion, State and Society* (London, 2007). Dr Bennison is a frequent guest on BBC radio discussions of historical themes in Muslim civilisations.

Gary R. Bunt is Senior Lecturer in Islamic Studies and MA Islamic Studies Programme Director at the University of Wales, Lampeter. His teaching and writing have focused on contemporary expressions of Islam, with particular regard to Muslims and the internet. He has also been active in various initiatives on Islam in higher education at the national and global levels. Dr Bunt's publications include *Virtually Islamic* (Cardiff, 2000), *Islam in the Digital Age* (London, 2003) and *i-Muslims* (London, 2009). His 'Islamic Studies Pathways' website was started in 1996 as an entry point and guide to Islamic resources online. Dr Bunt's research website and blog can be found at *virtuallyislamic.com*

Azizah Yahia al-Hibri is professor of law at the University of Richmond in Virginia, USA. She is founding editor of *Hypatia: a Journal of Feminist Philosophy*, and founder and president of *KARAMAH: Muslim Women Lawyers for Human Rights*. Dr al-Hibri has written extensively on women's rights, and on Islam and democracy, and is completing a book on Muslim marriage contracts in the courts. Her article on 'Muslim Women's Rights in the Global Village: Opportunities and Challenges' in *The Journal of Law and Religion* (Fall, 2001) evolved into her chapter in this volume. She was the recipient of the Virginia First Freedom Award presented by the Council of America's First Freedom in 2007, the Dr Betty Shabazz Award presented by Women in Islam in 2006, and the University of Richmond's Distinguished Educator Award in 2004.

Amir Hussain is associate professor in the Department of Theological Studies at Loyola Marymount University in Los Angeles, where he lectures on world religions. His specialty is the study of contemporary Muslim societies in North America; he co-chairs the 'Contemporary Islam' consultation of the American Academy of Religions, as well as serving on the steering committee of the Academy's 'Religion in South Asia' section. Dr Hussain is the author most recently of *Oil and Water: Two Faiths, One God* (Kelowna, BC, 2006), and is working on two other books, *Canadian Faces of Islam*, and *Muslims: Islam in the West in the 21st Century*. In 2008, he was voted Professor of the Year by students at Loyola Marymount.

Shainool Jiwa specialises in Shi'i history and thought at The Institute of Ismaili Studies, where she also heads the Community Relations department. Her forthcoming book, *Towards a Shi'i Mediterranean Empire: Fatimid Egypt and the Founding of Cairo*, offers a portrait of the reign of the Imam-caliph al-Muizz, which she draws upon for her chapter here. Dr Jiwa is also a chief examiner in Islamic history for the International Baccalaureate Organization. Prior to joining the Institute, she served as a counsellor and manager for Saheliya, a mental health project for Edinburgh's ethnic minority women. In 1998, she was appointed as a part-time Commissioner for the Mental Welfare Commission in Scotland.

Anil Khamis is lecturer in education and international development at the University of London's Institute of Education. Dr Khamis specialises in education and development with special regard to Muslim communities and societies, as well as education for disadvantaged/at-risk communities. He previously taught at the Aga Khan University in Pakistan, and has worked in East Africa and Central Asia for over a decade, notably on issues of educational access and alternatives to formal education. Dr Khamis has contributed to several leading texts and journals on themes in Muslim education and effectiveness in teaching and learning.

Hasan-Uddin Khan is Distinguished Professor of Architecture and Historic Preservation at Roger Williams University and Visiting Professor of Architecture at the Massachusetts Institute of Technology. His architectural practice has ranged over the United Kingdom, Pakistan and the United States. He has served with the Aga Khan Award for Architecture, the Rockefeller Foundation and the Getty Grant Program for architectural conservation. Professor Khan was founder and editor of the quarterly journal, *Mimar: Architecture in Development*, and his publications include *The Mosque and the Modern World* (London, 1997, with Renata Holod), *Modernities and Memories: Recent Works from the Islamic World* (New York, 1997), and *The Mosque: History, Architecture, Development and Regional Diversity* (London, 1994, with Martin Fishman).

Bruce Lawrence is the Nancy and Jeffrey Marcus Humanities Professor at Duke University, where he also directs the Duke Islamic Studies Center. His research ranges from institutional Islam to Indo-Persian Sufism; it also encompasses the comparative study of religious movements. His recent books include *Messages to the World: The Statements of Osama Bin Laden* (London, 2005); *The Qur'an: A Biography* (Toronto, 2006), and *Muslim Networks: From Hajj to Hip Hop* (Chapel Hill, NC, 2005, with Miriam Cooke), which his chapter here draws upon. Professor Lawrence was named a Carnegie Scholar in 2008, and will explore why religious minorities remain a crucial index to the success of pluralism and social comity, with particular regard to Egypt, Ethiopia, Indonesia and the Philippines.

Abdullah Saeed is director of the Asia Institute at the University of Melbourne, where he also serves as the Sultan of Oman Professor of Arab and Islamic Studies, and co-director, Centre for Islamic Law and Society. While the focus of his teaching and writing is the interpretation of the Quran, he also engages with issues in Islamic law reform, modernity and human rights. Professor Saeed has been active in interfaith dialogue both in Australia and abroad. His publications include *Interpreting the Qur'an: Towards a*

Contemporary Approach (London, 2006), *Islamic Thought: An Introduction* (London, 2006), *Contemporary Approaches to the Qur'an in Indonesia* (London, 2005), and *The Qur'an: An Introduction* (London, 2008), which he draws upon in his chapter here.

Amyn B. Sajoo lectured at Simon Fraser University and the University of British Columbia before joining The Institute of Ismaili Studies in 2007, where he lectures and leads projects on Muslim modernities and heritages. He has held visiting appointments at Cambridge and McGill universities. Dr Sajoo is the author/editor of *Muslim Modernities: Expressions of the Civil Imagination* (London, 2008), *Muslim Ethics: Emerging Vistas* (London, 2004), *Civil Society in the Muslim World* (London, 2002), and *Pluralism in Old Societies and New States* (Singapore, 1994), and is a frequent contributor to the news media on both sides of the Atlantic. He earlier served with the Canadian departments of Justice and Foreign Affairs in Ottawa, and as Canada-ASEAN Fellow at the Institute of Southeast Asian Studies (ISEAS) in Singapore.

List of Illustrations

Fig. 1: Map of World Distribution of Muslims
          © Quantum Publishing, 2004   xviii
Fig. 2: Sketch of mosque types
          © Hasan Khan, 1998   186

Plate Section located between pages 204 and 205

PL. 1:   Southeast view of the Great Mosque of Djenne, Mali.
          © AKTC/Amir-Massoud Anoushfar, 2007.
PL. 2:   The Phoenix Pavilion in the Fourth Court, Great Mosque of
          Xian, China.
          © Cherie Wendelken and You-Huan Zhu, 1984, courtesy of
          the Aga Khan Visual Archive, MIT.
PL. 3:   The Hassan II Mosque, Casablanca, Morocco.
          © Emilio Suetone/Hemis/Corbis, c. 1993–1994.
PL. 4:   Woman in mihrab at al-Azhar Mosque, Cairo, Egypt.
          © Pascal Deloche/Godong/Corbis, 2004.
PL. 5:   Dar al-Islam Abiquiu, New Mexico.
          © Hasan Khan, 2007.
PL. 6:   Ismaili Jamatkhana and Centre, Burnaby, Canada.
          © AKTC, Gary Otte.
PL. 7:   The Great Mosque and bridge, Cordoba, Spain.
          © Patrick Ward/Corbis, 1995.
PL. 8:   Bab al-Futuh Cairo, Egypt.
          © John A. and Caroline Williams, c. 1977.
PL. 9:   Maydan-i Shah (Maydan-i Imam) complex, Isfahan, Iran.
          © Richard Ross/Getty Images.
PL. 10: Aerial view, the dome of the Friday Mosque and view of Old
          Delhi, India.
          © Jeremy Horner/Corbis, 1996.
PL. 11: Djemaa el-Fna (main square) and Kutubiyya Mosque,
          Marrakesh, Morocco.
          © Gavin Hellier/JAI/Corbis, 2005.

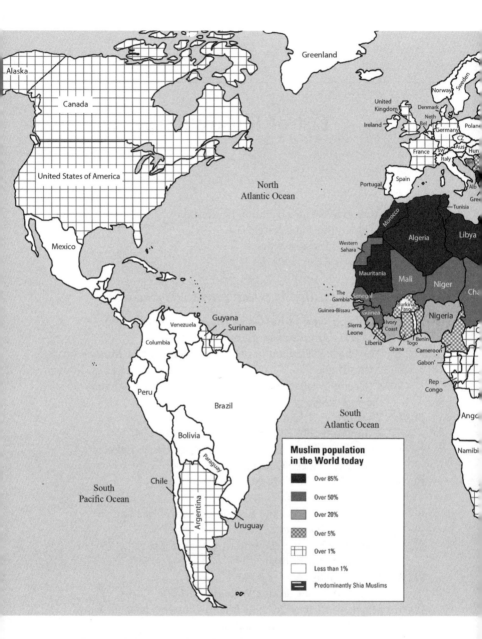

Fig. 1: Map of World Distribution of Muslims

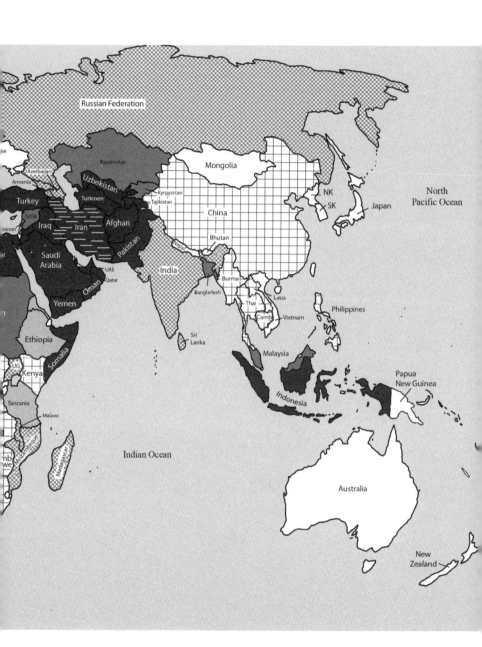

Introduction

Amyn B. Sajoo

This *Companion* begins a fresh initiative – the Muslim Heritage Series – which aims to bring insightful essays on key themes in the civilisations and cultures of Islam to a general readership. There are exciting challenges in doing so, of the kind that confront any such venture today. Scholars in every discipline have a language that has become specialised over time, and is perhaps suitable for dialogue within the discipline. Alas, this can make it impenetrable even to highly intelligent readers from outside the field. One recalls George Bernard Shaw's quip that 'all professions are a conspiracy against the laity'.

Beyond a specialised vocabulary or jargon, other practices deepen the feeling of a professional code that seems to be aimed at excluding the lay reader. There are multiple dating systems that relate to various calendars, such as the Muslim lunar in addition to western solar dating. Then there are the diacritic marks, or signs attached to letters in transliteration, which give the text a look unlike anything that one usually encounters in books, newspapers or on the internet. Too often, scores of footnotes which rather than effectively explaining matters, speak of obscure sources to back this or that opinion can add to the gloom.

These conventions certainly have their place in texts that are situated within a particular scholarly discourse. But they can also get in the way of a non-specialised reader who is already grappling with theories about how to understand a line of scripture or legal rule or artistic expression. Nor is this a plea for what is commonly referred to as 'dumbing down'. Rather, it is an argument for readability – indeed, reasonable access – to ideas and discussions that have a profound impact on society, by way of influencing the individual reader and the people with whom he or she is in conversation. The issue is perhaps better recognised in the sciences. Skilled journalists as well as scientists are called upon, in the public interest, to explain new developments in genetics or nuclear physics or astronomy, and receive prizes for doing so effectively. This plain speaking coexists happily with science journals and books that remain as technical as ever. Why should we expect less when it comes to discussing ethics or gender in Muslim societies, where the public interest is hardly less pressing?

Our response in the Muslim Heritage Series is to offer texts that are readable in several practical ways. Jargon and footnotes will be kept to a minimum, and diacritic marks avoided altogether. Where technical language cannot reasonably be avoided, it will be explained to the reader as plainly as possible. Dates will tell of the birth and death years of key figures to give a fuller picture of their flourishing, and follow the western calendar. Our scholars will seek to refrain from straying into the kind of abstract theoretical talk that can drive the lay reader, and sometimes even fellow specialists, to distraction. Footnotes will appear only where they give essential information in support of a claim in the text. A list of 'further readings' directs the reader to books and articles that are readily available to extend the appreciation of each theme.

If readability is a priority, so is the quality of scholarship, which we have no wish to compromise in this venture. The integrity of what is on offer with regard to each theme – the accuracy, balance and clarity of the writing – remains vital. It must, if this series is to achieve its avowed purpose of making accessible the best knowledge and thinking on the heritages of Islam as experienced and understood today. This *Companion* features writers who are Muslim and non-Muslim, women and men, selected for their academic expertise. Many are well-known names internationally, while other younger scholars have made valuable contributions. The series is firmly committed to this approach.

Understanding the Muslim World

Our task would surely be easier were it not for the events and aftermath of September 11, 2001, which cast long shadows on the perception of Islam and Muslims. In our globalised world, it matters little
whether one inhabits the Muslim-majority societies of Asia, Africa
and the Middle East, or those of the rest of the world. From daily
reports in the news media, including the internet, to the hundreds
of books and articles (from sources of varying reliability), 'Islam'
is news. A significant portion is simply off the mark, whether in
getting the facts right about Muslims and their faith traditions, or
drawing rational conclusions about them. The tone is more often
than not alarmist and the consequences can be serious. At the
everyday level, the impact of the 'war on terror' is felt by individuals and communities the world over, but especially by Muslims.

Easy generalisations and stereotypes that link Islam to violence,
gender abuse, uncivil politics and an aversion to science and modernity have been common since at least the colonial period. But
recent events have heightened prejudice, as well as fear. Both are
often tied to ignorance. Those who violate the most basic ethical
principles while claiming to act in the name of religion are taken
at their word – and the resulting view of that religion is then
foisted on all its adherents. When such claims and behaviour take
centre stage in the news media, so do the prejudice and fear. The
situation is not improved when politicians and instant experts
with axes to grind get into the game. Yet there is no lack of
evidence in the public domain to counter this: a rich array of acts
of charity, solidarity, artistic and cultural expression, passion for
learning and political innovation, inspired by a view of Islam that
is boldly humanistic. Much is obscured by the smoke and noise
of our post-September 11 world.

History reminds us that all major civilisations and cultures
have gone through their 'dark ages', when the tide seems to have
turned forever. It was a Muslim scholar, Ibn Khaldun (1332-1406),
who first wrote of the cycles of rise and fall that afflict societies
and empires. This was not long after the Mongol invasions that

destroyed much of the glory of Muslim civilisations in the east, including those of Central Asia, Iraq, Iran and Syria. A symbol of the new darkness was the razing of Baghdad in 1258 by Hulegu, grandson of Genghis Khan, with the slaughter of tens of thousands and the burning of the city's magnificent library. But the Muslim east was to recover, with a creative energy that proved nothing short of astonishing. With the rise of the Mughals, Safavids and Ottomans, the tide had turned again. 'In the sixteenth century of our era,' notes Marshall Hodgson in *Rethinking World History* (1993), 'a visitor from Mars might well have supposed that the human world was on the verge of becoming Muslim'. This was not merely about the frontiers of empire. From the art of governance and law-making to commerce, urban planning and architecture, to painting, poetry and the sciences, the post-Mongol Muslim world was a thriving space. It certainly had plenty to teach Europe in its Renaissance, which was built on the shoulders of knowledge societies across the Muslim Mediterranean and beyond.

A Void of Knowledge

That heritage was hastily forgotten once colonial rule prevailed over the Muslim east, west and south. Images of a cultural, social and political backwardness tied to race and religion (of the non-Christian kind) became commonplace. In the postcolonial era, this tendency was exposed and challenged, especially with the publication of Edward Said's *Orientalism* in 1978 and *Covering Islam* (1981). But the old prejudice seems to have found new impetus. One prominent avenue is the idea of a 'clash of civilisations' between the West and the Rest, though mainly between the West and the Muslim world. In this influential view,[1] values such as equality and freedom

---

[1] Put forward most famously by Samuel P. Huntington, *The Clash of Civilizations and the Remaking of World Order* (New York, 1996). In the same vein, Bernard Lewis reduces modern civic values to the generalised cultures of 'East' and 'West' in *What Went Wrong? Western Impact and Middle East Response* (New York, 2002). Again, Francis Fukuyama insists that 'something about Islam' makes 'societies particularly resistant to modernity': 'The West has won', *The Guardian*, 11 October 2001.

of thought are exclusively Euro-American, at fateful odds with Islamic (as well as Chinese) civilisation. Many in the West and beyond have pointed out the historical and logical flaws in such claims, including the idea that diverse peoples can be reduced to 'a civilisation' whose behaviour is determined by their religious beliefs. Surely what is most worrying in the present political and social climate is a 'clash of ignorance' in a shrinking world.[2]

By their own account, nearly 60 per cent of Americans know little or nothing about Islam, the religion of one-fifth of mankind today and of millions in the United States itself.[3] Heavy media coverage and the sudden proliferation of books on all matters Islamic since 2001 have failed to better inform Americans about a faith that also explicitly affirms the sanctity of the Judeo-Christian revelation. More than two-thirds of Americans believe that Christianity has very little in common with Islam. Half of all Americans hold prejudicial views about Islam and Muslims – a situation not helped by the fact that leading Christian ministers have repeatedly made derogatory remarks about Islam as a faith. This against a background in which 46 per cent say that the Bible should be a source of legislation in the United States, and 42 per cent want religious leaders to have a role in drafting a constitution. In Europe, a 2008 survey showed growing prejudice against both Jews and Muslims.[4] The worst figures were in Germany, Poland, Russia and Spain, with France and Britain faring only slightly better. As in the United States, Europeans with a lower level of education were more likely to hold such prejudices, whether against Jews or Muslims.

Yet according to the *New York Times*, the level of basic knowledge of Islam and Muslims is strikingly poor even among elite officials

---

[2] See Edward Said, 'The Clash of Ignorance', *The Nation*, 22 October 2001.
[3] As reported in two separate opinion surveys in 2007, respectively by the Pew Research Centre, available at http://pewforum.org/surveys/religion-views07/, and the Gallup World Poll, reported in John L. Esposito and Dalia Mogahed, *Who Speaks for Islam?* (New York, 2007).
[4] Pew Research Centre poll, available at http://pewresearch.org/pubs/955/unfavorable-views-of-both-jews-and-muslims-increase-in-europe.

of United States security agencies and politicians in Congress. Most had no idea about the difference between Shia and Sunni.[5] 'Wouldn't British counterterrorism officials responsible for Northern Ireland know the difference between Catholics and Protestants?', asks the report. The then head of the FBI's national security branch thought Iran was a Sunni nation. In another recent episode, an army official delivering a press briefing about cultural deficits in the education of the United States military claimed that the official language in Baghdad was 'Iraqi'. At present, then, having a higher education seems to offer no assurance of even a minimal grasp of the world of Islam. Alas, to those of us who are educators in the humanities and social sciences on both sides of the Atlantic, it comes as no surprise.

This 'current void of knowledge' was broached by His Highness Prince Karim Aga Khan IV – a leading international figure and imam of the Shia Ismaili Muslims – speaking to a gathering of German ambassadors in Berlin. The way forward lay not in a focus on theology, he urged, but an appreciation of the culture and civilisation of the Other:

> Today, theological interpretation and proselytisation continue to divide among Catholic, Orthodox and Protestant interpretations in the Christian world, as in the Islamic world between Sunni and Shia and their various sub-divisions. I would hope to see the day when the definition of an educated person in Judaeo-Christian culture would include an intelligent understanding of the Muslim world. That would include an understanding of their tradition of research and achievements, from philosophy and the arts, to the sciences, architecture and engineering. You cannot build a dialogue based upon ignorance. Without meaningful dialogue, you cannot construct coherent and sustainable foreign policy. How would the handling of the situations in Kashmir, Afghanistan, Iraq and the wider Middle East, or the Philippines, have been different if the

---

[5] Jeff Stein, 'Can You Tell a Sunni From a Shiite?' *New York Times*, 17 October 2006.

main players had benefited from a thorough understanding of the history and culture of those regions?[6]

Indeed, this wider approach would be enormously valuable to Muslim societies as well, the Aga Khan pointed out, in bringing home the rich pluralism of their own civilisational heritage, including 'interpretations of Islam'. A major initiative in that regard was taken in 2005 with the Amman Declaration by scholars and emissaries from across the Muslim world, affirming the diversity of Muslim traditions of law and worship, as well as committing Muslims to interfaith dialogue.[7]

Mutual ignorance gives plenty of fuel to the idea that the West and Islam are entirely separate worlds that are destined to clash. One powerful myth is that the attacks of September 11 were about hatred of the West for its freedoms and democracy. This is thought to show in a popular anti-Americanism, which can turn to outright militancy of the kind engineered by al-Qaeda. Hence, 80 per cent of Americans told a Gallup poll in 2002 that Muslim dislike of the United States was simply about 'misinformation'; the figure was down to 57 per cent in 2007, but only 26 per cent felt that this might have to do with their country's foreign policies.[8] Yet the polls found that most Muslims in Egypt, Jordan, Saudi Arabia and elsewhere strongly admired and desired the values of political freedom and democracy, which were associated with the modern West. Large majorities back equal rights for women and freedom of speech. But 75 per cent expressed strong dislike of the

---

[6] Abbreviated quote. Full text available at http://www.akdn.org/speech/583/ Annual-Conference-of-German-Ambassadors; and 'Underwriting human progress', 6 September 2004, HH the Aga Khan, *Where Hope Takes Root: Democracy and Pluralism in an Interdependent World* (Vancouver, 2008), pp. 65-66.

[7] The Declaration was adopted by some 180 scholars and emissaries from 45 Muslim states, and representing key Sunni and Shia institutions. Texts available at http://ammanmessage.com/index.php?option=com_content& task=view&id=20&Itemid=34

[8] Esposito and Mogahed, *Who Speaks for Islam?*, p. 159.

actions of the United States – an attitude that was widely shared among those polled in Western Europe.

Again, while each side believes that the other side just does not care, the polling evidence says otherwise. Most Muslims and Americans are highly concerned about relations with each other. Muslims who were asked what should be done about the future wished for mutual respect; unlike most Americans, they were critical of their own side, and urged greater understanding for western concerns about extremist violence and liberty. However, a key apprehension for Muslim societies was the perceived insensitivity of the West to Islam as a faith. An obvious example would be the controversy about political cartoons of the Prophet Muhammad, first published by the Danish newspaper *Jyllands-Posten* in September 2005. The matter was cast as one of freedom of expression, directed at militancy among Muslims. If so, why did they not choose to depict a figure such as Osama bin Laden? Why were earlier cartoons directed at the figure of Jesus Christ turned down by *Jyllands-Posten*? Would anti-Jewish cartoons be regarded as legitimate? In the face of obvious distress among Muslims, other western newspapers chose to reproduce the cartoons in 2008. Was this about principles or profits? Diplomacy, peaceful protest and legal action on the part of Muslims yielded no results. Sharing their distress, France's Grand Rabbi, Joseph Sitruk, noted that freedom of expression 'is not a right without limits', and saw no gain in 'lowering religions, humiliating them and making caricatures of them'.[9] A majority of those polled by Gallup in Britain and France agreed that printing the cartoons was not legitimate free speech.

Overlapping Worlds

It turns out, then, that disagreement about the *scope* of civil liberties, even something as basic as free speech, is not evidence of a clash of religious traditions or civilisations. Opinion on vital issues

---

[9] Quoted in Ibrahim Barzak 'Protests over Prophet Muhammad cartoons escalate in Islamic world', *Associated Press*, 2 February 2006.

varies not only among and within western societies but also the world's 1.3 billion Muslims who live in 57 countries as majorities or sizable minorities. Most do not live in the Middle East or speak Arabic. Aside from the majority living in South and Southeast Asia, there are large indigenous communities in China and Central Europe, and migrant communities in France, Spain and the United Kingdom. It remains the principal faith tradition of West Africa, and is a major religion not only in the rest of Africa but also, increasingly, in Western Europe, Canada and the United States. This vast spread of the 'Muslim world' can only mean that there are diverse social, economic and political factors that shape identities. Equally, there have always been plural ways of being Muslim: communities of interpretation flourish among both Shia and Sunni, each bringing to Islam its own set of experiences in time and locale. True, religion has a place in the lives of Muslim individuals and communities that is more central than in the secular societies of modern Europe. Yet, this aspect of Muslim modernity is shared with the United States where public religion is also vital.

Globalisation has indeed put peoples and cultures – and therefore faith traditions – in closer proximity than ever before. Streets and neighbourhoods in Dubai, Singapore, Manchester, Perth, San Francisco and Vancouver offer the global in the local, from architecture, dress, food and music to spaces of worship. This proximity is made tighter still by technology and especially the internet. But the intensity of it all does not change the fact that overlapping worlds have long been a reality. The societies of the Mediterranean and South Asia are obvious examples, while the Silk Road from Xian to Istanbul was a medieval internet, a channel for ideas as well as goods and peoples across civilisations. Cosmopolitan cities like Bukhara, Khotan, Peshawar and Samarkand dotted the Silk Road, vying with Baghdad, Istanbul and Xian.

Muslims drew some of the most authoritative early maps of the world, such as those of al-Khwarazmi (c. 780-850), al-Idrisi (1100-1166), Zheng He (1371-1433) – and Piri Reis (1465-1554) whose mapping of the Americas and the Antarctic had a precision all new in the old world. Others ventured to the far ends of the Islamic world and beyond, like Ibn Battuta (1304-1368) in Beijing and Hangzhou, leaving us an account of the familiar struggle to come to terms with human and social difference. This is equally evident in the writings of Leo Africanus, alias Hassan al-Wazzan (1485-1554), even if they were the outcome of capture by Spanish pirates and becoming a prisoner of Pope Leo X in Rome. Or consider the shock and awe of the young Egyptian imam Rifaa al-Tahtawi (1801-1873) on his visit to Paris. 'If Islam had not been protected by the might of God, it would be nothing compared to their prowess, population, wealth, skills ... their knowledge of astronomy and geography, their appetite for business and trade, and their love of travel', he noted.[10] His writings and public career were to have an enormous impact on political and social reform in Egypt. By contrast, the sojourn of Sayyid Qutb (1906-1966) in the United States was less happy. He found American ways to be overly loose and trivial, apparently without the redeeming qualities that Tahtawi found in France. The experience helped turn Qutb into a political and religious militant.

As the reality of overlapping worlds becomes clearer, so may the need to hold on to that which is found to be distinctive. This is especially so when the Other is seen as dominant. In the aftermath of World War II, America was for Qutb a threatening presence, as was France in the 1820s for Tahtawi. Yet Tahtawi was keen – as were reformers like Muhammad Abduh (1814-1905), Sayyid Ahmed Khan (1817-1898) and Jamal al-Din al-Afghani (1838-1897) – to absorb what they saw as the best of the West. There was confidence not only that this could be done but also that it *must* be done. After all, had Muslims not once carried the torch in the sciences and humanities, from which was lit the fire of the Renaissance that led to Modernity? Tahtawi evokes the image of the Prophet as a model seeker of wisdom earthly and divine,

---

[10] From his account of 1834, quoted in Roxanne L. Euben, *Journeys to the Other Shore: Muslim and Western Travellers in Search of Knowledge* (Princeton, 2006), p. 101.

coupled with his own love of homeland (*watan*), as a moral base from which to engage with the Other. For Qutb, fear leads to a rejection of all voices outside his own 'authentic' vision as corrupt, including other Muslim voices. This is an old tension, felt across history: what one welcomes as cosmopolitan and enriching, another sees as a loss of heritage and identity. Steering through the waters is no easy task, yet the stakes are high enough, as Marshall Hodgson notes in *The Venture of Islam*:

> If the realities of the Islamic heritage can be frankly faced – its historical actuality good and bad, the problems which it presents as well as the spiritual opportunities it offers – then Islam as a heritage might conceivably prove able to serve flexibly in the Modern crisis. Facing up to their history in this way might help Muslims – and possibly others as well – to overcome the cultural dislocations of our time and provide a basis for creativity in the midst of lettered mass culture, a basis consistent with, but able to transcend, the 'democratic virtues'. More generally, it might show that Islam was able to fill the modern need for moral vision, for a creative illumination of the human conscience in a technicalistic world ... [I]f Islam can be shown to be capable of providing a fruitful vision to illuminate the Modern conscience – then all mankind, and not only Muslims, have a stake in the outcome; even those who explicitly or even militantly reject any religious tradition.[11]

This *Companion*

What is distinctive about Islam, amid all the emphasis on values and experiences that are said to overlap with those of other civilisations and societies? Many will point to the 'five pillars' that Muslims regard as central, since they were articulated in a well-attested account or hadith which involved an encounter in Medina between Muhammad and the archangel Gabriel. The pillars are

---

[11] Marshall G.S. Hodgson, *The Venture of Islam* (Chicago, 1974), vol. 3, pp. 440-441.

the *shahada* or affirmation that there is only one God and Muhammad is His messenger; *salat* or daily recital of ritual prayers; *zakat* or the giving of alms; *sawm* or keeping the fast during the month of Ramadan; and *hajj* or the pilgrimage to Mecca. Along with these outward acts of submission – *islam* – the Gabriel hadith has the Prophet stating the importance of faith or *iman*, and virtuous conduct or *ihsan* done with the consciousness of God's presence.

From the outset, Muslims have understood and practised the pillars in a variety of ways. There have been multiple schools of law as well as of theology among Sunni and Shia alike, in interpreting what the central doctrines actually entail. The foremost of the five pillars, the *shahada*, involves for Shia Muslims an affirmation also of the privileged status of Imam Ali (599-661) as rightful successor to Muhammad. For those who uphold the Sufi or mystical traditions of Islam, going back to the time of the Prophet, it is the Quran's spiritual aspect that matters most – beyond mere adherence to religious laws and customs. Women have figured prominently from the earliest days of the Sufi traditions. At the same time, as many scholars have pointed out, Islam has always been more about how people act and the faith with which they do so, than what their creedal beliefs say. The letter of the law can be overridden by *maslaha*, the public good. The Quran holds 'the best' to be about conduct before all else (3:110). For Muhammad, the 'best Islam' was about spreading peace alike among those one knew and those that one did not.

In other words, it won't do to reduce Islam to creed or doctrine. We must inquire about the way that it is lived, both in terms of what Muslims do and their disposition or ethos. An inquiry that attends to civilisations and cultures tells us what Islam has actually meant in history, in its plural interpretations and realities, and what that heritage means today. This *Companion* sets out to capture some of the vital elements in that picture, always putting them in their social as well as moral context. The broad picture of the Muslim world is not, of course, something that can be conveyed and discussed in every detail, even by a volume several times the size of this one. The challenge for us is to leave the reader with a sense of the fullness, diversity and energy of the experience of Islam in the world, in a language and style that is accessible. What follows in this introduction is a map of the volume, which sets out the four main pathways that our contributors here have explored. These are 'foundations', 'expressions', 'inclusions' and 'networks', which take us through past and present as well as some possible pathways to the future.

Foundations

Muhammad and the Quran stand at the beginning of our journey, marking the birth of Islam in the Arabian peninsula of the early seventh century. They stay with us throughout the journey, in word and deed, for reasons that are explored in the opening chapters by Reza Aslan and Abdullah Saeed. The Prophet's earliest biographies were written long after his death in 632, and often reflect the later realities of a successful empire, as viewed from Baghdad or Damascus. So in taking us through the 'remote desert oasis' of Muhammad's time, Aslan sets out to sift history from ideology. There are encounters not only around the revelation that became the Quran, but more ordinary though often challenging ones with wives, Jewish traders and quarrelsome tribesmen. By situating the verses of the Quran which Muhammad received over a period of 22 years (a far shorter span, of course, than the extended revelations of the Bible) in the soil of the everyday, Aslan is able to give us more than a detailed narrative of the birth of a religion. In grasping the social *context* of that birth, where fundamental ideas come forth about how to live ethically and the proper treatment of women and minorities, one can see more clearly what principles are at stake rather than just what the rules are. Practices of veiling and worship are related intimately to custom and circumstance – which have a continuity with earlier religious and cultural traditions.

What is distinctive here is that far from proclaiming their uniqueness, Islam and its Prophet are adamant about not inventing new truths but affirming timeless ones in a fresh setting. The Quran itself asserts that all revealed scriptures come from a single source, the *Umm al-Kitab* or 'Mother of Books' (13:39). 'As far as Muhammad was concerned', notes Aslan, 'the Jews and the Christians were "People of the Book" (*Ahl al-Kitab*), spiritual cousins who, as opposed to the pagans and polytheists of Arabia, worshipped the same God, read the same scriptures, and shared the same moral values as his Muslim community.' What differences there were in theology and practice were a matter of divine plan, for did He not prefer in the Quran that 'every umma have its own Messenger'? Yes, there were wars to fight, since Muhammad's community was for most of his life a small minority at odds with the more powerful clans and interests around it; yet time and again he sought a compromise even with those whose beliefs he found deeply wanting.

What, though, is the Quran in the first place? How did its individual verses, existing only in oral form as they were spoken to a prophet said to be unlettered, come to form a single book? When did it become a vital feature of Muslim intellectual and legal life? These are among the questions that Saeed tackles en route to showing how 'reading the Quran' is a practice and an exercise that speaks to the essence of how one imagines being a Muslim. If the earliest interpretation came in the form of Muhammad's practical choices in giving life to the word of God, then a century after his death a tradition of sophisticated writing was already taking off. Surrounded by the complex legal and political heritages of the Byzantine and Sassanian empires that had come under Muslim rule, where else could one turn for guidance that had moral as well as pragmatic value? This also meant, of course, that varying situations called for a diversity of readings of the Quran. To be sure, there were leanings toward a more literal approach among Sunni groups, compared with a Shia preference for seeking out the inner essence of texts. But as the multiplicity of schools of law proves, there were mutually recognised differences in what the Quran was felt to imply on a whole range of secular and religious issues – for which the sharia or body of ethical principles was derived from the Quran.

Saeed draws out the exciting trends that appeared with the rise of learning in Islam. Greek rationalism shaped how thinkers like al-Farabi (870-950), Ibn Rushd (1126-1198) and the adepts of the Ikhwan al-Safa (Brethren of Purity, in 10th-century Basra) read the Quran; others like al-Tustari (818-896) and Ibn Arabi (1165-1240) coupled reason with a keen mysticism in their quest for meaning. There were also those like the Asharis who questioned the role of reason and favoured a conservative stance. All of which laid the groundwork for a richly varied tradition of exegesis or scriptural interpretation that has lived on across the Muslim world. As in the past, social context has plenty to do with how Muslims relate to the Quran as text and guide. Modern science, colonialism, debates about women's equality and human rights, and new ways of approaching literary texts have all left their mark. 'In the contemporary struggles for "authenticity", Quranic exegesis is at the forefront of debate', Saeed notes, not only among traditionalists but also Sufis and postmodernists.

Expressions

Fired by the images of scripture and the story of the rise of Medina from pagan oasis to the Prophet's 'Illuminated City', Muslims could hardly be content with living in old ways. Gardens are brought up no fewer than 120 times, whether as places of blissful retreat or secure refuge, in the Quran. Water, trees and animals abound. Ideas about cleansing, family life, collective and solitary prayer, pilgrimage and trade are part of a universe that emerges from the founding narratives of Islam. Although it draws on aspects from pre-Islamic times, there is fresh meaning attached to these ideas and practices, which are tied to moral purpose and accountability. It leaves behind the time of darkness, *jahiliyya*, when mere material ends were pursued by rulers and ruled, in ignorance of the proper ideals of community and civilisation. This shift is seen not only in codes of law and ways of worship but also in art, architecture, poetry, music and learning. The place where this can best be witnessed and experienced is the city. Here the gardens of paradise come to life, minarets and libraries jostle with markets, news is exchanged in public baths, courts and bureaucrats keep order, while travellers, traders and mystics find rest in caravanserais or *khanqahs*.

Amira Bennison's chapter, 'The Umma in the City', reminds us that the earliest shifts of the moral universe happened in Jerusalem, Mecca and Medina. 'Islam has often been characterised as an urban faith in the sense that its ritual, political and legal requirements are most easily met in cities', she notes – but also that cities are about 'culture, society and the environment, and how these different things intertwine to create a particular city and way of urban living at a specific time'. Over time, western scholars keen to write about the 'Islamic city' have developed a stereotype in which economic and social factors that shape urban spaces are ignored, making it all about religion. For example, the practice of ranging the city centre around a principal place of worship – a church or temple – with a marketplace nearby was common in medieval Europe; yet the expression of this with a mosque and bazaar at the heart of the *kasbah* is seen as peculiarly 'Islamic'. True, there were religious influences such as the need for spaces for cleansing before prayers, and the division of public and private spaces between men and women. But in taking us through five great centres – Cairo, Cordoba, Delhi, Isfahan and Marrakesh – Bennison shows that the character of urban life in Muslim societies has always been a lively mix of culture, geography, wealth and lived faith.

Surely, though, the mosque is an entirely distinctive expression of Islam? Only to a point, as Hasan-Uddin Khan notes in his account of its art and architecture. The minaret and the dome are optional; neither was present in the Prophet's own mosque; the Dome of the Rock in Jerusalem has no minaret. There are Chinese mosques built with pagodas rather than domes, West African mosques with high mud walls that look like exotic fortresses, North American mosques that recall Navajo and other indigenous styles, and robust Indian ones that draw on Hindu and Victorian features. Khan shows that what is most universal are themes such as the threshold or entrance 'that marks a symbolic change of mind from one state to another', the space for ablutions 'both practical and inspirational, for it marks another threshold', and the niche (*mihrab*) that marks the direction of prayer. He sees two issues dominating how Muslims today think about mosques: expressions of local and global identity, and the status of women. These often interface, as when some North American Muslims choose to have a woman lead the ritual prayer – a reflection of how the congregation wishes to see itself, and be seen by others. In the dialogue of tradition and modernity, with sensitivity toward the environment, initiatives like the Aga Khan Award for Architecture have encouraged bold innovation in how Muslims express their aspirations.

Such innovation was once commonplace, when Muslim approaches to the body of knowledge as well as to cities, mosques and the Quran itself were dynamic. It is in these 'cultures of learning' that Anil Khamis locates his chapter on institutions of education. The rise of the world's oldest universities, al-Azhar in Cairo (969) and the Nizamiyya in Baghdad (1091), was accompanied by the vigorous building of libraries and centres for translation and research across the Islamic Mediterranean. What's now thought of as the lowly *madrassa* was then not merely a 'Quran school' but a thriving place of secular and religious learning. These once-innovative institutions became 'traditional' when the lead in fostering 'knowledge societies' passed to the West. In many Muslim countries, education today lags on every score, from basic literacy to the quality of higher learning in the natural and social sciences, to a degree that is only partly explained by poverty. Khamis finds that some of the most creative solutions in bridging the gap, for females and males, aim to rehabilitate older institutions like the *madrassa* and make them into 'hybrid' schools that tackle *all* learning seriously. At the same time, formal as well as alternative types of schools and universities need to foster more effectively an ethic of civil belonging, one that is rooted but pluralist in outlook.

No encouragement on that score is needed when it comes to poets, at least the good ones, of whom the Muslim world has surely had a fair share. But does poetry really matter in our impatient age – and what are the wider prospects for verse written in Persian, Urdu or Arabic? There is a clue in the fact that Jalal al-din Rumi (1207-1273) is today among the most widely read poets in the world, in all his rooted yet cosmopolitan spirituality that poured forth in classical Persian. Among the most effective modern renditions in English is that of Raficq Abdulla, whose chapter here offers spirited reasons for taking poets seriously. They speak to our displacement both internal and external, to longings that the rest of us have difficulty putting into coherent language, or which we may not even consciously recognise. 'Poetry matters because, like music, it removes us from the mundane, it teaches us to sense the unseen influences that mould us and mature us', says Abdulla. 'Like prayer, it opens us to deeper layers of the self.' Secular and sacred themes alike figure in his exploration here, and so they must since poets have a way of dwelling between worlds – cultural, religious and political – rather than being shut in. A leading contemporary poet who captures these many worlds while also explaining them in prose (scholarly and fiction) is Salma Jayussi. Like her fellow Palestinian poet, Mahmoud Darwish (1941-2008), Jayussi writes from exile that becomes more than just political; it is also about the dislocation and journeying of the human soul, in a modern echo of Rumi.

Inclusions

Women have figured prominently among Muslim poets and mystics, but less so among those who have determined the course of political and religious life. The Prophet himself leaned heavily on Khadija as his wife, counsellor and even employer, while women played vital roles in attesting to the hadith and other essential narratives of the community. Indeed, the Quran addressed them directly as moral equals of men, and set the foundation for laws that could treat them as such. Yet the patriarchal societies of the Middle and Near East were hard on the status of Muslim women, as they were on their Christian, Jewish and Zoroastrian sisters. The legacy of those cultural realities is the focus of Azizah al-Hibri's chapter, in which she notes (as activist and scholar) that gender equity has a powerful basis within Islam. In matters of inheritance, economic independence, choice of spouse and security from abuse, she finds that the practice of Islamic law has veered far from what the underlying norms actually say. What influential male jurists have done, she argues, is to distort the Quranic sensitivity to step-by-step change in matters of deep social reform, and to freeze the laws at stages that suit their own conservatism. Thus, even though the Quran limited to four the number of wives that a man could marry and placed a heavy burden on having more than one, polygamy became the favoured practice, legitimated in law.

For al-Hibri, each generation must exercise *ijtihad* or interpretation in the light of its social context, which today is 'a world that takes as non-negotiable the rights of women as full and active citizens'. That is certainly the spirit in which reformist women have sought to deal with those for whom 'tradition' is tied to a fixed reading of religion and identity. Anxieties about the loss of patriarchal power attached to fixed versions of tradition/religion can unleash strong reactions to preserve old forms of dominance. In Afghanistan, the Taliban's version of tradition means that female legislators and activists risk life and limb to advocate a reading of the sharia that is true to its liberating spirit. Elsewhere, from Iran and Pakistan to Nigeria and Saudi Arabia, women's groups are using the language both of tradition and modern human rights in pushing for legal reform and effective participation.

Inclusion within the wider governance of society extends not only to women, of course, but also to those from various ethnic and religious backgrounds. The template was cast at the very birth of Islam, when the Constitution of Medina brought a *civic* umma together, with Muhammad as guardian of all faiths. Even his religious umma sought to break with prior affinities to clan and tribe, defining itself in terms only of its ethical ideals. Shainool Jiwa's chapter offers another example of inclusive governance, that of the Fatimids in Egypt (969-1171), who traced their lineage as well as their inspiration in this regard to Muhammad. In particular, the Fatimids proclaimed a warrant of general safety and civic well-being or *Aman*, which Jiwa sees as 'the blueprint' for their two centuries' rule as a Shii regime in the midst of a Sunni majority as well as Christian and Jewish minorities. Under the *Aman*, citizens could freely practice their faith and follow any of the religious schools of law; the state would ensure the upkeep of places of worship and of their administrators. One is reminded of Cyrus II of Persia's celebrated assurance of relief and security for all subjects upon his conquest of Babylon in 539 BC. But Fatimid Egypt went much further: skilled individuals of all persuasions could gain a place in the highest levels of government, as well as in the military. Women played important public roles in politics and culture, with many receiving an advanced education. The broad setting for all this was one of extraordinary success in the arts, commerce, learning and development, including the founding of the city of Cairo and al-Azhar university.

This was but one of several such epochs of liberal governance in settings as diverse as Moorish Andalusia, Mughal India and Ottoman Turkey. It would, of course, be ahistorical to expect these settings to have all the elements of contemporary pluralist democracy, such as constitutional neutrality on religion and a separation of powers among the legislature, judiciary and executive. What they do offer, though, is evidence that Muslims have taken very seriously the values of tolerance and inclusion – which Amir Hussain extends to a larger interweaving of religious traditions. For just as the 'Muslim world' has long included and drawn upon Buddhist, Christian, Hindu, Jewish and other faith traditions in its cultural and intellectual life, so too has Islam penetrated the lifeworlds of those Others. In the Americas, Hussain notes that Arab travellers, African slaves and Christian converts brought their assorted 'Islams' long before today's waves of migrants. When we seek a sensible pluralism, then, we ought to look not only at inclusive theologies but also at dense histories of cultural and civilisational sharing. This can give us a cosmopolitanism that has both cultural and religious roots. There are lessons here, Hussain says, for the troubles in Afghanistan, Iraq and elsewhere. Minorities and majorities that feel excluded will take what is presented to them as a sole marker of their identity, like ethnicity, region or religion. What sits under these labels is real or feared exclusion in economic, social or political life. If an 'ethic of inclusion' is to be more than a slogan, it should 'find its way into constitutions, codes of law and institutions of governance'.

Networks

Hussain's theme of 'Islams in the Plural' is for Bruce Lawrence best understood, in history and today, as a matter of how *social networks* express the bonds of faith, trade, travel and more. 'Precisely because Islam is not homogeneous, it is only through the lens of Muslim networks, whether they be historical or commercial, academic or aesthetic, that one can see how diverse groups contest and articulate what it means to be Muslim.' There are the more obvious webs that have marked the flourishing of secular and religious bonds, like those of the Silk Road, guilds and brotherhoods of artists, craftsmen, clerics and Sufis, the sojourns of Ibn Battuta, pilgrimages to Mecca, and scholarly associations. They are rooted, for Lawrence, in the founding idea of the umma itself, which sets 'the broadest boundaries defining Muslim collective identity'. Muhammad's own life and message thrived on existing webs of clan, commerce and pilgrimage that criss-crossed Arabia, and which defined pre-Islamic solidarities and identities on the basis of trust. The umma cast these anew as global and also local. Today's umma has multiple threads that include sisterhoods of solidarity for equity, as well as networks for migrants, musicians and political causes. In negotiating trust, such networks must grapple with inclusions (and exclusions) of class, gender, nationality and ways of understanding and practising the faith – which reminds us of the tension of 'universality and uniformity' that mark globalisation.

Nowhere is that tension, and indeed contemporary networking, played out more visibly than in the 'cyberworld', the universe of the internet in all its energetic sprawl. Here we have opportunities and spaces not only for direct communication and networking among individuals and groups, but also for images and sounds, for points of view and debate, and for archives that can range back to the founding sources of Islam. The 'digital umma', as Gary Bunt calls it, is now a transforming reality for those with and also those without access to the internet. Cyberspace allows for authoritative judgments on issues of faith in the form of *fatwas* to be asked for and delivered, for details about ritual prayers and fasts to be posted, for pious images and sounds to be carried, and for 'Islamically approved' arrangements for dating and marriage. The digital umma engages in daily shopping, chat and social networking – outside the radar of media and intelligence agencies on the watch for online jihad. As the internet becomes ever more vital both as a tool and a space, so do questions of access and participation. Bunt points out that while countries like Bahrain, Qatar and the United Arab Emirates rank relatively high in terms of internet access, the overall picture in 2005 was that 50 per cent of those in developed countries as against nine per cent in less developed ones, and just one per cent in the least developed nations, had access. The cost of individual access tends to be much higher in poorer countries, and there are disparities also of gender and region within societies. Still, Africa and the Middle East rank highest in growth of usage as of 2008, and many Muslim countries are fast becoming emerging markets for information technology. When it comes to social networking, young Iranian females and males rank among the most active in the world; they are quickly being joined by Muslim youth elsewhere.

Today's 'networked Islam' may not be entirely new. Webs of information and solidarity on the basis of trust have long been part of human society. But cyber networks challenge the way we experience the world, including 'old, exclusive divisions between East and West', notes Lawrence. Geography itself is collapsed by overlapping cyber cultures and civilisation. This also means, says Bunt, that the Muslim diaspora in Europe and North America is highly visible in every form of cyber expression, from websites to databases on history and religious practice, to the point of reversing the old divide of 'centre' and 'periphery'. This is hardly surprising, of course, given the access to advanced information technology in these regions. At the same time, the wide terrain of cyber space is not without its dangers, byways that stray from the civil or the ethical. 'The open-ended nature of the internet makes the boundaries of digital Islam at once more porous and more subject to change', Lawrence observes. So the 'familiar guideposts' of faith and ethics are still needed as the umma strives, in the cyber as in the social world, to keep along the *sirat al-mustaqim*, the Straight Path.

The finest of journeys – by adventurers and pilgrims, scholars and mystics – are as much passages within the self as they are outward travels. This is captured with much flair in epic poetry, such as Attar's *The Conference of the Birds*, where dialogue on the perils and prizes of a long journey is really all about the character of the questing self. Since maps of internal travel are harder to draw, the outward ones must serve as a symbolic guide. So it is with mapping the 'Muslim world' over time. The pathways discussed in this introduction tell us broadly of the landscape, and suggest what aspects are not fully covered. But they can barely hint at the internal journeys that Muslims have made in their evolving appreciation of the founding sources and of the manifold ways that faith is lived in the secular world. In this, we rely much on the reader's imaginative generosity, with a little help from the suggestive gifts of our contributors. Future publications in the Muslim Heritage Series will focus more specifically on ethics, the sciences, philosophy, mysticism, the arts and public culture. In this exploration of heritage we must give history its due – but also inquire into how and why that heritage matters. Traditions should be 'sought as shelters and avoided as prisons', observes the Iranian intellectual Abdolkarim Soroush.[12] As the Muslim world grapples with globalisation, the knowledge society and the fostering of pluralist civil society, both change and continuity will characterise the choices that are to be made.

---

[12] Abdolkarim Soroush, *Reason, Freedom and Democracy in Islam*, tr. and ed. M. Sadri and A. Sadri (Oxford, 2000), p. 53.

Further Reading

An-Naim, Abdullahi A. *Toward an Islamic Renaissance*. Syracuse, 1990.

Arkoun, Mohammed. *Rethinking Islam: Common Questions, Uncommon Answers*. tr. Robert D. Lee. Boulder, Colorado, 1994.

Esack, Farid. *On Being a Muslim: Finding a Religious Path in the World Today*. Oxford, 1999.

Hillenbrand, Robert. *Islamic Art and Architecture*. London, 1999.

Hodgson, Marshall G.S. *Rethinking World History: Essays on Europe, Islam, and World History*. ed. Edmund Burke III. Cambridge 1993.

Nasr, Seyyed Hossein. *Ideals and Realities of Islam*. Rev. ed., Chicago, 2000.

Norris, Pippa and Ronald Inglehart. *Sacred and Secular: Religion and Politics Worldwide*. Cambridge, 2004.

Rahman, Fazlur. *Islam and Modernity: Transformation of an Intellectual Tradition*. Chicago, 1982.

Rippin, Andrew, ed. *The Islamic World*. London, 2008.

Safi, Omid, ed. *Progressive Muslims: On Justice, Gender, and Pluralism*. Oxford, 2003.

Sajoo, Amyn B., ed. *Muslim Modernities: Expressions of the Civil Imagination*. London, 2008.

Taji-Farouki, Suha and Bashir Nafi, ed. *Islamic Thought in the Twentieth Century*. London, 2004.

The Prophet's City

Reza Aslan

I

In the evening, the sun in the desert is a glowing white orb set low in the sky. It dips into the horizon, and its light is eclipsed by the dunes, making them appear as heaving black swells in the distance. At the edge of Yathrib, a hedge of lofty palm trees forms a boundary separating the oasis from the advancing desert. Here the small band of Emigrants wait, hands shading their eyes, staring out over the vast expanse for any sign of their Prophet. They've been standing at the edge of the desert for days and nights. What else can they do? Many of them have no homes in Yathrib. Most of their possessions were left behind in Mecca. Their journey was not a grand exodus through the desert, camels laden with goods. The Hijra, as the migration from Mecca to Yathrib is known, was a secret operation: daughters sneaking out of their fathers' homes at night, young men gathering whatever provisions they could carry on their backs for the arduous week-long journey through the barren wilderness. The few possessions they brought with them have become communal property and will not last.

The problem is that the Meccan Emigrants or *Muhajirun* (those who have made the Hijra) are primarily traders and merchants, but Yathrib is not a city built on trade. Yathrib is not a city at all. It is a loose federation of villages inhabited by farmers and orchardists, tillers of the earth, nothing like the bustling, prosperous city the Emigrants left behind. Even if they could transform themselves from traders to farmers, all the best agricultural lands in Yathrib are already occupied. How are they to survive here except on the charity and goodwill of the *Ansar* or 'Helpers', the handful of Yathrib's villagers who have also accepted the Prophet Muhammad's message and converted to his movement? What is to happen to them now that they have abandoned the protection of the Quraysh, Mecca's ruling tribe? Will the most powerful tribe in Arabia simply allow them to leave Mecca without consequences? Have they really chosen to cast off their homes, their families, their very identities, all at the command of an extraordinary but untested prophet who is now nowhere to be found?

Just before the sun vanishes, two smouldering silhouettes are spotted in the desert, lurching toward Yathrib. A cry spreads among the Emigrants: 'The Messenger is here! The Messenger has come!' The men jump up and run out to meet Muhammad and his companion, Abu Bakr, as the two cross into the oasis. The women join hands and dance in circles around the two men, their ululations rolling from house to house, announcing the Prophet's arrival.

Muhammad, parched and blistered from the journey, sits back in his saddle and lets the reins of his camel hang loose. A crowd gathers, offering food and water. A few of the Ansar struggle to grab hold of the camel's reins and steer it toward their villages. They shout, 'Come, O Messenger of God, to a settlement which has many defenders and is well-provisioned and impregnable.' But Muhammad, not wishing to ally himself with any particular clan in Yathrib, refuses their offers. 'Let go her reins', he commands. The crowd backs off, and Muhammad's camel staggers forward a few more steps. It circles an abandoned burial ground now used for drying dates, then stops and kneels, lowering its neck for the Prophet to dismount. Of the owners of the land, Muhammad asks a price.

'We do not want money for it', the owners reply. 'Only the reward we shall receive from God.'

Grateful for their generosity, Muhammad orders the land to be levelled, the graves dug up, and the palm trees cut down for timber to build a modest home. He envisions a courtyard roofed in palm leaves, with living quarters made of wood and mud lining the walls. But this will be more than a home. This converted drying-ground and cemetery will serve as the first *masjid* or mosque of a new kind of community, one so revolutionary that many years later, when Muslim scholars seek to establish a distinctly Islamic calendar, they will begin not with the birth of the Prophet, nor with the onset of the Revelation, but with the year Muhammad and his band of Emigrants came to this small federation of villages to start a new society. That year, 622, will forever be known as Year 1 AH (After Hijra). And the oasis that for centuries was called Yathrib will hence be celebrated as *Madinat al-Nabi*, The City of the Prophet, or more simply, Medina.

There exists an enduring mythology about Muhammad's years in Medina, a mythology that has defined the religion and politics of Islam for 1,400 years. It is in Medina that the Muslim community was born. 'Muhammad in Medina' became the model for the Muslim empires that expanded throughout the Middle East after the Prophet's death, and the standard that every Arab kingdom struggled to meet during the Middle Ages. The Medinan ideal inspired the various Islamic revivalist movements of the 18th and 19th centuries, all of which strove to return to the original values of Muhammad's unadulterated community as a means to wrest control of Muslim lands from colonial rule (though they had very different ideas about how to define those original values). With the demise of colonialism in the 20th century, it was the memory of Medina that launched the Islamic state.

Today, Medina is the archetype both of democracy and the impetus for militancy in the Muslim world. Modernists like the Egyptian writer and political philosopher Ali Abd al-Raziq (1888-1966) pointed to Muhammad's community in Medina as proof that Islam advocated the separation of religious and temporal powers. Extremists in Afghanistan and Iran have used the same community to fashion models of theocracy. In their struggle for equal rights, Muslim feminists have consistently drawn inspiration from the legal reforms Muhammad instituted in Medina. At the same time, traditionalists have construed those same legal reforms as grounds for maintaining the subjugation of women in society. For some, Muhammad's actions in Medina serve as the model for Muslim-Jewish relations; for others, they demonstrate the insurmountable conflict that has always existed, and will always exist, between the two sons of Abraham, Isaac and Ismail. Regardless of whether one is labelled a modernist or a traditionalist, a reformist or a fundamentalist, a feminist or a male chauvinist, all Muslims regard Medina as the model of Islamic polity. Put simply, Medina is what Islam was meant to be.

As with all mythologies of this magnitude, it is often difficult to separate factual history from sacred history. Part of the problem is that the historical traditions dealing with Muhammad's time in Medina were written long after the Prophet's death by Muslim historians who were keen to emphasize the universal recognition and immediate success of his divine mission. Muhammad's biographers were living at a time in which the Muslim community had already become a powerful empire. As a result, their accounts more often reflect the political and religious ideologies of ninth-century Damascus, or 11th-century Baghdad, than of seventh-century Medina.

To understand what really happened in Medina and why, one must sift through the sources to uncover not the holy city that would become the capital of the Muslim community, but rather the remote desert oasis originally called Yathrib, which nurtured and cultivated that community in its infancy.

II

Yathrib in the seventh century was a thriving agricultural oasis thick with palm orchards and vast arable fields, most of which were dominated by some 20 Jewish clans of varying sizes. Unlike the Jews who had settled throughout most of the Hijaz, who were mainly immigrants from Palestine, Yathrib's Jews were primarily Arabs who had converted to Judaism. Apart from their religious designation as Jews, little differentiated them from their pagan neighbours. Like all Arabs, the Jews of Yathrib considered themselves first and foremost members of their own individual clans – each of which acted as a sovereign entity – rather than as a single community of Jews. And while a few Jewish clans may have had alliances with one another, even these in no way constituted a united Jewish tribe.

As the earliest settlers in the region, the Jews occupied Yathrib's most fertile agricultural lands, called 'the Heights', quickly becoming masters of Arabia's most prized crop: dates. The Jews were also skilled jewellers, clothiers, arms makers and vintners (Jewish wine was considered the best in the Peninsula). But it was Yathrib's dates, coveted throughout the Hijaz, that had made them rich. As a matter of fact, five of the largest Jewish clans in the oasis – the Banu Thalabah, the Banu Hadl, the Banu Qurayza, the Banu Nadir and the Banu Qaynuqa (who also controlled the city's only market) – enjoyed an almost complete monopoly over Yathrib's economy.

By the time a number of Bedouin tribes gave up their nomadic existence and also settled in Yathrib, all the most fertile lands had been claimed. What remained were the barely cultivable lots situated in a region termed 'the Bottom'. The competition over limited resources had not only created some conflict between the pagan and Jewish clans, it had also resulted in a gradual decline of the Jews' authority and influence in Yathrib. For the most part, however, the two groups lived in relative peace through strategic tribal affiliations and economic alliances. The Jews regularly employed the Arabs to transport their dates to nearby markets (especially in Mecca), while the Arabs maintained a high esteem for the learning, craftsmanship and heritage of their Jewish neighbours who were, in the words of the Arab chronicler al-Waqidi, 'a people of high lineage and of properties, whereas we were but an Arab tribe who did not possess any palm trees nor vineyards, being people of only sheep and camels'.

The real conflict in the oasis was not between the Jews and Arabs, but among the Arabs themselves, and more specifically between Yathrib's two largest Arab tribes, the Aws and the Khazraj. While the origins of this conflict have been lost to history, what seems clear is that the Law of Retribution, the purpose of which was to deter precisely this kind of ongoing tribal conflict, had failed to solve the long-standing quarrel. By the time Muhammad arrived in Yathrib, what had probably begun as a disagreement over limited resources had escalated into a bloody feud which had spilled over even to the Jewish clans, with the Banu Nadir and the Banu Qurayza supporting the Aws, and the Banu Qaynuqa siding with the Khazraj. In short, this conflict was splitting the oasis in two.

What the Aws and the Khazraj desperately needed was an arbiter or *hakam*. Not just any *hakam*, but an authoritative, trustworthy and neutral party who was totally unconnected with anyone in Yathrib, someone who had the power – better yet, the divine authority – to arbitrate between the two tribes. How fortunate, then, that the perfect man for the job was himself in desperate need of a place to live, having been forced out of Mecca by the Quraysh.

That Muhammad came to Yathrib as little more than the *hakam* in the quarrel between the Aws and the Khazraj is certain. And yet the traditions seem to present Muhammad arriving in the oasis as the mighty prophet of a new and firmly established religion, and as the unchallenged leader of the whole of Yathrib. This view is partly the result of a famous document called the Constitution of Medina, which Muhammad may have drafted some time after settling in the oasis. This document – often celebrated as the world's first written constitution – was a series of formal agreements of non-aggression among Muhammad, the Emigrants, the Ansar and the rest of Yathrib's clans, both Jewish and pagan. The Constitution appears to assign to Muhammad unparalleled religious and political authority over the entire population of the oasis, including the Jews. Under it, Muhammad had sole authority to arbitrate all disputes in Yathrib, and not just that between the Aws and Khazraj. It declares him to be Yathrib's sole war leader (*qaid*) and recognizes him as the Messenger of God. While it implies that Muhammad's primary role was as 'shaykh' of his 'clan' of Emigrants, it also clearly endows him with a privileged position over all other tribal and clan shaykhs in Yathrib.

When exactly was the Constitution of Medina written? The traditional sources, including al-Tabari and Ibn Hisham, place its composition among the Prophet's first acts upon entering the oasis: that is, in 622. But that is unlikely, given Muhammad's weak position during those first few years in Yathrib. He was, after all, forced to flee Mecca and was sought throughout the Hijaz. As Michael Lecker has shown in his *Muslims, Jews, and Pagans*, (1995), it was not until after the Battle of Badr in 624, and perhaps not even until 627, that the majority of the Aws tribe converted to Islam. Before then, few people outside the Ansar (then only a small number of the Khazraj) would have known who Muhammad was. His movement represented the smallest fraction of Yathrib's population; the Jews alone may have totalled in the thousands. When Muhammad arrived in the oasis, he had brought fewer than a hundred men, women and children with him.

The Constitution of Medina may reflect several early pacts of non-aggression among Muhammad, the Arab clans and their Jewish clients. It may even reproduce certain elements of Muhammad's arbitration between the Aws and the Khazraj. But it could not have been completed as it has been preserved before 624. Only after Badr could Muhammad have enjoyed the powers attributed to him by the Constitution of Medina; only after Badr could Yathrib even be thought of as Medina.

Muhammad's role during those first couple of years in Yathrib was likely that of a *hakam* – albeit a powerful and divinely inspired one – whose arbitration was restricted to the Aws and Khazraj, and whose authority as a shaykh was confined to his own 'clan' of Emigrants. Muhammad's claim to be the Messenger of God would not have had to be either accepted or rejected for him to function properly in either of these two roles. Both the pagan Arabs and the Jews of Yathrib would have considered his prophetic consciousness to be proof of his supernatural wisdom, especially since the ideal *hakam* was almost always also the *kahin* (a soothsayer or ecstatic poet in pre-Islamic Arabia), whose connection to the spirit world was indispensable in especially difficult disputes like the one between the Aws and Khazraj.

Yet, while the other inhabitants of Yathrib may have viewed Muhammad as little more than a *hakam* and a shaykh, that was not at all how the Emigrants saw him. To his small band of followers, Muhammad was the Prophet/Lawgiver who spoke with the authority of the one God. He had come to Yathrib to establish a new kind of socio-religious community, though how that community was to be organised, and who could be considered a member of it, was yet to be defined.

It may be tempting to call the members of this new community Muslims, 'those who submit' to God. But there is no reason to believe that this term was used to designate a distinct religious movement until many years later, perhaps not until the end of Muhammad's life. It would perhaps be more accurate to refer to Muhammad's followers by the same term the Quran uses: the umma. But no one is certain what this term meant or where it came from. It may be derived from Arabic, Hebrew, or Aramaic; it may have meant 'a community', 'a nation' or 'a people'. A few scholars have suggested that umma may be derived from the Arabic word for mother (*umm*); while this idea may be aesthetically pleasing, there is no linguistic evidence for it. To complicate matters further, umma inexplicably ceases to be used in the Quran after 625 when, as Montgomery Watt has noted, it is replaced with the word *qawm*, Arabic for 'tribe'.

But there may be something to this change in terms. Despite its ingenuity, Muhammad's community was still an Arab institution based on Arab notions of tribal society. There was simply no alternative model of social organisation in seventh-century Arabia, save for monarchy. Indeed, there are so many parallels between the early Muslim community and traditional tribal societies that one is left with the distinct impression that, at least in Muhammad's mind, the umma was indeed a tribe, though a new and radically innovative one.

For one thing, the reference in the Constitution of Medina to Muhammad's role as shaykh of his clan of Emigrants indicates that, despite the Prophet's elevated status, his secular authority would have fallen well within the traditional model of pre-Islamic tribal society. What is more, just as membership in the tribe obliged participation in the rituals and activities of the tribal cult, so did membership in Muhammad's community require ritual involvement in what could be termed its 'tribal cult': in this case, the nascent religion of Islam. Public rituals like communal prayer, almsgiving and collective fasting – the first three activities mandated by God – when combined with shared dietary regulations and purity requirements, functioned in the umma in much the same way that the activities of the tribal cult did in pagan societies.

They provided a common social and religious identity that allowed one group to distinguish itself from another.

What made the umma a unique experiment in social organisation was that in Yathrib, far away from the social and religious hegemony of the Quraysh, Muhammad finally had the opportunity to implement the reforms he had been preaching to no avail in Mecca. By enacting a series of radical religious, social and economic reforms, he was able to establish a new kind of society, the likes of which had never before been seen in Arabia. For instance, whereas power in the tribe was allocated to a number of figures, none of which had any real executive authority, Muhammad united all the pre-Islamic positions of authority unto himself, making his authority as Prophet/Lawgiver absolute. Also, while the only way to become a member of a tribe was to be born into it, anyone could join Muhammad's community simply by declaring, 'There is no god but God, and Muhammad is God's Messenger.' The *shahada*, as this profession of faith is called, was thus transformed in Yathrib from a theological statement with explicit social and political implications into a new version of the oath of allegiance, the *baya*, which members of a tribe gave to its shaykh. And because neither ethnicity nor culture nor race nor kinship had any significance to Muhammad, the umma, unlike a traditional tribe, had an almost unlimited capacity for growth through conversion.

The point is that one can refer to Muhammad's community in Yathrib as the umma, but only insofar as that term is understood to designate what the Orientalist explorer Bertram Thomas has called a 'super-tribe', or what the historian Marshall Hodgson more accurately describes as a 'neo-tribe', that is, a radically new kind of social organisation but one that was still based on the traditional Arab tribal model. As was the case with all tribal shaykhs, Muhammad's primary function as head of the umma was to ensure the protection of every member in his community. This he did through the chief means at his disposal, the Law of Retribution. But while retribution was maintained as a legitimate response to injury, Muhammad urged believers toward forgiveness: 'The retribution for an injury is an equal injury', the Quran states, 'but those who forgive the injury and make reconciliation will be rewarded by God' (42:40). Likewise, the Constitution of Medina sanctions retribution as the principal deterrent for crime, but with the unprecedented stipulation that the entire community may be 'solidly against [the criminal] and may do nothing except oppose him', a stark reversal of tribal tradition and a clear indication that Muhammad was already beginning to lay the foundations of a society built on moral rather than utilitarian principles. But this was only the beginning.

To further his egalitarian ideals, Muhammad equalized the blood-worth of every member of his community, so that no longer could one life be considered more or less valuable (materially speaking) than another. This was yet another innovation in the Arabian legal system. An injury to a victim's eye in pre-Islamic Arabia would have, according to the Law of Retribution, required an equal injury to the criminal's eye. But no one would have considered a shaykh's eye to be worth the same amount as an orphan's. Muhammad changed all that, but not without seriously disrupting the social order. The traditions recount a particularly amusing story about an aristocratic tribesman named Jabalah ibn al-Ayham who was struck in the face by a humble man from the Muzaynah, a modest tribe in Arabia. Expecting that a stern penalty would be imposed on the lowly offender – one that would signify his inferior status in society – al-Ayham was shocked to learn that all he could expect as retribution was the opportunity to strike the humble man back. So outraged was he by this 'injustice' that al-Ayham immediately abandoned Islam and became a Christian. Nor did Muhammad's move toward equality end there. In Yathrib, he categorically outlawed usury, the abuse of which was one of his chief complaints against the Meccan religio-economic system. To facilitate the new economy, he established his own market which, unlike the one controlled by the Banu Qaynuqa, charged no tax on transactions and no interest on loans. While this tax-free market eventually became a point of conflict between Muhammad and the Banu Qaynuqa, the Prophet's move was not a means of antagonizing the Qaynuqa, but a further step toward removing the divide between the ridiculously wealthy and the absurdly poor.

Using his unquestioned religious authority, Muhammad initiated a mandatory tithe called *zakat* that every member of the umma had to pay according to his or her means. Once collected, the money was redistributed as alms to the neediest members. *Zakat* means 'purification' and was not an act of charity but of religious devotion. Benevolence and care for the poor were the first and most enduring virtues preached by Muhammad in Mecca. Piety, the Quran reminds believers, lies 'not in turning your face East or West in prayer. . . but in distributing your wealth out of love for God to your needy kin; to the orphans, to the vagrants and to the mendicants; it lies in freeing the slaves, in observing your devotions and in giving alms to the poor' (2:177).

Perhaps nowhere was Muhammad's struggle for economic and social justice more evident than in the rights and privileges he bestowed upon the women in his community. Beginning with the un-Biblical affirmation that men and women were created together and simultaneously from a single soul (4:1; 7:189), the Quran goes to great lengths to emphasize the equality of the sexes in the eyes of God:

God offers forgiveness and a great reward,
For men who surrender to Him, and women who surrender to
    Him,
For men who believe, and women who believe,
For men who obey, and women who obey,
For men who speak truth, and women who speak truth,
For men who persevere, and women who persevere,
For men who are humble, and women who are humble,
For men who give alms, and women who give alms,
For men who fast, and women who fast,
For men who are modest, and women who are modest,
For men who remember God, and women who remember God
(33:35).

The Quran acknowledges that men and women have distinct and separate roles in society; it would have been preposterous to claim otherwise in seventh-century Arabia. Thus, 'men are to take care of women, because God has given them greater strength, and because men use their wealth to provide for them' (4:34). With a few notable exceptions such as Khadija, Muhammad's first wife, women in pre-Islamic Arabia could neither own property nor inherit it from their husbands. Actually, a wife was herself considered property; both she and her dowry would be inherited by the male heir of her deceased husband. If the male heir was uninterested in the widow, he could hand her over to his kin – a brother or a nephew – who could then marry her and take control of her dead husband's property. But if she was too old to marry again, or if no one was interested in her, she and her dowry would revert to the clan. The same was true for all female orphans, as well as those male orphans who, like Muhammad when his parents died, were considered too young to inherit property from their fathers.

However, Muhammad – who had benefited greatly from the wealth and stability provided by Khadija – strove to give women the opportunity to attain some level of equality and independence in society by amending Arabia's traditional marriage and inheritance laws in order to remove the obstacles that prevented women from inheriting and maintaining their own wealth. The exact changes Muhammad made are far too complex to discuss in detail here; suffice it to note that women in the umma were, for the first time, given the right both to inherit the property of their husbands and to keep their dowries as their own personal property throughout their marriage. Muhammad also forbade a husband to touch his wife's dowry, forcing him instead to provide for his family from his own wealth. If the husband died, his wife would inherit a portion of his property; if he divorced her, the entire dowry was hers to take back to her family.

As one would expect, Muhammad's innovations did not sit well with the male members of his community. If women could no longer be considered property, men complained, not only would their wealth be drastically reduced, but their own meagre inheritances would now have to be split with their sisters and daughters – members of the community who, they argued, did not share an equal burden with the men. The historian al-Tabari recounts how some of these men brought their grievances to Muhammad, asking, 'How can one give the right of inheritance to women and children, who do not work and do not earn their living? Are they now going to inherit just like men who have worked to earn that money?'

Muhammad's response to these complaints was unsympathetic and unyielding: 'Those who disobey God and His Messenger, and who try to overstep the boundaries of this [inheritance] law will be thrown into Hell, where they will dwell forever, suffering the most shameful punishment' (sura 4:14).

If Muhammad's male followers were disgruntled about the new inheritance laws, they must have been furious when, in a single move, he limited how many wives a man could marry and granted women the right to divorce their husbands. In some ways, pre-Islamic Arabian custom was extraordinarily lax when it came to marriage and divorce. In Bedouin societies, men and women practised polygamy and both had recourse to divorce: men simply by making a statement such as 'I divorce you!' and women – who remained with their father's family during marriage – by turning their tent around so that its entrance would no longer be available to the husband when he came for a 'visit'. Because paternity was unimportant in Bedouin societies (lineage was passed mainly through the mother), it made no difference how many husbands a woman had or who fathered her children. But in sedentary societies like Mecca, where the accumulation of wealth made inheritance and, therefore, paternity much more important, matrilineal society had slowly given way to a patrilineal one. As a result of this trend, women in sedentary societies were stripped of their right to divorce and their access to polyandry (the practice of having more than one husband). Although Muhammad's views on marriage seem far more influenced by Jewish tradition than by the traditions of pre-Islamic Arabia, he was still a product of Meccan society. While he limited the rights of men to divorce their wives – forcing upon them a three-month reconciliation period before the statement of divorce could take effect – and while he gave women the right to divorce their husbands if they feared cruelty or ill-treatment, he still consolidated the move toward a patrilineal society by putting an end to all polyandrous unions. Never again could a Muslim woman have more than one husband. Whether a Muslim man may have more than one wife (polygyny), however, remains a contested issue to this day.

On the one hand, Muhammad clearly accepted polygyny (within limits) as necessary for the survival of the umma, especially after war with the Quraysh resulted in hundreds of widows and orphans who had to be provided for and protected by the community. 'Marry those women who are lawful for you, up to two, three, or four', the Quran states, '*but only if you can treat them all equally*' (4:3; emphasis added). On the other hand, the Quran makes it clear that monogamy is the preferred model of marriage when it asserts that, 'no matter how you try, *you will never be able to treat your wives equally*' (4:129; again, emphasis added). This seeming contradiction offers some insight into a dilemma that plagued the community during its early development. The individual believer was to strive for monogamy, yet the community that Muhammad was trying to build in Yathrib would have been doomed without polygyny. For the vast majority of Muslims throughout the world, there is little doubt that the two verses cited above, when combined and considered in their historical context, should be interpreted as rejecting polygyny. But there are those Muslims, especially in tribal societies, who justify their polygynous marriages not necessarily by citing the Quran but by pointing to the example of Muhammad.

After having lived a monogamous life with Khadija for more than 25 years, Muhammad, in the course of 10 years in Yathrib, married nine different women. With very few exceptions, though, these marriages were political. As shaykh of the umma it was his responsibility to forge links within and beyond his community through the only means at his disposal: marriage. His unions with Aisha and Hafsah linked him to the two most important and influential leaders of the early Muslim community – Abu Bakr and Umar respectively. His marriage to Umm Salamah a year later forged an important relationship with one of Mecca's most powerful clans, the Makhzum. His union with Sawdah, by all accounts an unattractive widow long past the age of marriage, was an example to the umma to marry those women in need of financial support. His marriage to Rayhana, a Jew, linked him with the Banu Qurayza, while his marriage to Mariyah, a Christian and a Copt, created a significant political alliance with the ruler of Egypt.

Nevertheless, for 1,400 years – from the medieval Popes of the Crusades to the Enlightenment philosophers of Europe to evangelical preachers in the United States – Muhammad's wives have been the source of numerous lurid attacks against the Prophet and the religion of Islam. In response, contemporary scholars, Muslim and non-Muslim alike, have done considerable work to defend Muhammad's marriages, especially his union with Aisha, who was nine years old when betrothed to the Prophet. While these scholars should be commended for their work in debunking the bigoted and ignorant critiques of anti-Islamic preachers and pundits, the fact is that Muhammad needs no defence on this point.

Like the great Jewish patriarchs Abraham and Jacob; like the prophets Moses and Hosea; like the Israelite kings Saul, David and Solomon; and like nearly all of the Christian/Byzantine and Zoroastrian/Sassanian monarchs, and all tribal shaykhs in Arabia, Muhammad had either multiple wives, multiple concubines, or both. In seventh-century Arabia, a shaykh's power and authority was largely determined by the size of his harem. Muhammad's union with a nine-year-old girl may be shocking to our modern sensibilities, but his betrothal to Aisha was just that, a betrothal. Aisha did not consummate her marriage to Muhammad until after reaching puberty, which is when every girl in Arabia without exception became eligible for marriage. What is surprising about Muhammad's marriages is not his 10 years of polygyny in Yathrib but his 25 years of monogamy in Mecca, something practically unheard of at the time. If there is anything interesting or unusual about Muhammad's marriages, it is not how many wives he had but the regulations imposed on them, especially with regard to the veil.

Although long seen as the most distinctive emblem of Islam, the veil is, surprisingly, not enjoined upon Muslim women anywhere in the Quran. The tradition of veiling and seclusion (known together as hijab) was introduced into Arabia long before Muhammad, through Arab contacts with Syria and Iran where the hijab was a sign of social status. Only a woman who need not work in the fields could afford to remain secluded and veiled. In the umma, there was no tradition of veiling until around 627, when the so-called 'verse of hijab' suddenly descended upon the community. That verse was addressed not to women in general, but exclusively to Muhammad's wives: 'Believers, do not enter the Prophet's house. . . unless asked. And if you are invited . . . do not linger. And when you ask something from the Prophet's wives, do so from behind a hijab. This will assure the purity of your hearts as well as theirs' (33:53).

This restriction makes perfect sense when one recalls that Muhammad's house was also the community's mosque: the centre of religious and social life in the umma. People were constantly coming in and out of this compound at all hours. When delegations from other tribes came to speak with Muhammad, they would set up their tents for days at a time inside the open court-yard, just a few feet away from the apartments in which Muhammad's wives slept. And new emigrants who arrived in Yathrib would often stay within the mosque's walls until they could find suitable homes. When Muhammad was little more than a tribal shaykh, this constant commotion could be tolerated. But by the year 627, when he had become the supremely powerful leader of an increasingly expanding community, some kind of segregation had to be enforced to maintain the privacy of his wives. Thus the tradition, borrowed from the upper classes of Iranian and Syrian women, of veiling and secluding the most important women in society from the peering eyes of everyone else.

That the veil applied solely to Muhammad's wives is further demonstrated by the fact that the term for donning the veil, *darabat al-hijab*, was used synonymously and interchangeably with 'becoming Muhammad's wife'. For this reason, during the Prophet's lifetime, no other women in the umma observed hijab. Of course, modesty was enjoined on all believers, and women in particular were instructed to 'draw their clothes around them a little to be

recognized as believers and so that no harm will come to them'
(sura 33:60). More specifically, women should 'guard their private
parts . . . and drape a cover (*khumur*) over their breasts' when in
the presence of strange men (24:31–32). But nowhere in the whole
of the Quran is the term hijab applied to any woman other than
the wives of Muhammad.

It is difficult to say with certainty when the veil was adopted
by the rest of the umma, though it was most likely long after
Muhammad's death. Muslim women probably began wearing the
veil as a way to emulate the Prophet's wives, who were revered as
'the mothers of the umma'. Yet, the veil was neither compulsory
nor widely adopted until generations after Muhammad's death,
when a large body of male scriptural and legal scholars began
using their religious and political authority to regain the dominance men had lost in society as a result of the Prophet's egalitarian reforms.

III

The era immediately after Muhammad's death was a tumultuous
time for the Muslim community. The umma was growing and
expanding in wealth and power at an astounding rate. A mere 50
years after his death, the tiny community that Muhammad had
founded in Yathrib burst out of the Arabian Peninsula and swal-
lowed whole the massive Sassanian empire of Iran. Fifty years after
that, it had secured most of northwest India, absorbed all of North
Africa and reduced the Christian Byzantine empire to little more
than a deteriorating regional power. Fifty years after that, Islam
had pushed its way deep into Europe through Spain and southern
France.

As Muhammad's small community of Arab followers swelled
into the largest empire in the world, it faced a growing number
of legal and religious challenges that were not explicitly dealt with
in the Quran. While Muhammad was still in their midst, these
questions could simply be brought to him. But without the Prophet,
it became progressively more difficult to ascertain God's will on
issues that far exceeded the knowledge and experiences of a group

of Hijazi tribesmen. At first, the umma naturally turned to the early Companions for guidance and leadership. As the first generation of Muslims, the people who had walked and talked with the Prophet, the Companions had the authority to make legal and religious decisions by virtue of their direct knowledge of Muhammad's life and teachings. They were the living repositories of the hadith, the oral anecdotes recalling the words and deeds of Muhammad.

The hadith, insofar as they addressed issues not dealt with in the Quran, would become a vital tool in the making of Islamic law. However, in their earliest stages, the hadith were muddled and unregulated, making their authentication almost impossible. As the first generation of Companions passed on, the community had to rely increasingly on the reports that the second generation of Muslims had received from the first. When the second generation died, the community was yet another step removed from the actual words and deeds of the Prophet.

In the ninth and tenth centuries, a solid effort was made to sift through the massive accumulation of hadith to separate the reliable from the rest. Nevertheless, for hundreds of years, anyone who had the power and wealth necessary to influence public opinion on a particular issue – and who wanted to justify his own ideas about, say, the role of women in society – had only to refer to a hadith which he had heard from someone, who had heard it from someone else, who had heard it from a Companion, who had heard it from the Prophet. It would be no exaggeration to say that quite soon after Muhammad's death, those men who took upon themselves the task of interpreting God's will in the Quran and Muhammad's will in the hadith – men who were, coincidentally, among the most powerful and wealthy members of the umma – were less concerned with the accuracy of the chains of transmission, or the objectivity of their exegesis, than with regaining the financial and social dominance that the Prophet's reforms had taken from them. As Fatima Mernissi notes, one must remember that behind every hadith lie the power struggles and clashing interests one would expect in a society 'in which social mobility [and] geographical expansion [were] the order of the day'.

Hence, when the Quran warned believers not to 'pass on your wealth and property to the feeble-minded' or *sufaha*, the early Quran commentators – all of them male – declared, despite the Quranic warnings on the subject, that 'the *sufaha* are women and children . . . and both of them must be excluded from inheritance.' When a wealthy and notable merchant from Basra named Abu Bakra (not to be confused with Abu Bakr) claimed, 25 years after Muhammad's death, that he once heard the Prophet say 'Those who entrust their affairs to a woman will never know prosperity', his authority as a Companion was unquestioned. And when Ibn Maja reported in his collection of hadith that the Prophet, in answer to a question about the rights a wife has over her husband, replied rather incredibly that her only right was to be given food 'when you [yourself] have taken your food', and clothed 'when you have clothed yourself', his opinion, though contrary to all the demands of the Quran, went uncontested.

When Abu Said al-Khudri swore he had heard the Prophet tell a group of women, 'I have not seen anyone more deficient in intelligence and religion than you', his memory was unchallenged, despite the fact that Muhammad's biographers present him as repeatedly asking for and following the advice of his wives, even in military matters. Finally, when the celebrated Quranic commentator Fakhr al-din al-Razi (1149–1209) interpreted the verse '[God] created spouses for you of your own kind so that you may have peace of mind through them' (30:21) as 'proof that women were created like animals and plants and other useful things [and not for] worship and carrying the Divine commands . . . because the woman is weak, silly, and in one sense like a child', his commentary became (and still is) one of the most widely respected in the Muslim world.

This last point bears repeating. The fact is that for 14 centuries, the science of Quranic commentary has been overwhelmingly the domain of Muslim men. And because each one of these exegetes inevitably brings to the Quran his own ideology and his own preconceived notions, it should not be surprising to learn that certain verses have most often been read in their most misogynist interpretation. Consider how the following text on the

obligations of men toward women (sura 4:34) has been rendered
into English by two different but widely read contemporary translators of the Quran. The first is from the Princeton edition, translated by Ahmed Ali; the second is from Majid Fakhry's translation,
published by New York University:

> Men are the support of women [*qawwamuna ala an-nisa*] as God
> gives some more means than others, and because they spend of
> their wealth (to provide for them) . . . As for women you feel are
> averse, talk to them suasively; then leave them alone in bed (without
> molesting them) and go to bed with them (when they are willing).

> Men are in charge of women, because Allah has made some of
> them excel the others, and because they spend some of their wealth
> . . . And for those [women] that you fear might rebel, admonish
> them and abandon them in their beds and beat them [*adribuhunna*].

Because of the variability of the Arabic language, both of these
renditions are technically correct. The phrase *qawwamuna ala an-
nisa* can be understood as 'watch over', 'protect', 'support', 'attend
to', 'look after', or 'be in charge of' women. The final word in the
verse, *adribuhunna*, which Fakhry has rendered as 'beat them', can
equally mean 'turn away from them', 'go along with them', and,
remarkably, even 'have consensual intercourse with them'. If religion is indeed based on interpretation, then which meaning one
chooses to accept and follow depends on what one is trying to
extract from the text: if one views the Quran as empowering
women, then Ali's; if one looks to the Quran to justify violence
against women, then Fakhry's.

Throughout Muslim history, there have been a number of
women who have struggled to maintain their authority as both
preservers of the hadith and interpreters of the Quran. Karima
bint Ahmad and Fatima bint Ali are regarded as two of the most
important transmitters of the Prophet's traditions, while Zaynab
bint al-Shari and Daqiqa bint Murshid, both textual scholars, occupied an eminent place in early Islamic scholarship. It is hard to
ignore the fact that nearly one sixth of all 'reliable' hadith can be

traced back to Muhammad's wife Aisha. But celebrated as they are, these women were no match for the authority of early Companions like Umar, the young, brash member of the Quraysh elite whose conversion to Islam was a particular source of pride to Muhammad. The Prophet had admired Umar not just for his physical prowess as a warrior, but for his impeccable moral virtue and the zeal with which he approached his devotion to God. In many ways, Umar was a simple, dignified and devout man. He also had a fiery temper and was prone to anger and violence, especially toward women. So infamous was he for his misogynist attitude that when he asked for the hand of Aisha's sister, he was flatly rebuffed because of his rough behaviour toward women.

Umar's misogynist tendencies were apparent from the moment he ascended to the leadership of the Muslim community. He tried without success to confine women to their homes and wanted to prevent them from attending worship at the mosque. He instituted segregated prayers and, in direct violation of the Prophet's example, forced women to be taught by male religious leaders. Incredibly, he forbade Muhammad's widows to perform the pilgrimage rites and instituted a series of severe penal decrees aimed mainly at women. Chief among these was the stoning to death of adulterers, a punishment that has no foundation at all in the Quran but which Umar justified by claiming it had originally been part of the Revelation, and had somehow been left out of the authorized text. Umar never explained how a verse such as this 'accidentally' could have been left out. Then again, he didn't have to, for he spoke with the authority of an early Companion.

There is no question that the Quran, like all scriptures, was deeply affected by the cultural norms of the society in which it was revealed – a society that did not consider women to be equal members of the tribe. As a result, there are numerous verses in the Quran that, along with the Jewish and Christian scriptures, clearly reflect the weak position of women in the male-dominated societies of the ancient world. But that is precisely the point which the growing Muslim feminist movement has been making over the last century. These women argue that the religious message of the Quran – one of revolutionary social equity – must be separated from the cultural prejudices of seventh-century Arabia. For the first time in history, they are being given the audience necessary to include their views into the male-dominated world of Quranic interpretation.

IV

Just as they reversed many of Muhammad's social reforms aimed at empowering women, the Muslim scriptural and legal scholars of the following centuries rejected the idea that Jews and Christians were part of the umma and instead marked both groups as unbelievers. These scholars read the Revelation to say that the Quran had superseded, rather than added to, the Torah and the Gospels, and called on Muslims to distinguish themselves from the People of the Book. To understand Muhammad's actual beliefs regarding the Jews and Christians of his time, one must look not to the words that chroniclers put into his mouth hundreds of years after his death, but rather to the words that God put into his mouth while he was alive.

The Quran, as a holy and revealed scripture, repeatedly reminds Muslims that what they are hearing is not a new message but the 'confirmation of previous scriptures' (12:111). In fact, the Quran proposes the remarkable idea that all revealed scriptures are derived from a single divine source called the *Umm al-Kitab*, or 'Mother of Books' (13:39). That means that as far as Muhammad understood, the Torah, the Gospels and the Quran must be read as a single narrative about humanity's relationship to God, in which the prophetic consciousness of one prophet is passed spiritually to the next, from Adam to Muhammad. For this reason, the Quran advises Muslims to say to the Jews and Christians:

> We believe in God, and in that which has been revealed to us,
> which is that which was revealed to Abraham and Ismail, Isaac and
> Jacob and the tribes [of Israel], as well as that which the Lord
> revealed to Moses and to Jesus and to all the other Prophets.
> We make no distinction between any of them;
> we submit ourselves to God (3:84).

Muslims believe that the Quran is the final revelation in this sequence of scriptures, just as they believe Muhammad to be 'the Seal of the Prophets'. But the Quran never claims to annul the previous scriptures, only to complete them. While one scripture giving authenticity to others is an extraordinary event in the history of religions, the concept of the *Umm al-Kitab* may indicate an even more profound principle.

As the Quran suggests over and over again, and as the Constitution of Medina clearly affirms, Muhammad may have understood the concept of the *Umm al-Kitab* to mean not only that the Jews, Christians, and Muslims shared a single scripture but also that they constituted a single umma. As far as Muhammad was concerned, the Jews and the Christians were 'People of the Book' (*Ahl al-Kitab*), spiritual cousins who, as opposed to the pagans and polytheists of Arabia, worshipped the same God, read the same scriptures and shared the same moral values as his Muslim community. Although each faith comprised its own distinct religious community (its own individual umma), together they formed one united umma, a concept that Mohammed Bamyeh calls 'monotheistic pluralism'. The Quran promises that 'all those who believe – the Jews, the Sabians, the Christians – anyone who believes in God and the Last Day, and who does good deeds, will have nothing to fear or regret' (5:69).

It was his belief in a unified, monotheistic umma that led Muhammad to link his community to the Jews, not that he felt either the need to emulate the Jewish clans, nor the desire to facilitate their acceptance of him as a prophet. Muhammad aligned his community with the Jews in Medina because he considered them, as well as the Christians, to be part of his umma. When he came to Medina, he made Jerusalem – the site of the Temple (long since destroyed) and the direction in which the diaspora Jews turned during worship – the direction of prayer or *qibla* for all Muslims. He imposed a fast on his community, to take place annually on the 10th day of the first month of the Jewish calendar, the day more commonly known as Yom Kippur. He set the day of Muslim congregation at noon on Friday so that it would coincide with, but not disrupt, Jewish preparations for the Sabbath. He adopted many of the Jewish dietary laws and purity requirements, and encouraged his followers to marry Jews, as he himself did.

Muhammad ultimately changed the *qibla* from Jerusalem to Mecca, and set the annual fast at Ramadan (the month in which the Quran was first revealed) instead of Yom Kippur. However, these decisions should not be interpreted as 'a break with the Jews', but as the maturing of Islam as a religion. Muhammad continued to encourage his followers to fast on Yom Kippur, and he never ceased to venerate Jerusalem as a holy city. Indeed, after Mecca and Medina, Jerusalem is the most sacred city in the Muslim world. Moreover, the Prophet maintained most of the dietary, purity and marriage restrictions he had adopted from the Jews. Until the day he died, Muhammad sought to engage in dialogue, not theological debate, with the Jewish communities of Arabia, just as the Quran commanded him to do: 'Do not argue with the People of the Book – apart from those individuals who act unjustly toward you – unless it is in a fair way' (29:46). Muhammad's example must have had a lasting effect on his early followers. Throughout the first two centuries of Islam, Muslims regularly read the Torah alongside the Quran.

Muhammad understood that there were theological differences between Islam and the other People of the Book. But he saw these differences as part of the divine plan, for God could have created a single umma if he wished to but instead preferred that 'every umma have its own Messenger' (sura 10:47). To the Jews, God sent the Torah, 'which contains guidance and light'; to the Christians, God sent Jesus, who 'confirms the Torah'; and finally, to the Arabs, God sent the Quran, which 'confirms the earlier revelations'. Hence, the differences among the People of the Book are explained as showing God's desire to give each people its own 'law and path and way of life' (5:42–48).

That being said, there were some differences that Muhammad found to be intolerable heresies created by ignorance and error. Chief among these was the idea of the Trinity. 'God is one', the Quran states definitively. 'God is eternal. He has neither begotten anyone, nor is he begotten of anyone' (112:1–3). Yet, this verse, and the many others like it in the Quran, is in no way a condemnation of Christianity but of imperial Byzantine (Trinitarian) Orthodoxy, which was neither the sole nor the dominant Christian position in the Hijaz. From the start of his ministry, Muhammad revered Jesus as among the greatest of God's messengers. Much of the Gospel narrative is recounted in the Quran, though in a somewhat abridged version, including Jesus' virgin birth, his miracles, his identity as Messiah and the expectation of his judgment over humanity at the end of time.

What the Quran does not accept is the belief of those Orthodox Trinitarians who argued that Jesus was himself God. These Christians Muhammad did not even consider to be People of the Book: 'It is the unbeliever who says, "God is the third of three,"' the Quran declares. 'There is only God the One!' (5:73). It was Muhammad's belief that Orthodox Christians had corrupted the original message of Jesus, who the Quran says never claimed divinity and never asked to be worshipped, but rather commanded his disciples to 'worship God, who is my Lord and your Lord' (5:72).

At the same time, Muhammad lashed out at those Jews in Arabia who had 'forsaken the community of Abraham' (2:130) and 'who were trusted with the laws of the Torah, but who fail to observe them' (62:5). Again, this was not a condemnation of Judaism. The reverence that Muhammad had for the great Jewish patriarchs is evidenced by the fact that almost every Biblical prophet is mentioned in the Quran, and Moses nearly 140 times! Rather, Muhammad was addressing those Jews in the Arabian Peninsula, and only there, who had in both belief and practice 'breached their covenant with God' (5:13). If the Jewish clans in Medina were any indication, there were many of them. Muhammad's complaints in the Quran were not directed at Judaism and Christianity, which he considered to be nearly identical to Islam: 'We believe in what has been revealed to us, just as we believe in what has been revealed to you [Jews and Christians]', the Quran says. 'Our God and your God are the same, and it is to Him we submit' (29:46). His grievance was over those Jews and Christians in Arabia who, in his opinion, had forsaken their covenant with God and perverted the teachings of the Torah and Gospels. These were not believers but apostates with whom the Quran warns Muslims not to ally themselves: 'O believers, do not make friends with those who mock you and make fun of your faith ... Instead say to them: "O People of the Book, why do you dislike us? Is it because we believe in God and in what has been sent down to us [the Quran], and what was sent down before that [the Torah and Gospels], while most of you are disobedient?"' (5:57–59).

When Muhammad reminded the Jews of Arabia of the 'favours [God] bestowed on you, making you the most exalted nation in the world' (2:47), when he raged against the Christians for abandoning their faith and confounding the truth of their scriptures, when he complained that both groups 'no longer follow the teachings of the Torah and the Gospel, and what has been revealed to them by their Lord' (5:66), he was merely following in the footsteps of the prophets who had come before him. He was, in other words, Isaiah calling his fellow Jews 'a sinful nation, a people laden with iniquity, offspring of evildoers' (Isaiah 1:4); he was John the Baptist lashing out against 'the brood of vipers' who assumed that their status as 'sons of Abraham' would keep them safe from judgement (Luke 3:7–8); he was Jesus promising damnation for the hypocrites who 'for the sake of tradition, have made void the word of God' (Matthew 15:6). After all, isn't this exactly the message a prophet is supposed to deliver?

The point is that although Muhammad recognised the irreconcilable differences that existed among the People of the Book, he never called for a partitioning of the faiths. On the contrary, to those Jews who say 'the Christians are wrong!' and to those Christians who say 'the Jews are wrong!' and to both groups who claim that 'no one will go to heaven except the Jews and Christians', Muhammad offered a compromise. 'Let us come to an agreement on the things we hold in common', the Quran says, 'that we worship none but God, that we make none God's equal, and that we take no other as lord except God' (3:64).

V

Once Medina was in his control, Muhammad again turned toward Mecca, not as the Messenger of God but as something the Quraysh in their role as Keepers of the Keys could not refuse: a pilgrim. In 628, the year following the Battle of the Trench, Muhammad suddenly announced that he was going to Mecca to perform the pilgrimage rites at the Kaaba. He was in the middle of a bloody and protracted war with the Meccans, and surely the Quraysh, who had spent the past six years trying to kill him, would not simply move out of the way while he and his followers prayed at the sanctuary. But Muhammad was undaunted. With more than a thousand of his followers marching behind him, he crossed the desert on his way to the city of his birth, uttering along the way the pilgrim's chant: 'Here I am, O Allah! Here I am!'

The sound of Muhammad and his followers, unarmed and dressed in pilgrim's clothes, proclaiming their presence to their enemies, must have rung like a death knell in Mecca. Surely the end was near if this man could be so audacious as to think he could walk into the sacred city unmolested. The Quraysh, who rushed out to halt Muhammad before he could enter Mecca, were confounded. Meeting him just outside the city, in a place called Hudaybiyyah, they made one last attempt to preserve their control of Mecca by offering the Prophet a ceasefire, the conditions of which were so against Muhammad's interests that it must have appeared to the Muslims to be a joke.

The Treaty of Hudaybiyyah offered that in return for his immediate withdrawal and the unconditional cessation of all caravan raids around Mecca, Muhammad could return in the following pilgrimage season, when the sanctuary would be evacuated for a brief time so that he and his followers could perform the pilgrimage rites undisturbed. Adding insult to injury, Muhammad would be required to sign the treaty not as the Apostle of God but only as the tribal head of his community. Given Muhammad's rapidly growing position in the Hijaz, the treaty seemed absurd. More than anything, it demonstrated the certainty of Mecca's impending defeat.

It is difficult to say why Muhammad accepted the Treaty of Hudaybiyyah. In any case, the decision to accept the ceasefire and return the year after turned out to be the most decisive moment in the battle between Mecca and Medina. When ordinary Meccans saw the respect and devotion with which their supposed enemy and his band of 'religious zealots' entered their city and circled the Kaaba, there seemed little incentive to continue supporting the war. A year after that pilgrimage, in response to what he regarded as a Quraysh violation of the ceasefire, Muhammad marched again toward Mecca, this time with 10,000 men behind him – only to find the city's inhabitants welcoming him with open arms.

After accepting Mecca's surrender, Muhammad declared a general amnesty for most of his enemies, including those he had fought in battle. Despite the fact that tribal law now made the Quraysh his slaves, Muhammad declared all of Mecca's inhabitants (including its slaves) to be free. Only six men and four women were put to death for various crimes, and no one was forced to convert to Islam, though everyone had to take an oath of allegiance never again to wage war against the Prophet. Among the last to take that oath was Abu Sufyan, the Shaykh of Quraysh, and his wife Hind who, even as she formally converted to Islam stayed defiant, barely masking her disgust with Muhammad and his 'provincial' faith.

When this business was complete, the Prophet made his way to the Kaaba. With the help of his cousin and son-in-law, Ali, he lifted the heavy veil covering the sanctuary door and entered the sacred interior. One by one, he carried the idols out before the assembled crowd and, raising them over his head, smashed them to the ground. The various depictions of gods and prophets were all washed away with water from the well of Zamzam; all, that is, except for the one of Jesus and his mother, Mary. Over this image the Prophet put his hands reverently, saying, 'Wash out all except what is beneath my hands'.

Finally, Muhammad brought out the idol of the great Syrian god, Hubal, who was the chief god of the Kaaba. As Abu Sufyan watched, the Prophet unsheathed his sword and hacked the idol into pieces, forever ending the worship of pagan deities at Mecca.

The remains of Hubal's statue Muhammad used as a doorstep leading up to the new, sanctified Kaaba. That sanctuary would henceforth be known as 'the House of God', the seat of a wholly new and universal faith: Islam.

Further Reading

Aslan, Reza. *No god But God: The Origins, Evolution and Future of Islam.* New York, 2005.

Bamyeh, Mohammed. *The Social Origins of Islam.* Minneapolis, MN, 1999.

Haddad, Yvonne Yazbeck and John L. Esposito, ed. *Islam, Gender, and Social Change.* Oxford, 1998.

Hodgson, Marshall G.S. *The Venture of Islam.* Chicago, 1974, 3 vols.

Lecker, Michael. *Muslims, Jews, and Pagans: Studies on Early Islamic Medina.* Leiden, 1995.

Lings, Martin. *Muhammad: His Life Based on the Earliest Sources.* Rochester, VT, 2006.

Mernissi, Fatima. *The Veil and the Male Elite.* Reading, MA, 1991.

Peters, Rudolph. *Jihad in Classical and Modern Islam.* Princeton, 1996.

Watt, W. Montgomery. *Muhammad: Prophet and Statesman.* Oxford, 1961.

3

Reading the Quran

Abdullah Saeed

'Quran' is an Arabic term which means 'recitation' or 'reading'. It comes from the Arabic root *qaraa*, which is also the root of the first word that the Prophet Muhammad received as revelation: *iqra*, meaning 'recite' or 'read'. Muhammad's role as a prophet began when he was commanded to 'recite'. Although the Quran uses a range of names to refer to itself, the name 'Quran' has become the most common one. Other names used by the Quran to refer to itself include the Revelation (*tanzil*), the Reminder (*dhikr*), the Criterion (*furqan*) or Scripture (*kitab*). The Quran also invokes attributes of itself as Blessed, Clear, Glorious and Noble (as in the widely used phrase 'the Noble Quran').

There are several Quranic verses which indicate that during the time of the Prophet, the Quran came to be conceived of as 'scripture', despite the fact that it had not yet been compiled into a complete written book. As shown above, the Quran often refers to itself as the Book or Scripture (*kitab*). For instance, the Quran says, 'God has sent down the Scripture and Wisdom to you, and taught you what you did not know' (4:113); and 'Now We have sent down to you [people] a Scripture to remind you' (21:10). In fact, the Quran uses *kitab* to refer to itself more than 70 times in various contexts, indicating that the concept of the Quran as a book, or scripture, was well established before the Prophet's death. It was not until the time of the third caliph of Islam, Uthman ibn Affan (r. 644-656), however, that the Quran was compiled as a book.

Structure of the Quran

The Quran is made up of 114 chapters (*suras*) of varying lengths. Each chapter comprises a number of verses (*ayas*), the length of which also varies significantly. Muslim tradition holds that the division of the Quran into *suras* and *ayas* goes back to the instructions provided by Prophet Muhammad himself. Some verses may consist of several sentences, while others may only be a short phrase or, in some cases, a single word. For example, '*al-Rahman*' (the Lord of Mercy) is the first verse of a chapter by the same name. In Arabic, it is one word. By contrast, verse 282 of the second chapter (*al-Baqara*) is longer than many of the Quran's shorter chapters. In English, this verse is over 300 words long; it discusses commercial transactions and the proper nature of a contract.

With the exception of the first chapter, *al-Fatiha* (the Opening), the Quran is generally organised according to the length of its chapters. The first chapter is in the form of a prayer, which is seven verses long and is recited several times by Muslims in their daily prayers (*salat*). In addition to *al-Fatiha*, a Muslim is expected to recite a few other verses of the Quran during prayer. Although not all verses are in the form of prayers – for instance, some are historical and others are ethical or legal in nature – any part of the Quran can be recited during prayer. Here are some examples.

Chapter 1: *al-Fatiha (the Opening)*

> In the name of God, the Lord of Mercy, the Giver of Mercy! Praise belongs to God, Lord of the Worlds, the Lord of Mercy, the Giver of Mercy, Master of the Day of Judgment. It is You we worship; it is You we ask for help. Guide us to the straight path: the path of those You have blessed, those who incur no anger and who have not gone astray.

Starting with the second chapter, *al-Baqara* (the Cow), which is the longest and comprises 286 verses, the chapters of the Quran gradually become shorter. Thus, the shortest chapters, 110, 108 and 103, all appear toward the end of the Quran and comprise only three verses each.

Chapter 97: Laylat al-Qadr (the Night of Glory)

This Meccan *sura* celebrates the night when the Quran was first revealed:

> In the name of God, the Lord of Mercy, the Giver of Mercy.
> We sent it down on the Night of Glory. What will explain to you what that Night of Glory is? The Night of Glory is better than a thousand months; on that night the angels and the Spirit descend again and again with their Lord's permission on every task; [there is] peace that night until the break of dawn.

Each chapter of the Quran has a very short name – in most cases, only one word – which Muslim scholars generally agree was assigned by the Prophet Muhammad under divine instruction. In many cases, this name refers to an issue, event or person found or mentioned in the chapter. 'The Cow' referred to in the name of Chapter 2 (*al-Baqara*) appears in connection with a story of the Prophet Moses and the Israelites. This story relates the response of the Israelites to God's command to sacrifice a cow. The name 'Cow' appears to have been chosen because of the significance of the story rather than its length, as the story comprises only eight out of the 286 verses in the chapter. Although this story is not mentioned elsewhere in the chapter, the theme of disobedience to God's commandments, to which the story relates, is touched on repeatedly.

Chapter 2: al-Baqara (the Cow)

> Remember when Moses said to his people, 'God commands you to sacrifice a cow.' They said, 'Are you making fun of us?' He answered, 'God forbid that I should be so ignorant.' They said, 'Call on your Lord for us, to show us what sort of cow it should be.' He answered, 'God says it should neither be too old nor too

young, but in between, so do as you are commanded.' They said, 'Call on your Lord for us, to show us what colour it should be.' He answered, 'God says it should be a bright yellow cow, pleasing to the eye.' They said, 'Call on your Lord for us, to show us [exactly] what it is; all cows are more or less alike to us. With God's will, we shall be guided.' He replied, 'It is a perfect and unblemished cow, not trained to till the earth or water the fields.' They said, 'Now you have brought the truth,' and so they slaughtered it, though they almost failed to do so (2:67–73).

At other times, the chapter's name may simply be a prominent word found in the chapter, in some cases the first word of the chapter, which may not be related to a particular narrative. For instance, the title of Chapter 36, *Ya-Sin*, comes from the two Arabic letters *ya* and *sin*, with which that chapter begins. Several chapters begin with such combinations of letters, which Muslim commentators believe to have an esoteric meaning.

Ever since it was revealed in the seventh century, Muslims have sought to understand the meaning of the Quran. The great importance placed on this arose from the belief that the Quran is God's Word, as revealed to the Prophet Muhammad in the Arabic language. Muslim laity and scholars have always used their knowledge of Arabic for exegesis – formal and informal interpretations of scripture. By drawing on the Quran, the example of the Prophet and interpretations of earlier generations as well as knowledge of Arabic language, each generation has sought to understand the Quran as it applies to their own context. This is true of Muslims today.

Beginning with the first recipients of the Quran, the Companions of the Prophet, Muslims recognised that it introduced new ideas and terms and also adapted a range of pre-Islamic concepts. This meant that interpretation was needed to clarify the Quran's teachings. It was the Prophet who first undertook this task and provided some insights into understanding the Quran. The interpretation of the Quran has fed the development of the sharia, the body of ethical principles in the text which inspired Muslims to develop a rich and pluralist legal tradition over the ages.

Early Quranic Interpretation

The Quran states that part of the Prophet's mission was to help explain the meanings of the Quran, which he did through words and actions. Although the Prophet's exegesis was highly important, history suggests that he may have verbally explained only small portions of the Revelation to his followers. Since most of the Companions were Arabic-speaking and were familiar with the broader context and meanings of the Quran, an explanation of much of the text would rarely have been required. Nonetheless, there would have been a need for some explanation of verses that expressed new concepts or used certain pre-Islamic terms in new ways, or where there were linguistic difficulties, especially for people who were not familiar with the Arabic dialect of Mecca.

Of the few explanatory comments provided by the Prophet, even fewer were actually recorded. Most of the Prophet's interpretation existed in the form of 'practical exegesis', that is, the Prophet's practical illustration of a specific Quranic term or idea. Fortunately, much of this 'practical exegesis' survived in the memory of the Companions and the practice of the community. A significant amount of this was later recorded in the hadith literature. An example is the Prophet's detailed demonstration of how the five daily prayers were to be performed.

After the death of the Prophet, only a small number of his immediate Companions are reported to have contributed to the new field of Quranic exegesis. Those Companions who engaged in exegesis drew on several sources for understanding and interpreting the Quran, including relevant sections of the Quran itself, oral and practical details received from the Prophet, and their own understanding of the language of the text. They also relied on the traditions of the People of the Book (Jews and Christians), especially in relation to narratives in the Quran about past prophets, peoples and events. Their exegesis remained largely oral and was transmitted through their students.

Islam's first century saw its expansion into what we call today the Middle East and North Africa. It was in the middle of this century that the second generation of Muslims began to grow in number and became significant as contributors to the emerging body of Islamic knowledge. This second generation, known as the Successors, included the children of the first generation as well as a large number of converts to Islam, mainly from Christian and Zoroastrian backgrounds.

The Successors were a much more heterogeneous group than the Companions. Given their different cultural and linguistic backgrounds, and the wider gap between themselves and the time of the Prophet, the community's need for interpretation of the Quran increased. Thus exegesis, though still informal, began to develop on a larger scale, mainly in key centres of learning in Mecca, Medina, Damascus, Yemen and Iraq. Muslims also began to find themselves interacting with the cultural, political and legal practices of the former Byzantine and Sassanid empires, whose lands they had by then conquered. Thus, many began to look to the Quran and its interpretation for guidance in the face of these new social contexts.

The expansion of Islam also resulted in greater interaction between Islam and other religious traditions of the region. Popular preachers and storytellers among Muslims began to fill in details of the stories of past prophets – usually only alluded to in the Quran – by drawing on Jewish and Christian sources. Other Quranic narratives related to early Islamic events, such as the battles between Muslims and their opponents, were also elaborated on, based on accounts of the time. Much of this information became part of early Quranic exegesis and was also used in popular storytelling.

As the Muslim community grew in its first century, interpretation and understanding of the Quran also became increasingly diverse. After the death of the Prophet, divisions among Muslims along religio-political and theological lines also began to emerge. There were heated debates about the extent to which human beings and their actions were free or predetermined, who should be considered a Muslim, and the rightful ruler of the growing Muslim community. The competing parties often used passages from the Quran to argue points. At the same time, Islamic disciplines such as hadith, law, the study of the Prophet's life and Arabic linguistics were also emerging. A basic form of the discipline of Quranic exegesis was beginning to develop. As all these disciplines emerged together, they were each influenced to varying degrees by the social and political environment of the time.

Although most of the earliest forms of Quranic exegesis were transmitted orally, recent research has confirmed that written exegesis had emerged by at least the early part of Islam's second century. The writings from this period did not consist of complete commentaries on the Quran. Initially, these works comprised brief explanatory comments regarding unclear, difficult or ambiguous words and phrases. They also discussed legal and ritual matters, such as how to perform prayer, calculate *zakat* (alms) or perform the pilgrimage, and dealt with certain commandments and prohibitions found in the Quran. In matters where the Quran only provided a general instruction, such as to perform daily prayers, these early exegetical writings tried to provide explanations and fill in the gaps based on the example of the Prophet and the practice of the earliest Muslims.

By the end of this century, works dealing with the entire Quran had emerged, and soon after (that is, by the ninth century in the western calendar) Quranic exegesis was an established discipline. Hence, the body of works became larger and more varied, and included theological, legal, religio-political and mystical writings. Distinct schools of thought within Islam now came to the fore, having matured from their origins in the mid-seventh century. Religio-political groupings such as Sunni, Shia and Khariji had developed their own approaches to legal and theological matters as well as Quranic exegesis.

In Sunni exegesis, the emphasis was on a literal, rather than allegorical reading of the Quran. Many Sunni exegetes have preferred to rely on hadith and exegetical traditions from the earliest Muslims (Companions) rather than adopt a reason-based approach to interpretation. They argue that one has to rely on the earliest authorities to determine what is acceptable and what is not in matters of interpretation. This reflects the high degree of respect bestowed on all Companions, who are considered to be the most important source of religious authority after the Prophet. In general, esoteric or inner meanings of the Quran are rejected as speculation.

An outstanding Sunni exegete was al-Tabari (838-923), whose 30-volume *Jami al-bayan* remains vital for scholars to this day. He approached the Quran from a linguistic standpoint, but made some theological and legal deductions from the text. As a scholar of hadith, law and history, al-Tabari sought to collect and refer to as many relevant hadith (traditional narratives) of the Prophet as possible. He also cited the views of many early Muslim authorities in relation to each Quranic verse.

Shii exegesis, by comparison, favoured a reason-based approach to Quranic interpretation, and stressed the esoteric or inner meaning of the Revelation. Since imams play a central theological role in Shiism, this becomes a defining feature of Shii readings of the Quran. The imams are descendants of the Prophet Muhammad, through his daughter Fatima and cousin and son-in-law Ali (also the fourth caliph after Muhammad) and one of their sons, Husayn or Hassan. While the recognition of the line of imams varies among Shii persuasions or *tariqas*, all regard the imams as inspired and specially equipped to provide proper guidance on the meaning of the Quran, especially with regard to its *batin* or inner meaning. The key exegetical figure was Imam Jafar al-Sadiq (702-756), after whom the main Shii tradition of law (the Jafari school) is named, and whose students included Sunni scholars of the Quran. His interpretive writings available today are more mystical in nature, though there are passages with a specifically Shii perspective.

Khariji exegesis – which represents a very small minority within Islam – is based primarily on a literal reading of the text and rarely considers deeper meanings. It is driven by theological beliefs that have often been described as 'puritanical', with a history of strong condemnation of those who do not share Khariji views of legitimate leadership and personal virtue. The earlier theological ideas are adhered to by a small number of Muslims today, most of whom are descendants of early Kharijis. Most of these descendants now live in Oman and North Africa and are known as 'Ibadis'.

They do not refer to themselves as Kharijis, as they regard this as
a pejorative term used by their opponents.

Several trends in interpretation emerged in the first three
centuries of Islam. Exegetes who were linked with these trends
– theological, legal, mystical and philosophical – were usually
also associated with one of the main branches of Islam (Sunni,
Shia or Khariji). However, labels such as 'theological', 'legal',
'mystical' or 'philosophical' indicate the emphasis of particular
works, not their attachment to the Sunni, Shia or Khariji
branches.

Theological Exegesis

Scholars of theological exegesis were often associated with the two
major theological schools of early Islam: Mutazilis and Asharis.
Some smaller theological schools, such as the Maturidis, also existed,
although their theology did not differ significantly from that of
the larger schools. The Mutazili school emerged first. It is best
known for its uncompromising interpretation of God's unity, and
consequent belief that the Quran is created, as it could not possibly
be co-eternal with God.[1] Other issues which were often addressed
in Mutazili theology included the definition of a true believer and
free will, the status of human beings in the hereafter, the nature
of Paradise and Hell, and God's attributes.

In their exegesis, the Mutazilis relied heavily on linguistic and
literary analysis of texts, particularly when literal readings contra-
dicted Mutazili theological positions. They emphasized rationalist
interpretations and the metaphorical nature of Quranic language,
particularly when it speaks about God. They used philosophical
arguments in defence of their theological positions and rejected
any hadith that conflicted with them.

Although most early Mutazili works are now lost, commentaries of the Quran are believed to have been compiled by scholars
such as Abu Bakr al-Asamm (d. 816) and Abu Ali al-Jubbai

[1] Sabine Schmidtke, 'Mutazila', in Jane McAuliffe, ed., *Encyclopaedia of the
Qur'an* (Leiden, 2001-2006), p. 467.

(849-915). From surviving fragments of al-Asamm's work, it appears that he attempted to produce a comprehensive Quranic theology that dealt with issues of abrogation, and also suggested that both clear and ambiguous verses of the Quran could be understood rationally, the latter merely requiring deeper reflection. In the early 10th century, the Ashari theological school emerged out of the Mutazili tradition. Towards the end of the ninth century, Abu al-Hasan al-Ashari (c. 873-935), the theologian after whom the Ashari school of theology is named, had produced works based on Mutazili theology. He later came to doubt key Mutazili beliefs and broke away from this group, teaching doctrines that denied his Mutazili past.

In addition to strongly questioning the original Mutazili understandings of God's essence and attributes, the Asharis also attacked Mutazili beliefs regarding free will, the nature of divine law, the definition of evil and the role of reason. In time, Ashari theology became the dominant theological school for Sunnis while Mutazili theology remained the dominant theological school for Shiism.

Legal Exegesis

Immediately after the death of the Prophet, there was a pressing need to understand the rulings, commandments, prohibitions and instructions of the Quran as they related to a Muslim's daily life. Thus, legal exegesis was among the first forms of exegesis to emerge. Approaches to legal exegesis varied considerably among early Muslims, and disagreements often arose about the intended meaning of concepts that were addressed in two or more seemingly contradictory verses of the Quran. If such disagreements could not be resolved by a close examination of the text and the context of its revelation, rulings based on later revelations were generally given precedence over earlier ones.

In the eighth and ninth centuries, as the discipline of hadith began to develop, an increasing number of reports of the Prophet's sayings and actions were collected. As the volume of these reports increased, differences in scholarly opinion as to which hadith held more weight also began to emerge. Thus, the Quran became one of the most important aids in determining the authenticity or weight of a given hadith. Despite the use of the Quran, differences in opinions continued to exist and eventually developed into the different classical schools of law: Hanafi, Maliki, Shafii, Hanbali and Jafari. Because of their primary focus on matters of law, these schools are also known as the Islamic legal schools or *madhhabs*.

Jurists from each of these schools produced many works of legal exegesis, many of which are still in circulation today. Scholars of legal exegesis often focused on what appeared to be legal texts of the Quran at the expense of other verses and provided exegesis in the form of legal opinions.

Mystical Exegesis

This type of exegesis is based on ideas that developed among Muslim mystics or Sufis from around the eighth century. Islamic mysticism (or Sufism) is thought to have emerged as a distinct movement around this time in reaction to the wider Muslim community's increasing emphasis on material aspects of life and the growing number of political and factional struggles. Proponents of mystical exegesis emphasised the spiritual aspects of Islam, rather than the political, legal and worldly dimensions. Sufi scholars often preferred to explore questions regarding knowledge of God or the nature of human existence and its relation to the Divine. They believed that the mystical allusions in the Quranic text were related most closely to the human spiritual condition and were impossible to understand through superficial readings or arguments over points of law and theology. Thus, in mystical exegesis, the spiritual and inner meanings of the Quran were considered paramount.

Major scholars from the early period of mystical exegesis include al-Hasan al-Basri (642-728), Jafar al-Sadiq (702-765), Sahl al-Tustari (818-896) and al-Sulami (c. 937-1021). The focus on spirituality in mystical exegesis shows in the titles of many exegetical works, for example *The Spiritual Realities of Exegesis*, written by al-Sulami, and *The Divine Openings and the Secret Keys*, by the Ottoman scholar al-Nakhjuwani (d. 1514). Another well-known mystical exegete was Ibn Arabi (1165-1240), who came from Muslim Spain. Known to Sufis simply as the *Shaykh al-Akbar*, the Greatest Master, Ibn Arabi is widely considered one of the most significant Sufi sages and contributed greatly to the tradition of mystical exegesis.

Philosophical Exegesis

As Muslim interest in Greek philosophical works began to develop in the early centuries of Islam, so too did arguments over the acceptability of philosophy and its place in Islam. While many Muslims argued against the use of philosophy in exegesis, those of a more rationalist orientation wholeheartedly adopted philosophy as a valuable part of the exegetical process. Such scholars preferred an allegorical interpretation of the Quran, as it enabled them to harmonize philosophical ideas more easily with those of the Quran. As such, philosophical interpretations of the Quran, particularly verses related to God, His nature and relationship to creation, and the concepts of Paradise and Hell, tended to differ greatly from more literal readings of Quranic verses.

The renowned Muslim philosopher al-Farabi (870-950) was known to many as the 'second teacher', the first being Aristotle. Although we do not know whether he produced a full commentary of the Quran, his views had a significant influence on philosophical exegesis. Al-Farabi believed that while philosophy had come to an end elsewhere, it had found its place again in the world of Islam. A similarly influential philosopher, Ibn Sina (980-1037), who was also a physician, produced a number of works, including a minor work of exegesis. The use of allegorical interpretation is a distinctive feature of philosophical exegesis of the Quran, and one of its most illustrious examples is the work of the philosopher Ibn Rushd (1126-1198), *The Decisive Treatise Determining the Nature of the Connection between Religion and Philosophy*, where he argues that the Quran and philosophical reasoning do not contradict each other, as both are paths to 'the Truth'.

The Quran in the Contemporary World

While all the above forms of exegesis are studied and used in the modern period, various new forms have also emerged. In response to global developments in politics, ecology, the sciences and ethics, Muslims are among those searching for a balance between traditional and modern ways of being. It is in this environment that new forms of exegetical thinking such as modernist, scientific, socio-political, feminist and thematic have emerged – along with the tussle today between 'contextual' and 'textual' readings of the Quran.

Modernist Exegesis

This form of exegesis is in certain respects a continuation of the Muslim reformist thought of the 18th century; it can also be seen as an active response by Muslims to the challenges posed by modernity while remaining faithful to the teachings of their religion. Among the first 'modernists' were Jamal al-din al-Afghani (1838-1897) and Muhammad Abduh (1849-1905), and scholars of the Indian subcontinent such as Sayyid Ahmad Khan (1817-1898) and Muhammad Iqbal (1877-1938). Since the movement began in the mid-19th century, a large number of scholarly works have been written by modernist scholars. One of the best-known modernist writings is Muhammad Abduh's *Tafsir al-manar*, which was compiled by Rashid Rida (1865-1935), a student of Abduh.

Central to the modernist approach is the idea of reform. Figures such as al-Afghani argued that Muslims should have a reform movement like the ones that had taken place in Christian Europe. Put another way, Muslims needed their own Martin Luther to initiate a major reform of the Islamic heritage. According to these thinkers, the modern context demanded a reappraisal of the intellectual heritage of Muslims; this process required giving up the practice of blind imitation or *taqlid*, which modernists claimed was common among earlier scholars. Other key ideas of modernist exegesis included the need for a flexible interpretation of Islam and its sources in order to develop ideas compatible with modern conditions. In particular, many modernists suggested the need to understand the Quran from a scientific worldview, which required a reinterpretation of Quranic ideas such as miracles.

Modernists proposed that a return to Islam as it was originally practised would inject into Muslim societies the intellectual dynamism required to catch up with the West. For that purpose, political, legal and educational institutions in particular had to be reformed. Part of this reform involved avoiding the use of earlier exegesis that contained too much jargon and had made the Quranic text seem obscure.

Modernist scholars also argued that accepting the concept of revelation did not clash with the use of reason. Thus, they tried to revive Islam's rationalist philosophical tradition, and some previously discounted ideas of the rationalist Mutazilis came into vogue again among some modernist scholars. Other popular topics to have undergone reinterpretation by proponents of modernist exegesis include the status of women, polygamy, war and peace, science, slavery and justice. The following passage demonstrates Muhammad Abduh's views on polygamy.

> Polygamy, although permitted in the Quran, is a concession to necessary social conditions which was given with the greatest reluctance, in as much as it is accompanied by the provision that a man may take more than one wife only when he is able to take equal care of all of them and give to each her rights with impartiality and justice. The sharia has, in requirement of circumstances, permitted the legality of four contemporaneous marriages with great reluctance. Since the proviso immediately following – if you fear that you cannot be equitable and just with all then (marry) only one – is given so much stress that [sic] the permission to contract four contemporaneous marriages becomes practically ineffective.[2]

---

[2] Muhammad Abduh, *Tarikh al-ustad al-imam*, vol. 2, *Egypt: Matbaat al-manar* (1906), quoted in Asghar Ali Engineer, *The Rights of Women in Islam* (London, 1992), p. 157.

Scientific Exegesis

This type of exegesis has been particularly influential in the 20th century, although its precursors can be found in the pre-modern period. For instance, the classical scholar al-Ghazali (1058-1111) could be described as an early proponent of 'scientific exegesis'. This is reflected in his description of the Quran as being the ocean from which all sciences emerged.

Similarly, early forms of scientific exegesis in the 20th century attempted to reconcile Quranic teachings with scientific knowledge. Today, scientific exegesis has come to be related to the idea that the Quran predicted many of the findings of modern science. The popular nature of this discourse is demonstrated by the large number of conferences, seminars and publications devoted to it. There are some Muslim thinkers, however, who criticize it for ignoring the open-ended nature of scientific discovery and as misreading the Quran. Notwithstanding these criticisms, scientific exegesis has become one of the most popular forms of exegesis in the modern period.

One of the most widely circulated works in this genre is by the French writer Maurice Bucaille. Bucaille provided a scientific reading of a number of Quranic verses that appear to have some relationship to science. For instance, in his discussion of the expansion of the universe, one of the most important discoveries of modern science, he cites the verse 'We built the heavens with Our power and We are expanding it' (51:47). Bucaille suggests that this verse can be linked to modern scientific understandings of the beginning of the universe. He goes on to provide an interpretation of two key phrases from this verse:

'Heaven' is the translation of the word *sama* and this is exactly the extra-terrestrial world that is meant. '[We] are expanding it' is the translation of the plural present participle *'musiuna'* of the verb *ausaa* meaning 'to make wider, more spacious, and extend, to expand'. Some translators who were unable to grasp the meaning of the latter provide translations that appeared to me to be mistaken…there are those who armed themselves with authorized scientific opinion in the commentaries and give the meaning stated here [the expansion of the universe in totally unambiguous terms].[3]

Commenting on scientific exegesis, Mustansir Mir, a modern scholar of the Quran, observes that this form of exegesis has risen out of a need to counter the challenge that modern science poses for all religions. Mir states:

> The project of establishing compatibility (*muwafaqah*) between the Divine Word and scientific findings is, by definition, defensive in character. Muslim thinkers first engaged in a similar exercise in *muwafaqah* during the Abbasid period, when they felt constrained to reconcile Greek thought with Islamic religion. The arena of discussion at that time was theology; today, it is science, but the nature of the exercise is essentially the same. The challenge that modern science initially posed to Christianity has now been posed to all religions – to the very idea of religion itself. Muslims naturally feel the force of the challenge, whether or not they understand its exact nature, and some of them think that it would be an adequate defence of Islam to demonstrate that there is no conflict between the Quran and science or, going a step further, that the Quran prefigures modern science.[4]

Socio-political Exegesis

Another modern approach to the Quran, known as 'socio-political exegesis', was developed by the Egyptian scholar, Sayyid Qutb (1906-1966). Qutb was a leader of the Muslim Brotherhood, one of the political Islamic movements of the 20th century. He remains a major source of inspiration for those who seek a closer connection between Islam and the state.

Qutb's approach to exegesis was highly political and many of his positions were controversial. Among his arguments was a

---

[3] Maurice Bucaille, *The Bible, The Qur'an and Science* (Indianapolis, 1979), p. 167.

[4] Mustansir Mir, 'Scientific Exegesis of the Qur'an – A Viable Project?', *Islam & Science*, 5 (2004), p. 33.

suggestion that many aspects of modern society were *jahili* (akin to pre-Islamic 'ignorance': the state of the Arabs before the emergence of Islam in the seventh century). He also uncompromisingly argued that Islam should be the guiding and dominant political force in nations with majority Muslim populations.

In his reading of one of the earliest Quranic chapters, 'Say [Prophet], "Disbelievers, I do not worship what you worship, you do not worship what I worship; I will never worship what you worship, you will never worship what I worship; you have your religion and I have mine"' (109:1–5), Qutb says in his work, *In the Shade of the Qur'an*:

> *Ignorance* is nothing but *Ignorance* and Islam is altogether different from it. The only way to bridge the gulf between the two is for *Ignorance* to liquidate itself completely and substitute for all its laws, values, standards and concepts their Islamic counterparts.
>
> The first step that should be taken in this field by the person calling on people to embrace Islam is to segregate himself from *Ignorance*....[A]ny agreement or intercourse between him and *Ignorance* is absolutely impossible unless and until the people of *Ignorance* embrace Islam completely; no intermingling, no half measures or conciliation is permissible....The chief basis of the personality of the person inviting others to Islam is... his solemn conviction of being radically different from them.... His task is to orientate them so that they may follow his path without any fraud or pretence. Failing this, he must withdraw completely, detach himself from their life and openly declare to them: 'You have your own religion, and I have mine.'[5]

Thematic Exegesis

A thematic method of enquiry emphasizes the unity of the Quran. It approaches interpretation as a study of the Quran as a whole.

---

[5] Sayyid Qutb, *In the Shade of the Qur'an* (1954), tr. M.A. Salahi and A.A. Shamis (London, 1979), p. 331.

This method allows an interpreter to identify all verses related to a particular theme, gather them and then study and compare them. Examples of themes might be women, trade and commerce, war, tolerance, People of the Book or the poor. Proponents of this method argue that it allows for a more objective approach to the Quran.

Prominent scholars of thematic exegesis include the Iranian Ayatollah Murtaza Mutahhari (1920-1979) and the Egyptian writer Abbas Mahmud al-Aqqad (1889-1964), both of whom have written on themes such as society and history, women's rights and fundamental liberties. The Pakistani scholar Fazlur Rahman (1919-1988) was also a proponent of this type of exegesis, as shown in his work *Major Themes of the Qur'an* (1994). This style of Quranic exegesis is particularly popular in Egypt and Indonesia.

Feminist Exegesis

Over the second half of the 20th century, the body of Muslim feminist exegesis grew considerably. Most feminist exegetes criticize traditional male-centred interpretations of the Quran, arguing that the gender biases of predominantly male exegetes have, until now, largely shaped our understandings of the Quran and Islam more generally. In contrast to secularist feminists, Muslim feminist scholars do not reject Islam itself. Instead, they refer to the Quran and the Prophet's Sunna to support their claim that the Quran needs to be reinterpreted. Some major scholars of feminist exegesis include Fatima Mernissi, Amina Wadud and Asma Barlas. Their ventures into this once taboo field of exegesis have met with staunch opposition from traditionalist scholars, men and women alike.

One example of such exegesis is that of Asma Barlas who has focused much of her scholarly work on examining the ways in which Muslims 'interpret and live' the teachings of the Quran. In particular, she has produced a number of works examining the origins of patriarchal Quranic exegesis. Barlas argues that ideas of inequality and patriarchy were read into the Quran in order to justify existing social structures. In her book *'Believing Women' in*

Islam: Unreading Patriarchal Interpretations of the Qur'an (2002), Barlas re-examines a number of these issues and suggests that the teachings of the Quran do not support patriarchy, but are highly egalitarian. She has also proposed that it is necessary to avoid 'masculinising' God, and that it is the right of every Muslim to read and interpret the Quran for themselves.

Although Barlas' work has been referred to by some as 'Islamic feminism', she prefers not to be referred to as a feminist and describes herself as 'a believer'. Given that Barlas does not seek to question the divine origin of the Quran, reactions to her work have not been as negative as those towards some other modern feminist scholars. That said, certain aspects of Barlas' work remain controversial, and her suggestions have not always been well received by many Muslims.

Text and Context

Much of Quranic scholarship in our time is based on a textualist approach – which also dominated exegesis in the pre-modern period. Textualist scholars interpret the Quran by relying mainly on linguistic rather than social or historical resources. Scholars who adopt this approach believe that the language of the Quran has concrete, unchanging references, and hence the meaning that a verse had at the time of revelation must hold for today. For most textualists, the meaning of the Quran is fixed: Muslims must adapt to this meaning.

The scholarship of contextualists is generally linked to Islamic reform. In comparison to textualist approaches, the contextualists have a more nuanced way of finding 'meaning' in the Quran – though the details of this approach will often vary among scholars. A common feature is that they see the meaning of a particular Quranic verse as in large part indeterminate. Meaning, in this sense, is said to evolve over time, and depends on the socio-historical, cultural and linguistic contexts of the text. This approach allows a scholar to consider a given word in the light of its setting, and to arrive at an understanding which is felt to be more sensitive to the circumstances of the text.

Contextualists further argue that it is difficult to arrive at a truly 'objective' meaning, and that subjective factors will always intervene in our understandings. That is, interpreters cannot approach the text without the experiences, values, beliefs and assumptions that influence their own understanding.

Modern contextualist scholars have sought in particular to engage with the ethical and legal teachings that can be derived from the Quran. From a contextualist perspective, the Quran is not considered to be a book of laws, but one which contains ideas and principles that can be applied over changing times and places. In order to arrive at these ideas and principles, a contextualist study of the Quran requires both narrow and broad settings of the Quran to be defined. A broad definition of context allows a single verse to be compared to the overall intention and context of the text, which includes not only the Quran itself, but also the life story of the Prophet Muhammad. In seeking to understand the narrow context, a study must consider what appears directly before and after the verse in question, and also the exact words of the verse itself.

Farid Esack, a South African Muslim scholar, has suggested that 'receiving a text and extracting meaning from it do not exist on their own', and so meaning is always partial. In his work *Qur'an: Liberation and Pluralism* (1997), Esack says that the discipline of hermeneutics – the 'science' of interpreting and explaining scripture – began to influence Islamic scholarship in the 20th century, and he argues for a Muslim 'hermeneutic of liberation' as the way forward. This idea will be reflected in the profiles below of key Muslim scholars of the Quran today. These profiles will also show that hermeneutics is linked to reformist and 'liberal' scholarship in Islamic thought. Such ideas directly confront the assertions of Muslim textualists, who do not assign any significant role to the reader in the identification of meaning.

Fazlur Rahman

Fazlur Rahman is best known for his contribution to modern discussions of reform in Islamic thought. He wrote on a wide range of subjects, including Islamic education, interpretation of the Quran, hadith criticism, early development of Islamic intellectual traditions and the reform of Islamic law and ethics.

Rahman was born in Pakistan in 1919, and spent most of his adult life studying and teaching in Pakistan, the United Kingdom, Canada and the USA. While living in England he wrote his dissertation at Oxford University on Ibn Sina and subsequently taught Islamic philosophy at Durham University. He then moved to Canada where he taught at McGill University's Institute of Islamic Studies. He returned to Pakistan to teach and then served as director of the Islamic Research Institute. From 1961 to 1968, while at the Institute, Rahman advised the president, General Ayyub Khan, on how Pakistan could best steer a middle path between modernist and traditionalist Islam.

During his time in Pakistan, Rahman was criticised by those who wanted to maintain the dominant socio-religious practices of the time. When this criticism led to death threats, he sought safety abroad. Rahman took up the position of Professor of Islamic Thought at the University of Chicago, a position he held until his death in 1988. One of Rahman's students at the University of Chicago was Nurcholish Madjid, a Muslim scholar who went on to become a leading Indonesian intellectual and played a major role in broadening Islamic studies and developing Islamic liberalism and democracy in Indonesia.

Rahman's methodology has been applied by scholars in areas such as women's rights, as is evident in the writing of the American scholar Amina Wadud. Although Rahman spent a large part of his life in the West, he remained an avowedly Muslim scholar, committed to reaching and influencing a Muslim audience. Similarly, although he served as an advisor to General Ayyub Khan, Rahman was active mainly in academia and did not pursue direct influence over a political movement.

For Rahman, a primary purpose of the Quran was to create a society based on justice. He saw the Prophet Muhammad as a social reformer who sought to empower the poor, weak and vulnerable. Thus he viewed the Quran as a source from which ethical principles could be derived, not a book of laws. One of the aims

of his scholarship was to help foster a society without exploitation of the weak. In this regard he says,

> [T]he implementation of the Quran cannot be carried out *liter-*
> *ally* in the context of today because this may result in thwarting
> the very purposes of the Quran, and that, although the findings
> of the *fuqaha* [jurists] or the *ulama* [scholars] of Islam during the
> past thirteen centuries or so should be seriously studied and given
> due weight, it may well be found that in many cases their find-
> ings were either mistaken or sufficed for the needs of that society
> but not for today.[6]

Rahman argued that the practice of family law in Islamic history
had not accorded females the equal rights to which they appear
to be entitled, based on the Prophet's example and teachings of
the Quran:

> The Quran insistently forbids the male [from] exploit[ing] the
> female on the strength of his stronger position in society, and Islam
> set[s] into motion the whole complex of measures – legal and
> moral – whereby sex exploitation would be completely eradicated.
> It forbade the recourse to polygamy under normal circumstances,
> allowed the woman to own and earn wealth, declared her to be
> an equal partner in the society – noting and allowing for the disad-
> vantages she had in the society of that age. It laid down the basis
> of matrimonial life to be mutual love and affection, and that spouses
> were like garments unto each other. It strictly regulated the law of
> divorce.[7]

Rahman's emphasis on context has had a far-reaching influence on contemporary Muslim debates on human rights and
social justice. Despite some criticisms, Rahman's approach is
increasingly being adopted by Muslims in their attempts to relate

---

[6] Fazlur Rahman, 'The Impact of Modernity on Islam', *Journal of Islamic
Studies*, 2, (1966), pp. 112-128, at p. 127.

[7] Fazlur Rahman, 'The Impact of Modernity on Islam', p. 111.

the Quran to contemporary needs, and it will likely continue to be influential among today's Muslim intellectuals. His argument for recognition of subjective elements in Quranic interpretation foreshadows the recent scholarship of figures like Amina Wadud and Khaled Abou El Fadl.

Amina Wadud

Amina Wadud is an African-American scholar of Quranic exegesis and gender. In 1992 she produced her first book, a Muslim feminist work of exegetical principles of the Quran entitled *Qur'an and Woman: Rereading the Sacred Text from a Woman's Perspective* (1999). The book was endorsed by a number of Arabic-speaking feminists, and included controversial ideas such as the need to use more gender-neutral language in understanding the Quran.

Wadud was born into a Methodist family in 1952 in Maryland, USA. While growing up, she felt like an outsider by virtue of both her ethnicity and gender. A fellow scholar of Islamic feminism, Asma Barlas, writes, 'If race is what defined her in the eyes of her White peers, gender is what seems to have defined her in the eyes of her Black ones.'[8] When she was at university, the 20-year-old Wadud decided to become a Muslim. According to Barlas, Wadud's position as an African American, and thus 'Western', convert to Islam has enabled her to engage with Islam with a 'specific consciousness shaped by her identity'. Wadud gained her PhD in Islamic studies from the University of Michigan in 1988 and at the time of writing is teaching at the Virginia Commonwealth University.

Wadud has a controversial position in Islamic thought today. A strong advocate of gender equality, she is considered to belong to the 'feminist' movement within Islam. She is perhaps most widely known for having delivered a Friday sermon in South Africa in 1994, and more recently for her controversial leading of

---

[8] Asma Barlas, 'Amina Wadud's Hermeneutics of the Qur'an: Women Rereading Sacred Texts', p. 99 in S. Taji-Farouki, ed., *Modern Muslim Intellectuals and the Qur'an* (London, 2006), pp. 97-123.

a group of men and women in Friday prayers in 2005, acting as the imam or prayer leader. This event was commented on internationally and led to *fatwas* insisting that leadership in prayer is for Muslim men only when both men and women are in congregation.

Wadud's belief that the Quran liberates and empowers women has fuelled her 'gender jihad'. She has criticized some common Muslim narratives as erroneous, like the claim that woman was created from man and is thus a secondary creature. She finds no Quranic support for this, and cites verses such as sura 4:1 in support of her argument for gender equity: 'People, be mindful of your Lord, who created you from a single soul, and from it created its mate, and from the pair of them spread countless men and women far and wide.'

Wadud emphasises that the Quran does not 'assign responsibility for the expulsion of this pair [Adam and Eve] from Paradise to the woman'. She also says that the Quran places men and women on the same level; the only basis for differentiation among human beings, both women and men, is their degree of 'God-consciousness' (*taqwa*). Wadud does not consider the verses which deal with polygamy to be evidence of the subordination of women to men. Instead, she considers the key teaching of the Quran to be about justice in dealings, managing funds and relating to orphans and wives.

Her contribution to the study of the Quran has been summarized by Asma Barlas as follows:

> Wadud's critique of traditional *tafsir* is meant not only to reveal the flaws in patriarchal readings of the Quran, but also to get Muslims to realize what is at stake in rethinking their textual strategies, in devising new interpretative methods, and in including women in the processes of knowledge creation. She believes this will not only allow the women to develop a more authentic Muslim identity, but also will reflect 'new levels of understanding and human participation' in religious life.[9]

---

[9] Asma Barlas, 'Amina Wadud's Hermeneutics of the Qur'an'.

Mohamad Shahrour

Mohamad Shahrour was born in 1938 in Damascus, Syria. A civil engineer and self-taught scholar of Islam, Shahrour has written extensively on Islam and the Quran. As an outsider by profession, he argues that contemporary Muslims need to reconsider and question Islam's holy books, an idea which he expresses in a major work, *The Book and the Quran* (1990). Shahrour has been influenced by a wide range of intellectuals, from those as early as the Muslim philosopher al-Farabi, to the philosopher of 'German idealism', Johann Gottlieb Fichter, and the English mathematician and philosopher, Alfred North Whitehead.

Shahrour argues that because of developments in science, scholars today are better placed than those in the past to understand the 'divine will'. As such, Shahrour seeks to create a new framework and methodology for understanding the Quran, and to this end has created his own categories for approaching the Quran. Andreas Christmann writes that Shahrour wants his readers to understand the Quran 'as if the Prophet has just died and informed us of this book', thus approaching the Quran as if reading it for the first time.[10]

Shahrour's books have attracted much criticism. The response to his work has been often negative, whether for its alleged naïveté or its political implications. Shahrour has responded to these criticisms by claiming that such comments are an easy way of avoiding the discussion he is trying to initiate. Still, Shahrour's insistence that studies or readings of the Quran should be informed by developments in the social and natural sciences, philosophy and linguistics finds wide resonance in reformist circles today.

---

[10] Andreas Christmann, "'The Form is Permanent, but the Content Moves": The Qur'anic Text and its Interpretation(s) in Mohamad Shahrour's *al-Kitab wal-Qur'an*', in S. Taji-Farouki, ed., *Modern Muslim Intellectuals and the Qur'an*, pp. 263-295.

Mohammed Arkoun

Mohammed Arkoun was born in Algeria in 1928 and is culturally Berber, French and Arab. After studying in Algeria, he gained a PhD from the Sorbonne in Paris. Arkoun is now widely known as a pioneering scholar of contemporary Islamic thought. He is credited with broadening the discipline of Islamic studies by borrowing and developing ideas from sources not generally associated with Islamic studies. This is evident in one of his major works, *The Unthought in Contemporary Islamic Thought* (2000).

Arkoun went to the Sorbonne just before Algeria's independence, and there his intellectual development was enriched by the general changes that the humanities were experiencing during the 1950s and 1960s. Arkoun's thinking was also inspired by his research on the Persian intellectual and Islamic 'humanist' Miskawayh (932-1030) and his study of Arab humanism of the 10th century, which was also the subject of his PhD thesis.

A key element of Arkoun's thinking is his questioning of Islamic orthodoxy, and his view that it amounts to an ideology, one that is linked to the state. Traditionalist scholars show little respect for Arkoun, due to his secularist approach to analysis of the Quran and the apparent influence on his work of intellectuals like Derrida, Baudrillard and Foucault. He is also criticised by some for his complex and often elusive language and a lack of systematisation.

Ursula Günther argues that Arkoun's humanist thinking displays the qualities of a rhizome, an idea closely associated with post-modernist thought. Günther states:

> [The rhizome] symbolises a shift of paradigm that has already occurred at different levels of modern life. It stands for integrity, wholeness and plurality in contrast to dualism, decomposition and particularism ... In this respect Arkoun's approach bears features of postmodernism.[11]

---

[11] Ursula Günther, 'Mohammed Arkoun: Towards a Radical Rethinking of Islamic Thought', in S. Taji-Farouki, ed., *Modern Muslim Intellectuals and the Qur'an*, pp. 125-167.

Khaled Abou El Fadl

Khaled Abou El Fadl was born in Egypt in 1958. He is a leading scholar of Islamic law and a traditionally trained Muslim jurist. Abou El Fadl is presently a law professor at the University of California. Although widely viewed as a respected scholar, his attacks on some movements within Islam – in particular 'Wahhabism', which he sees as an ideology – have led to numerous death threats. He is especially critical of the harsh Wahhabi restrictions on women. He has argued against the idea of the compulsory wearing of the veil (hijab), and speaks out strongly against cultural practices that make women occupy subordinate positions in society. For him such practices strike at the core of what it means to be a Muslim.

One of Abou El Fadl's major works is *Speaking in God's Name: Islamic Law, Authority and Women* (2001). It asks about the role of the 'authoritative' reader of religious texts, challenging the way in which self-proclaimed 'scholars' of the Quran assume the role of God. He argues that in many cases they displace God's authority, 'an act of despotism'. Abou El Fadl highlights the importance of focussing on the interaction between the author of the Quran (God) and the reader, and the authoritative reader's responsibility, by virtue of this special position as interpreter of the text, to act as a faithful 'agent' for the 'principal' (God). In seeking to clarify the position of the reader in understanding the Quran, Abou El Fadl proposes questions such as:

To what extent are my sensibilities and subjectivities determinative in constructing the text's meaning? May I or should I submit the text to my use, and permit my needs to be determinative in constructing a meaning for the text? If the peculiarities of the reader are determinative, what then happens to the intent of the author? Should the reader focus on the intent of the author and consider the author's intent determinative as to the meaning of the text? Isn't this more respectful towards the author, especially when the author is divine? But how can the intent of the author be ascertained if the author's motives are not accessible?

The framing of a debate in this way is clearly an attack on those who 'speak in God's name' by claiming the authenticity and infallibility of 'literalist' or 'textualist' approaches.

Like Arkoun, Abou El Fadl also promotes the idea that there are many possible interpretations of the Quran. However, Abou El Fadl argues that the idea of, for instance, a 'European Islam' that is somehow different from Islam in general is superfluous, as the classical sources of Islam provide sufficient basis and flexibility with which to engage with the issues of Muslims living in the West as minorities. For him, Islamic theology and law have all that a Muslim needs in a secular, pluralist and democratic society – including pluralism, tolerance and ethical participation in public life.

Indeed, Abou El Fadl sees the ideas and methods of postmodernism as coming from the social context and historical experiences of the West, and thus as not being particularly relevant to contemporary Islamic thought. He suggests that Muslim scholars and interpreters of the Quran should use an approach that is rooted in the traditions of Islam and the Muslim experience. Yet his strong criticisms of the puritanical elements that impose a rigid orthodoxy on Quranic exegesis tie him to movements which have developed in connection with postmodernism. Unlike Arkoun and Shahrour, however, Abou El Fadl's criticism of conservative scholars is firmly grounded in Islamic jurisprudential methodology.

Abdolkarim Soroush

Born in Iran in 1945, Soroush, whose real name is Hosein Dabbagh, is considered to be one of the most influential Muslim thinkers today. His writings cover Quranic hermeneutics, philosophy, Persian literature, ethics and political theory. A selection of his work has been published in *Reason, Freedom, and Democracy in Islam* (2002).

Soroush studied science in Iran before leaving for London to pursue his doctoral work in chemistry. In London he was active in the opposition to the then Shah of Iran. After the 1979 revolution, he returned to Iran and held various jobs in government and academia. In the 1990s he increasingly became critical of the political establishment, which led to an increase in his following and also to restrictions on his freedom. Since 2000 he has been teaching in major Western universities including Princeton, Harvard and Yale.

Soroush has played a pivotal role in reformist movements in Iran. His learning has drawn on the fields of jurisprudence, history of ideas, hermeneutics, epistemology, the philosophy of science and the sociology of knowledge. Soroush has argued that over the course of the Prophet's mission, he became better at conveying the words of God and fulfilling his role as prophet.

Among his key ideas is that knowledge is not static and all areas of knowledge are always in a state of change and transformation; each area of knowledge impacts other areas leading to changes in all areas of knowledge. In the Islamic context, no field is immune to this. Thus, permanence cannot be attributed to areas of knowledge like Islamic law. The same applies to Quranic exegesis. Soroush believes that Quranic exegesis and law are also in a state of change and transformation. The discipline and the views and opinions expressed in it are not final and may require ongoing refinement and improvement. He proposes a number of new ideas for engaging with such areas of knowledge today,

> [I]t is the religious understanding that will have to adjust itself to democracy, not the other way around; justice, as a value, cannot be religious. It is religion that has to be just. Similarly, methods of limiting power are not derived from religion, although religion benefits from them ... [I]n a religious society, it is not religion per se that arbitrates, but some understanding of religion which is, in turn, changing, rational, and in harmony with the consensual and accepted extra-religious criteria.[12]

The Quran is the foundational text of Islam and from the very beginning has been at the centre of Islamic thought, ethics and

---

[12] Mahmoud Sadri and Ahmad Sadri, ed., *Reason, Freedom and Democracy in Islam: The Essential Writings of Abdolkarim Soroush* (Oxford, 2000), pp. 131-132.

law. Its guidance was instrumental in the development of legal schools, theological schools as well as mystical orders. Indeed, the vitality of the Quran is expressed through its interpretation. Scholars of different persuasions have always found in the Quran the necessary guidance and principles for their thought, be it legal, theological, political or ethical and moral. While the text remains the same, its interpretation provides a multiplicity of voices and displays a range of approaches to understanding its meaning.

Quranic interpretation has always been one of the most versatile of disciplines. In the contemporary struggles for 'authenticity', Quranic exegesis is at the forefront of debate. Some scholars wish to maintain pre-modern readings of the Quran, in a vein that tends to equate the everlasting truths of revelation with 'traditional' ways of interpretation. Fresh approaches to exegesis are seen as challenging the authority of the latter – which is easier to defend by claiming that it is the truths rather than human readings that are at stake.

For scholars such as Fazlur Rahman and Soroush, the Quran speaks to contemporary societies in ways that require dynamic readings. Their approaches show an appreciation of the historicity of the revelation, which is not to say that they have abandoned belief in the divine origins of the text. Again, Sufi or mystical exegesis in both Shia and Sunni traditions has always challenged literal readings of the Quran in favour of deeper quests. It is easy to forget this enduring plurality of approaches when the claims of authority and truth take a militant turn that dominates the headlines.

Further Reading

Arkoun, Mohammed. *Rethinking Islam: Common Questions, Uncommon Answers*, ed. and tr. Robert D. Lee. Boulder, Colorado, 1994.

Berg, Herbert. *The Development of Exegesis in Early Islam: The Authenticity of Muslim Literature from the Formative Period.* London, 2000.

Calder, Norman, Jawid Mojaddedi and Andrew Rippin, ed. and tr. *Classical Islam: A Sourcebook of Religious Literature*. London & New York, 2003.

Esack, Farid. *Qur'an, Liberalism and Pluralism*. Oxford, 1997.

Rahman, Fazlur. *Islam and Modernity: Transformation of an Intellectual Tradition*. Chicago, 1982.

Saeed, Abdullah. *Interpreting the Qur'an*. London, 2005.

—— *The Qur'an: An Introduction*. London, 2007.

Stowasser, Barbara Freyer. *Women in the Qur'an, Traditions, and Interpretation*. New York, 1994.

Taji-Farouki, Suha, ed. *Modern Muslim Intellectuals and the Qur'an*. London, 2004.

Versteegh, C.H.M. *Arabic Grammar and Qur'anic Exegesis in Early Islam*. Leiden, 1993.

4

Islam in the Plural

Amir Hussain

It is hard to talk in public about religion these days, and that certainly goes for pluralism. One is readily tempted to think of pluralism as implying an 'anything goes' attitude, which aims to mix all religions into one – a form of moral relativism. My own view of pluralism is shaped by the experience of being a Muslim academic in North America, involved in interfaith dialogue at local, national and international levels for over two decades. My appreciation of pluralism as a scholar of Muslim communities owes much to thinkers such as Wilfred Cantwell Smith and Diana Eck, who have championed the necessity of thinking deeply about religious pluralism. In her book *A New Religious America* (2001), Diana Eck identifies three important themes about pluralism:

1. Pluralism is not simply the same thing as diversity. People from different religious and ethnic backgrounds may be present in one place, but unless they are involved in an active engagement with one another, there is no pluralism. In other words, pluralism is not and cannot be a non-participant sport.

2. The goal of pluralism is not simply 'tolerance' of others, but rather an active attempt to arrive at an understanding. The very language of tolerance in fact keeps us from the type of engagement we are speaking of here. One can tolerate a neighbour about whom one remains thoroughly ignorant. That stance, while no doubt preferable to outright conflict, is still far from genuine pluralism.

3. Pluralism is not the same thing as relativism. Far from simply
   ignoring the profound differences among religious traditions,
   a genuine pluralistic perspective would be committed to
   engaging the very differences that we have, to gain a deeper
   sense of each other's commitments.[1]

Issues of pluralism and interfaith dialogue are of crucial importance to Muslims. After all, the diversity of Islam in matters of
law, ritual and theology is a reality in Muslim societies the world
over. Moreover, Islam is emerging as the second largest religious
tradition in a number of European and North American countries. In those settings, amid a plurality of belief systems, Muslims
have a responsibility to articulate their understanding and practice of Islam in its many expressions. The events of September 11,
2001, have underscored the urgency of that need. As Muslims, we
can help in the making of a world in which it is safe to be human.

Our discussion here will begin with Muslim thought and practice in inter-religious relations during the lifetime of the Prophet
Muhammad before moving to a broad survey of how this has
unfolded in the course of history. Then, I will situate those reflections in present-day settings, drawing upon my own experience
as mentioned at the outset. Mindful that this volume is intended
for non-specialists in the study of Islam or religion, I shall try to
avoid using jargon or theoretical models (which can be found in
some of the suggested readings at the end of this chapter).

Foundations

Islam began as a minority tradition in a non-Muslim setting. When
the Prophet Muhammad received his first revelations in Mecca in
610, the people around him were largely tribal and polytheistic.
Even though the people of Mecca knew of Christianity, Judaism,
Zoroastrianism and other religious traditions, large concentrations

---

[1] See Diana Eck, *A New Religious America: How a Christian Country Has
Now Become the World's Most Religiously Diverse Nation* (San Francisco,
2001).

of Christians or Jews were only to be found in other cities in Arabia. As with any new religious tradition, Islam would not have developed had it not been for interfaith dialogue. After Muhammad received his revelations, he began to speak about them publicly, first to his own family and then to other people.

The Quran, as the revelations to Muhammad from God came to be called, assumed that the first hearers of the revelation were familiar with the stories of Judaism and Christianity. For example, a verse in the Quran begins, 'Recite to them in truth the story of the two sons of Adam' (5:27). The implication is that the hearers are already familiar with aspects of the story, but that the Quran affirms and represents, and at times modifies, the previous versions of narratives. Another example is the mention of Gabriel and Michael in the context of angels and prophets (2:98). The verse does not specify that Gabriel and Michael are angels and not prophets, but assumes that the hearers are familiar with the Jewish and Christian traditions around them. A third example is the Quranic account of Joseph, referred to as 'the most beautiful of stories' (12:3), and the longest sustained narrative in the Quran. It does not go into detail about the family background of Joseph, but it does speak of Joseph being sold into slavery by his brothers out of jealousy. Presumably, the first hearers of this revelation were familiar with the story in the book of Genesis about Joseph and Benjamin – who are sons of Jacob and his wife Rachel, while the other brothers have different mothers. A fourth example is found in a verse about Jesus: 'And God said: "O Jesus, I am gathering you and causing you to ascend unto Me, and cleansing you of those who disbelieve, and making those who follow you above those who disbelieve, to the day of resurrection. Then to Me, shall be your return, and I will decide between you concerning that in which you differed"' (3:55). Presumably, the early Muslim community which heard these verses had some idea that, besides the Quranic presentation of Jesus, there was a range of interpretations of the life and nature of Christ in Christian communities. The Quran was revealed in a world that knew about various other faith traditions.

Many people are aware of the emigration of Muhammad and his earliest followers from Mecca to Medina in the year 622.

However, there was an earlier emigration to Abyssinia that under-scored the value of interfaith dialogue to Muhammad. The earliest biographer of the Prophet, Ibn Ishaq (c. 704-767) and the famed Muslim historian al-Tabari (838-923) discuss this migration. As people began to accept Islam they met with opposition from others in Mecca. This opposition turned to physical persecution of certain members of the early Muslim community. Muhammad gathered a group of those most vulnerable and instructed them to go across the Red Sea to Abyssinia, a Christian country ruled by a Christian king. There, the emigrants were welcomed and accepted. Indeed, the Christian king protected the Muslims against demands of extradition by the polytheists of Mecca. The emigrants stayed in Abyssinia until they rejoined the larger Muslim commu-nity in Medina.

Muhammad's act represents the first time that Muslims, as Muslims, dealt with Christians as a community. There was no sense of enmity against the Christians of Abyssinia; instead, they were seen as a people that would protect members of the nascent Muslim community. This is a very early example in Islam of the importance of pluralism and interfaith dialogue, and the debt that Muslims owe to Christians.

As mentioned earlier, Islam arose in an environment where the first converts were persecuted by polytheists for their beliefs. Later, there were tensions among Muslims and Jews, as well as tensions between Muslims and Christians. Not surprisingly, there are passages in the Quran that say positive things about other tradi-tions as well as passages that are critical of them. One of the chal-lenges faced by Muslims in an honest interfaith dialogue is to come to terms with the full range of verses that address the issue of relationships between Muslim and non-Muslim communities. Given that the Quran was revealed over a period of 23 years in changing historical settings, it is not surprising that there are different sets of guidance given to the young Muslim community. For instance, there are passages in the Quran which advise against taking 'non-believers' as protectors; most pointedly, sura 5:82 reads, 'You will find among the people the Jews and the Polytheists to be the strongest in enmity to the Believers.'

At face value, those passages seem quite different from other verses, such as the rest of sura 5:82 which continues, 'nearest among them in love to the Believers will you find those who say "We are Christians"'. While it is important to recognize that the Quran never sanctions the killing of Jews and Christians, it is also essential for Muslims to be aware of how the various strands in the Quran can be used both to build bridges and to justify mutual exclusivism. Moreover, there are passages that are critical of Muslims who show disregard for others in practice. 'The small kindness' of sura 107 is succinct on this score:

In the Name of God, the Compassionate, the Caring.
Do you see him who calls the reckoning a lie?
He is the one who casts the orphan away,
who fails to urge the feeding of one in need.
Cursed are those who perform the prayer
unmindful of how they pray, who make of themselves a display
but hold back the small kindness.

It is crucial for contemporary Muslim and non-Muslim readers of the Quran to know something of the contexts of the original revelations to Muhammad.

In a remarkable passage, the Quran speaks about creation and difference in a moral context: 'O humanity! Truly, We created you from a male and a female, and made you into nations and tribes that you might know each other. Truly, the most honoured of you in the sight of God is the most God-conscious of you. Truly, God is All-Knowing, All-Aware' (49:13). There are four key points in this verse. First, the passage is addressed to all of humanity and not specifically limited to Muslims. Second, the passage mentions that the creation of humanity into distinct groupings comes from God and is a positive value. Third, it encourages people to transcend their differences and learn from each other. Finally, the passage does not say that Muslims are better than other people, but rather that the best people are those who are aware of God.

Early History

Islam remained a minority tradition until two years before the death of Muhammad. From the time that Muhammad received his first revelations in 610 to the year 622, Islam was a persecuted minority religion in Mecca. In the year 622, Muhammad emigrated with his community to the city of Medina where Islam was also a minority tradition. However, in Medina, free from the persecution of the Meccans, the Muslim community could exist openly as a community. The number of Muslims greatly increased in Medina. Through conversion, the majority of the citizens of Medina became Muslim. In 630, Muhammad was able to return to Mecca in triumph, and much of the Arabian peninsula was converted to Islam by the time of his death in 632.

Islam has been, to be sure, a missionary religion. The three largest religious traditions in the world, Christianity, Islam and Buddhism, are all religions that encourage and engage in conversion. All three believe that there is a proper way to live in the world, and that it is incumbent upon believers to spread information about this proper way. This conviction gives rise to mutually exclusive truth claims: only Jesus' death saves us from sin; only Muhammad is the final Prophet of God; only the Buddha teaches us how we can attain enlightenment. All three of these religious traditions have, tragically, gone through phases where the 'other' was converted to the truth through force and violence.

The Quran is clear about not forcing people to convert: 'There is no compulsion in religion: the truth stands clear from the wrong' (2:256). When Muhammad returned to Mecca in the year 630 as the conquering ruler, he gave Muslims a clear example to follow. The psychological tensions in Muhammad's consciousness must have been extraordinary when one remembers just what was about to occur. Muhammad was born in Mecca in a branch of the noblest family in that city. He established a reputation for himself as a trustworthy and honest businessman, had a loving wife and four daughters. Then at the age of 40 he began to receive revelations from God, revelations that challenged the status quo. Muhammad was at first tolerated for his public preaching and then persecuted. Little more than a decade after receiving his revelations he had to leave the city of his birth and migrate with his followers to another city.

Eight years later, Muhammad was able to return to Mecca as the conquering ruler. He literally had the power of life and death over those who years earlier had tormented and persecuted him and had killed several of his followers. By pre-Islamic Arab custom, he had the power to seek revenge, even massacre his enemies. Instead, in this most triumphant of earthly moments, Muhammad chose to display the utmost mercy and declared an amnesty. In this extraordinary act, he came to those who had persecuted him and recited to them the words from the Quran that Joseph had first spoken to his brothers when they came to him in Egypt, humbled after having sold him earlier into slavery: 'This day let no reproach be upon you. May God forgive you, and God is the most merciful of those who show mercy' (12:92). There would be no slaughter or forced conversion of the Meccans.

For many converts, it is a message of justice that brings them to Islam. There is an emphasis on social justice in the Quran, and on siding with the poor, the orphaned and the oppressed. The ethical monotheism of the Quran requires that obligations be fulfilled, whether they are due to God or to other people. In this vein, Farid Esack's *Qur'an, Liberation and Pluralism* (1997) offers a brilliant account of the role of Muslims in the struggle to end apartheid in South Africa. On the matter of conversion, however, there is an old stereotype of Muslims forcing people to accept Islam. Images persist of Arab warriors on horseback with the

---

[2] In a tongue-in-cheek comment, a historian friend talks about the fallacy of this myth. Owing to the Semitic notion of ritual purity, many Muslims do not hold the sacred scripture of the Quran with their left hand, since the left hand is reserved for cleansing oneself. If there were an army of Muslims with the Quran in one hand and a sword in another, they would all have the Quran in the right hand and the sword in the left. No doubt the vision of an entire left-handed army is enough to give the lie to that myth. Furthermore, manuscripts of the Quran were far too rare (owing to the low rate of literacy) for every soldier to have had his own copy of the sacred text.

Quran in one hand and a sword in the other, chopping off the heads of those who refused to convert.[2] The reality was very different. For example, the first place that Islam spread to outside of Arabia was Iran. The dominant religious tradition in Iran before Islam was Zoroastrianism. It took about 200 years for Iran to transform from a country where there were almost no Muslims to a country where the majority were Muslim. Often it was the Sufis, the mystics of Islam, who spread Islam by living among the people and providing them with an example of how to live their lives as Muslims. In this way, they were no different from those Christians who lived out their lives as faithful witnesses, not active instigators of the conversion process. There have, certainly, been episodes in which Muslims abused the power that they had when they were able to dictate the discourse. But the dialogues of power corrupt any noble idea, whether it be Islam, Christianity, freedom or democracy.

I have pointed to a few incidents in the life of Muhammad because that life – the Sunna – is considered exemplary for Muslims. In Islamic history, a number of people sought to live out the model of tolerance that Muhammad lived. One instance is that of the Caliph Umar, the second successor to Muhammad. Umar ruled the Muslim community from 634 to 644. In 638 Muslims arrived at Jerusalem. Far from being a ruthless imperial conqueror, the traditions hold that Umar walked into Jerusalem because it was his servant's turn to ride the mount that they shared. While in the city, Umar was given a tour of the existing religious sites by the Christian Patriarch of Jerusalem. As the time approached for prayer, Umar asked for a place where he might offer his. Through translators, the Patriarch offered Umar the opportunity to pray where he stood, in the Church of the Holy Sepulchre, one of the most important of Christian sites. Umar refused, saying that wherever he, the first Muslim ruler in Jerusalem, was to offer his prayers, his followers would build a *masjid* or mosque. He would not let that place be inside a spot that was of crucial importance to Christians. Instead, he prayed outside of the church on what was then the Porch of the Martyrs. Sure enough, if one goes to the Church of the Holy Sepulchre today, across the street is the small Mosque of Umar, commemorating his prayers.

There have been times in various Islamic civilisations when there were good relations between Muslims and Christian and Jewish minorities. One thinks for example of the city of Baghdad in the eighth and ninth centuries. Baghdad was built on the banks of the Tigris River as the capital city of the Abbasid empire (750-1258) by Caliph al-Mansur, who ruled from 754 to 775. Baghdad truly was a metropolis with links to Persia, India, China, Byzantium and the Latin West. One sees this cosmopolitan nature in the great literary classic to emerge from Baghdad, *The Thousand and One Nights*, with its mix of diverse characters and stories from various locations. Baghdad was also home to the House of Wisdom (*Bayt al-Hikma*), built by Caliph al-Mamun (r. 813-833) as a centre of learning and translation for scholars from around the world. A Christian, Hunayn ibn Ishaq, was appointed as the director of the translation academy. This research institute was at the centre of the movement to bring the philosophical heritage of the Greeks, Persians and Indians within the fold of the Islamic quest for wisdom.

It is important here to emphasise that Islam has long existed within the culture of the West, first in Europe and later in North America. The pluralism that we see in the modern western world has ancient roots. From the eighth to the 15th century, much of Spain was Muslim, and al-Andalus (the Arabic term for Muslim Spain, Andalucia) was a high point of Islamic civilisation. In the ninth and 10th centuries, Cordoba in Muslim Spain became one of the most important cities in the history of the world. Christians and Jews were involved in the Royal Court and in the intellectual life of the city. Historically, there was also an Islamic presence in southern France, Italy, and Sicily, with Arabic being a language known to the highly educated. And of course, under Ottoman rule, there was a profound Muslim presence in Turkey, the Balkans and Eastern Europe. The Mughal empire was also known for its pluralism.

The Arabic language (especially via Spanish and French) has contributed to the vocabulary of English. Common English words such as 'coffee', 'sofa', 'genie' and 'alcohol', technical terms such as 'algebra' and 'alkaline', and even archaic words such as 'alchemy' and 'lute', have their roots in Arabic. Arabic words such as hajj, hijab and, of course, jihad, have become commonplace enough not to require translation. Clearly, Muslims influenced and were influenced by the people with whom they lived.

What really changed the way that Muslims, Christians and Jews understood each other in history was the succession of wars known as the Crusades (1096-1270). Before the Crusades, Muslims were relatively unknown to the European public. After the Crusades, with the making of enemy images on both sides, there was a great deal of polemic in European texts about Muslims. Norman Daniel has written the classic study of this time, his magisterial *Islam and the West: The Making of an Image* (1997). But there were also opportunities to counter the negative stereotypes. The ordinary European might come into contact with Muslims as merchants, traders or seafarers. The educated classes came to be exposed to works of Islamic philosophy, and classics of Greek philosophy (such as Aristotle) translated into Arabic and then into Latin. Maimonides, the great medieval Jewish philosopher, wrote *The Guide of the Perplexed* in Arabic. Other counter examples included the fact that Muslim physicians were among the best of their day, and Muslim scientists and mathematicians (in collaboration with non-Muslims) made great advances in the sciences. Anybody familiar with Thomas Aquinas's *Summa Theologica* has felt the hovering presence of medieval Muslim scholars. This powerful presence was beautifully represented by the great Renaissance painter, Raphael, who included Ibn Rushd (Averroes) in his painting *School of Athens*.[3]

Muslim civilisations had contact with the Americas well before the time of Christopher Columbus. The historian al-Masudi, writing around 956, mentions a sailor from Cordoba returning from a trip across the Atlantic. There is also a report from the geographer al-Idrisi (1099-1166) of sailors who reached the

---

[3] For an image of this painting and a further discussion of the link between Thomas Aquinas and Ibn Rushd, see Majid Fakhry, 'Philosophy and History', in *The Genius of Arab Civilisations: Source of Renaissance* (2nd ed., London, 1983).

Americas. Columbus himself, centuries later, brought with him on his voyage Luis de Torres, a *converso* (a Jew who had to convert to Christianity during Spain's *Reconquista*) who could speak Arabic with the people that he met in the Americas. This strengthens the case for a much earlier Arabic presence where the native peoples could have learned the language. María Rosa Menocal writes in *Shards of Love: Exile and the Origins of the Lyric* (1994): 'the first official diplomatic conversation in the New World took place between Luis de Torres, a Jew of recent conversion, speaking in the lovely Romance-accented Arabic that was the language of both high culture and stunning nostalgia, and a Taíno chief in the hinterlands of Cuba'.

Another root of dialogue was the transatlantic slave trade. Scholars estimate that between 10 and 20 per cent of slaves brought to the Americas were Muslim, the majority of whom were forced to convert to Christianity, but some of whom retained their Islamic identity. Job Ben Solomon, for example, was brought to Maryland in 1730. Solomon engaged with Christian missionaries (including his biographer, Thomas Bluett) and helped to explain his Muslim beliefs to them.

A key figure in early dialogue was Alexander Russell Webb, an American born in the Hudson River Valley in 1846. In 1888, while US Consul to the Philippines, Webb converted to Islam. He gave several lectures in India about Islam in 1892 and founded a monthly magazine in America the next year entitled *The Moslem World*. Also in 1893 he published a short book, *Islam in America*. He then issued a separate publication called *The Voice of Islam*. Between 1895 and 1896, the two journals were published together as *The Moslem World and Voice of Islam*, with the stated purpose 'to spread the light of Islamic truth in the United States and to assist in uniting under a common brotherhood all who accept the Moslem faith, intelligently, honestly, unselfishly and sincerely'. He published several other booklets about Islam. Webb was present for the defining moment of interfaith dialogue in the United States: the First World's Parliament of Religions held in Chicago in 1893. Prefiguring the state of affairs today, Webb noted that Islam was the most misunderstood religion in America.

Contemporary Experience

Perennial tenets of humane interfaith behaviour were set forth in the Quran. In particular: 'for every one of you did We appoint a law and a way, and if God had pleased God would have made you a single people, but that God might try you in what God gave you, therefore strive with one another to hasten to virtuous deeds; to God you will all return, so God will let you know that in which you differed' (5:48). Muhammad and other early leaders left Muslims with edifying examples of cooperative relations with religions other than Islam. Throughout history, Muslims have existed in dialogue with others. Whether the relationships have been productive or disastrous, Muslims have defined themselves in dialogue. They have always understood – and constructed – their 'Islams' in a pluralist context.[4]

One is surely reminded of early Muslim history when considering the modern situation of Muslim communities in North America. The first public prayer service in Ottawa was held in 1963 in the basement of a Christian church. According to a former President of the Ottawa Muslim Association, 'we have to acknowledge the help we got from Christians, especially the United Church'.[5] Since 1980, the National Christian Muslim Liaison Committee has existed as an official vehicle of dialogue. Under the leadership of the largest Protestant denomination in Canada, the United Church of Canada, there have been a number of conferences and workshops on interfaith dialogue. Several useful community resources have been produced as a result of these workshops.[6] This interfaith work also involves the attendance of non-Muslims at Muslim

---

[4] I use 'Islams' in the plural because there are multiple ways of being Muslim in any given context.

[5] Zulf M. Khalfan, 'Ottawa Muslims: Growing Pains', Islamic Horizons, 24 (1995).

[6] Examples include Susan L. Scott, ed., Stories in my Neighbour's Faith: Narratives from World Religions in Canada (Toronto, 1999); Faith in My Neighbour. World Religions in Canada: An Introduction (Toronto, 1994); and Stories of Interfaith Families: A Resource for Families and Congregations (Toronto, 1994).

rituals and celebrations, and the attendance of Muslims at non-Muslim religious ceremonies. The result is 'Islams' that influence and in turn are influenced by the other traditions with which they come into contact. As members of a minority religious tradition, Muslims in North America are aware of the dominant religious tradition, Christianity. While the majority tradition has not always had to be aware of the minority traditions in its midst (a situation that no doubt is changing because of our shrinking world), minorities must always understand the majority culture in order to survive.

Yet, there is the issue of what the underlying assumptions of religious pluralism mean for theology in North America. Are we teaching matters that are old news, or that our listeners are not prepared to hear? When I observe, 'I have said Friday prayers in the al-Aqsa Mosque and in the Dome of the Rock in Jerusalem, and I have prayed in the sweat lodge in Manitoba with my Cree elders, and I do not think that Allah distinguishes between these prayers', I get some very interesting reactions. Some want to hear more about each of these occasions, and are genuinely interested in connections between Islam and the religious traditions of First Nations. Others are horrified that I have prayed with non-Muslims or that I have linked the lodge with the mosque.

As a teacher, I often have Muslim students who are zealous 'defenders' of Islam. In hearing their rhetoric of intolerance, I think back to one of my own esteemed teachers, Professor Wilfred Cantwell Smith, one of the greatest North American scholars of Islam in the past century. Smith was, for many of us who study religion, the epitome of critical scholarship. From his deep knowledge, he was able to offer critique when it was needed. Of his scholarship, John Hick wrote: 'An outstanding feature of Wilfred's work is that it is on the highest level of technical historical scholarship and yet it is at the same time driven by involvement in and concern for the worldwide human community, with a keen sense of the threatening disasters and the amazing possibilities before us. This human involvement goes back to his work in India before Partition and has continued ever since, as a constant thread running through all his writings.'

Smith was a committed Christian, deeply concerned about the issues facing Muslims. He was not an apologist for Islam. Yet his critique never did violence to what it meant for other people to be Muslim. In *Islam in Modern History* he wrote, 'A true Muslim, however, is not a man who believes in Islam, especially Islam in history, but one who believes in God and is committed to the revelation through His Prophet.' Those words were published in 1957. In his 1963 book *The Meaning and End of Religion*, he continued: 'the essential tragedy of the modern Islamic world is the degree to which Muslims, instead of giving their allegiance to God, have been giving it to something called Islam.' Those words could have been written yesterday with equal force and validity.

Like others of his Muslim students, I often felt that Smith was a better muslim (one who submits to God) than I was, a fact that inspired me more than I can express. Smith and his wife, Muriel, spent six years as missionaries in Lahore before the partition of India and the creation of Pakistan. When we first met, he commented that he had lived in Lahore, my birthplace, longer than I had lived there, six years to my four. But Professor and Mrs Smith were no ordinary missionaries. I don't know that they ever converted a single person, but I am sure that they taught and influenced thousands. They were splendid exemplars of the kind of Christianity that I came to know and love.

Dr Bruce McLeod, a former Moderator of the United Church of Canada, told me an extraordinary story about Smith. Someone once asked him, 'Professor Smith, are you Christian?' After a characteristic pause, Professor Smith repeated the question, 'Am I Christian?' He then answered, 'Well, maybe I was, last week, at lunch, for about an hour. But if you really want to know, ask my neighbour.' For many of us who see ourselves as progressive Muslims, Smith's comment captures our own various Islams. We strive to be Muslim, meaning that we *live out* our submission to God in a way that can be felt by those whom we encounter. Not that we put on a pretence for the benefit of others, but that our lives are lived as an integrated whole, with no easy teasing out of our individual Islam from the poetry of our ordinary lives.

In the aftermath of the events of September 11, 2001, major

Muslim groups in North America were quick to condemn the terrorist attacks – a fact that was not widely reported in the news media in the early days. Many individual Muslims took the initiative to undertake civic dialogue for the first time, and speak to their friends and neighbours about Islam. Academics who study Islam were in great demand to address groups, large and small, across North America.[7] At one of the many churches at which I spoke, one of the audience members asked me why I thought I worshipped the same God that he worshipped. He mentioned to me that his minister had taught him that Muslims worshipped a different god than the One God worshipped by Jews and Christians. And having heard from his minister what Muslims believed, no argument from me, a believing Muslim, could persuade him otherwise! David Benke, a minister in the Lutheran Church-Missouri Synod, was suspended for participating in an interfaith event on the grounds that, 'Instead of keeping God's name sacred and separate from every other name, it was made common as it was dragged to the level of Allah.'

Amid an onslaught in the media from assorted quarters after September 11 about the perils of Islam,[8] one of the few groups to immediately show solidarity with Muslims were Japanese-Americans, many of whom were Christian. Having experienced racism and discrimination during their internment in the Second World War, Japanese Americans were sensitive to such a fate befalling their fellow Muslim citizens. In turn, Muslim Americans have joined Japanese-Americans on their annual pilgrimage to Manzanar National Historic Site in California's Owens Valley. Manzanar was one of the camps where Japanese-Americans were interned after the attacks on Pearl Harbor in 1941.

This is a reminder of the civic aspects of pluralism – in addition

---

[7] A fine web resource was created by Dr Omid Safi: http://groups.colgate.edu/aarislam/response.htm. All of us who teach Islam in North America are indebted to him for creating and maintaining this site.

[8] See the commentary by Nicholas Kristof, 'Bigotry in Islam – and Here', *New York Times*, 9 July 2002, http://www.nytimes.com/2002/07/09/opinion/09KRIS.html.

to matters that we think of as strictly 'religious'. Shared citizen-ship and the solidarity that goes with it in civil society are where pluralism finds actual expression. Muslims can draw inspiration for their civic commitments in the ethics of their faith tradition, as discussed earlier. But one cannot escape into an abstract 'theology of pluralism' outside the civic spaces where Muslims and their fellow citizens live their daily lives. Indeed, the Quran itself reminds us of the social aspects of a shared revelation, in the form of peaceful co-existence: 'And argue not with the People of the Book unless it be in [a way] that is better, except with such of them as do wrong; and say: "We believe in that which has been revealed to us and revealed to you; our God and your God is One, and to God do we surrender"' (29:46).

There is also the danger that by casting issues of tolerance chiefly in terms of theology or religion, we ignore the social realities that can cut away at civil society. Take the example of the country with the largest Muslim minority in the world, India. There are uncivil tensions among the various religious traditions there – commonly referred to as 'communalism' – a sectarian hatred with a tragic record. Much of this has to do with economic and social realities: exclusions of class, income and gender from participation in the mainstream of local and national life. Yet religion has become a political symbol and force in the violence among Hindus, Muslims, Sikhs and Christians – rather like the 'troubles' in Northern Ireland. And like the communities in Northern Ireland, the 'clashing cultures' of India overlap so heavily in terms of language, family and religious values, and preferences of dress, food and music, that distinctions can often fade in practice.[9] This truth has not, of course, come in the way of demagogues who are happy to manipulate (and even invent) differences for political gain.

The lessons here for other Muslim contexts such as Afghanistan and Iraq are critical. Minorities as well as majorities that feel excluded from the mainstream will often rally around what is presented to them as a key marker of their identity – such as their

[9] See Dominique-Sila Khan, *Crossing the Threshold: Understanding Religious Identities in South Asia* (London, 2004).

region, ethnicity or religious tradition. What usually sits under these markers is real or feared exclusion in economic, social or political life. Thinking of the conflict among Iraq's Kurds, Shia, Sunnis and Christians in these terms is surely more convincing than reducing it all to 'Islam' – and much the same is true of Afghanistan, with its long history of ethnic and regional imbalance. An inclusive civic ethic reduces the risk of manipulation, giving all citizens a stake in the success of the whole society. Such an ethic must find its way into constitutions, codes of law and institutions of governance if pluralism is to be more than just a slogan. After all, even the Prophet sought to frame the founding principles of the Quran's message in the inclusive Constitution of Medina, with the support of the consultative *shura*, in pursuit of an umma that was both religious and civic.

Conclusion

Religion and interfaith dialogue have a vital role in motivating individuals and groups to commit to the rule of law and civil society. There is much evidence of the success of such a partnership of sacred and secular – *din wa duniya* – in our time. Mohandas Gandhi, Martin Luther King, Oscar Romero and Desmond Tutu are among the luminaries in this regard. So are Zaina Anwar, Shirin Ebadi, Abdullahi An-Naim, Chandra Muzaffar, Abdolkarim Soroush, Tariq Ramadan and Azizah al-Hibri, to name but a few. Their inspiration is much needed by Muslims and non-Muslims alike in a world where tolerance alone is not enough. Fear and suspicion can make a false virtue of tolerance by allowing it to create walls behind which people live in passive ignorance; only dialogue gets beyond the barriers.

To engage in effective dialogue one must not only have a deep grasp of one's own faith but also an understanding and appreciation of the faith of the dialogue partner. This best happens in a diverse setting where one is more likely to see one's own beliefs and practices through the eyes of others – and to have first hand encounters with the belief and practices of the *real* rather than the imagined Other. It takes confidence in one's own faith to engage the generously with another person, and to see him/her as a fellow traveller in a shared quest. Pluralism, in other words, is a sign not of weakness but of courage. Indeed, in the ultimate sense, Muslims need to commit to pluralism, not because we have to but because we should, in order, as the Quran puts it, 'to know each other'.

This applies not only to relations between Muslims and non-Muslims, but also among Muslims themselves. This is sometimes easier to achieve in the diaspora where commonalities may be cherished over differences and fresh beginnings made. As a Sunni, I had the privilege in Toronto of performing the Friday afternoon prayer side by side with a Shii colleague, the prayers being led by a Bosnian imam, in a mosque built by Albanians. This may be somewhat harder in ancestral countries where Sunni and Shia have been in conflict. There is also, of course, the sheer cosmopolitanism of the diaspora in terms of both Muslim and non-Muslim diversity, which opens the way to fresh knowing of each other. In this regard, there is much leadership that Muslims in the West can offer to those in the traditional Muslim world. The Ismaili community has taken the lead here, as perhaps the most integrated Muslim community in North America. Their leader, Aga Khan IV, has spoken out repeatedly on the pressing need for a pluralist ethic against the 'clash of ignorance' that currently exists both within and among societies.[10]

The Quran is clear that God could well have created people with no differences among them, yet chose not to do so (11:118). Our differences are not to be feared, denied or eradicated. It is through dialogue that we learn about ourselves, about others – and in so doing, perhaps also about God.

---

[10] HH The Aga Khan, *Where Hope Takes Root: Democracy and Pluralism in an Interdependent World* (Vancouver, 2008).

Further Reading

Bulliet, Richard W. *Islam: The View from the Edge.* New York, 1994.
Cragg, Kenneth and R. Marston Speight. *The House of Islam.* 3rd ed. Belmont, CA, 1988.
Daniel, Norman. *Islam and the West: The Making of an Image.* Edinburgh, 1960; reprinted, Oxford, 1997.
Esack, Farid. *Qur'an, Liberation and Pluralism: An Islamic Perspective of Interreligious Solidarity against Oppression.* Oxford, 1997.
Gervers, Michael and Ramzi Jibran Bikhazi, ed. *Conversion and Continuity: Indigenous Christian Communities in Islamic Lands, Eighth to Eighteenth Centuries.* Toronto, 1990.
Hick, John. 'On Wilfred Cantwell Smith: His Place in the Study of Religion', *Method and Theory in the Study of Religion,* vol. 4:1–2 (1992), pp. 5-20.
Ramadan, Tariq. *Radical Reform: Islamic Ethics and Liberation.* Oxford, 2009.
Safi, Omid, ed. *Progressive Muslims: On Justice, Gender and Pluralism.* Oxford, 2003.
Smith, Wilfred Cantwell. *Islam in Modern History.* Princeton, 1957.
_____ *The Meaning and End of Religion.* New York, 1963; reprinted, Minneapolis, MI, 1991.
Turner, Bryan S., ed. *Religious Diversity and Civil Society: A Comparative Analysis.* Oxford, 2008.
Yazbeck Haddad, Yvonne and Wadi Z. Haddad, ed. *Christian-Muslim Encounters.* Gainesville, FL, 1995.

5

Networks of Solidarity

Bruce Lawrence

From the first umma in the seventh century to modern pilgrimages to Mecca and the Silk Road of times past, Muslims have thrived in networks of faith, family, trade and travel. To be networked means choosing to be connected across recognised boundaries. To be Muslim refers not only to a faith orientation but also to a social world in which Islam is not necessarily dominant. Networks are similar to social relations that are institutionalised, such as tribal ties and political dynasties, but also distinct from them. This chapter aims to show that the networked nature of Islam and the impact of Muslim networks on world history are pivotal – indeed, that networks are key to understanding the flourishing of the umma and its subsets not only in the past but also the future.

Why Networks?

Precisely because Islam is not homogeneous, it is only through the lens of Muslim networks, whether they be historical or commercial, academic or aesthetic, that one can see how diverse groups contest and articulate what it means to be Muslim. Humanists and social scientists look at different elements of the diversity within Islam. Some focus on individual Muslims who live and work in far-flung parts of the globe, yet are frequently in touch with one another. Others examine the multiple expressions of Muslim piety all over the world. Humanists tend to stress language and subjectivity; their goal is to understand and interpret the lives of individuals and communities, and the specific histories and texts that shape their identities. Social scientists, on the other hand, generally look at collective actors, for example, Muslims vs. non-Muslims. Their aim is to clarify – and if possible predict – social, cultural, political and economic change as well as conflict. Studying networks puts humanists and social scientists into conversation with each other. What it reveals is the great variation in Muslim cultural, linguistic and political exchanges.

One key word frames the medium for building Muslim networks, even as it suggests a method for their understanding. That word is umma, commonly translated as 'global Muslim community'. Umma is flexible rather than static; it signifies all Islam but within the broadest boundaries defining Muslim collective identity. The history of the umma has no single narrative but its many branches stretch back to seventh-century Mecca. The first Muslim networks overlay the trading routes of pagan Arabia that linked a merchant named Muhammad to the metropolitan world of Mesopotamia and beyond. Networks of negotiations made possible the exchange of material goods, ideas and people; they defined cultural practices in the earliest phases of Islamic civilisation. In our time, advances in technology have generated fresh networks in cyberspace. These new networks link formerly marginal Muslims with one another, and they also provide forums for new groups, whether in Arabia or America, to assert their understanding of Islam.

Until the 20th century Muslim networks privileged men. Whether they were networks of travel, pilgrimage or preaching, they were mainly networks of men on the move. The only network in which women's participation has been traditionally acknowledged is the annual hajj. It brings Muslims from across Africa and Asia to the Hijaz region in western Arabia. Clad in the *ihram*, the plain cloth wound around their bodies, both male and female pilgrims worship together. The hajj is limited to one month, yet pilgrimage routes function throughout the year. The hajj routes overlay the multiple networks of traders, travellers and seekers of knowledge that connect Muslims to each other. Other pilgrimages may take Muslims to places like Tanta, Ajmer, Touba and Karbala, but each models itself on the hajj network.

The most durable feature of the hajj is travel. Through literature we learn about the networked nature of Muslim mobility that accents the hajj, but also extends beyond it to privilege travel of all kinds to many places. Between the 10th and the 15th century, *adab al-rihla* or travel literature was established. Professional writers were commissioned to write *rihla*s. These became so popular that some of the later *rihla*s seem to have relied on earlier versions to fill in descriptions of places that their authors had not visited. Such *rihla*s were not so much fictions as recycled accounts. By the 14th century the style was so well established that the armchair travel writer could obtain narratives from far-flung corners of the Muslim world and adapt them to his purposes.

The travel writer often required a patron. For instance, the Moroccan Sultan Abu Inan was so impressed with the nomadic career of his countryman, the famous traveller Ibn Battuta (1304-1368), that he wanted to preserve its memory. He commissioned Ibn Juzayy, an eminent man of letters, to record colourfully the adventures of Ibn Battuta. The resulting *Rihla* tells the legendary travels of a Moroccan religious scholar who journeyed throughout the 14th-century Muslim world. It was a Muslim world hardly recognisable today. Ibn Battuta's journeys included a lengthy stay in Andalusia, as Muslim Spain was known from the eighth till the 16th century. His journeys also included a considerable stopover in West Africa long before the Atlantic slave trade emerged and devastated that part of the sub-Saharan African umma.

Among Ibn Battuta's contemporaries and co-religionists was the celebrated North African historian Ibn Khaldun (1332-1406). Jurist, philosopher, litterateur and historian, Ibn Khaldun circulated in the same regional network as Ibn Battuta, drawing on centuries-old connections that were moral as well as physical. His major work, the *Muqaddimah* or *Introduction to History*, shows how Arabic had become the lingua franca, and Mecca and Medina the geographic centres of a vast pre-modern Muslim network. The network was at once political and apolitical. In Albert Hourani's words, Islamic civilisation rested on 'a body of knowledge transmitted over the centuries by a known chain of teachers that preserved a moral community even when rulers changed'.[1] The moral community persisted even when individuals were uprooted from their countries of origin; the sense of shared experience stirred and sustained those like Leo Africanus who were compelled to move. An exile from Spain at the outset of the 16th century, the historical geographer Leo trod the paths of Ibn Battuta and Ibn Khaldun, traveling from southern Spain to northern Africa to Arabia, even enduring a 'conversion' to Christianity while a prisoner of the Vatican.

Leo's case is instructive. An involuntary Muslim traveller who was not a trained jurist, he began his journeys when he was forced to leave his homeland by the Reconquista of Spain's King Ferdinand and Queen Isabella. A reluctant migrant, Leo was the victim of a turbulent history. Ibn Battuta, by contrast, revelled in the opportunities that travel enabled. Wherever he went, he found himself integrated more and more into Dar al-Islam (the domain of Islam). To be Muslim and to be a Muslim judge opened for him the full benefits offered by 'a networked civilization'.[2]

Through Ibn Battuta's account we are given a model for understanding Muslim networks. His Rihla demonstrates how a religiously defined network can become a model of early cosmopolitanism. It reveals a world identified as Muslim that spanned continents and oceans. Dar al-Islam included non-Muslims as well as Muslims within its borders. It was an urban-based cosmopolitan world, at once diverse and plural. It was connected from West Africa to China through waterways, port cities and centres of political and religious power. Berbers, Arabs, Indians and Sudanese could travel to the outer limits of Dar al-Islam. Whatever obstacles they faced, they could rely on the hospitality of their co-religionists; everywhere they found food and lodging simply because they were Muslims. From the caravanserai

[1] Albert Hourani, History of the Arab Peoples (Cambridge, MA, 1991), p. 4.
[2] See David Gilmartin, 'A Networked Civilization?', in Miriam Cooke and Bruce Lawrence, ed. Muslim Networks: From Hajj to Hip-Hop (Chapel Hill, NC, 2005), pp. 51-68.

to the Sufi *zawiya* or lodge and the generosity of a local ruler, the traveller versed in Islamic sciences expected to find a welcome wherever he went. Often it was travel itself that conferred prestige and wealth. During his 24 years on the road and at sea, Ibn Battuta was honoured with more than a maintenance allowance: as he moved further and further away from his North African home, he found himself materially rewarded and also encumbered. En route to India, he describes being surrounded by a large retinue of companions, slaves and richly laden beasts of burden that he had acquired from his latest patron.

But how did this 14th-century network become so pervasive and so effective? There are several factors that have distinguished the Muslim world, making its networks at once more interlinked and interactive than those of other contemporary communities. They include trade, language, Sufism and scholarship, but above all, common moral ideals and social codes.

Trade, Talk and Trust

Prior to the rise of Islam trade networks had been widespread, extending across the Mediterranean to the Indian Ocean and to the South China Seas. Muslim traders built on these networks and gave them added value. In China, for instance, there were trading links with the Arab world traceable back to the second century BCE. This commercial connection had overland networks that cut across what became known as the Silk Road, as well as a southern sea route. Not long after Muhammad's death in 632, Muslim envoys crossed the Asian continent using these established networks of trade and cultural exchange to bring the message of Islam. Well armed and trained but not aggressive toward the Chinese state, Muslim soldiers helped the emperors quell local rebellions while they strengthened existing commercial and cultural ties. They and their young religion basked in imperial favour.

Their experience anticipated that of later Muslim traders who made the perilous sea journey to the southern ports of China. These traders settled in major Chinese cities and, like their co-religionists in the north, benefited from the patronage of a state that recognised effective allies in these trading Muslims. The trust was transferable: the Mongols were enemies of Chinese royalty, yet during the 13th and 14th century they singled out local Muslims for their commercial experience and expertise. Mongol leaders appointed Muslim traders to administrative office. They consolidated Muslim networks throughout imperial China, while also helping to incorporate them into a trans-regional system of Muslim networks. Most famously, they appointed Zheng He (1371-1431), a Muslim from Yunan, to head expeditions of trade and diplomacy across half the known world.[3]

Communication was facilitated by the fact that Arabic and Persian were the languages used by most elites. Some command of one or both helped individuals to integrate easily and quickly into a local Muslim trading network. Yet, the lynchpin for Muslim networks was not language per se but a double emphasis on reciprocity and hierarchy. Reciprocity or *taskhir* implied mutual gain for ruler and ruled, patron and scholar. Hierarchy was indispensable to reciprocity. Muslim society of the 14th century, for example, had four categories: men of the pen, men of the sword, men of negotiation and men of husbandry, ranked from the highest (men of the pen) to the lowest (men of husbandry). Though justice itself was the paramount virtue, it was justice less as equality than as equity or fairness through the balance of reciprocal obligations. While the ruler may have been privileged, he was not exempt from the rules of society as a whole, being dependent on each of these four groups as they were on him. Nor did the ruled automatically support the ruler. Ibn Battuta was linked to those like himself who were men of the pen rather than attached to those unlike him who were men of the sword or rulers.[4]

Though the cohesion created by shared values was not limited to men of the pen or ulama, they were its primary exemplars.

---

[3] Edward Dreyer, *Zheng He: China and the Oceans in the Early Ming Dynasty, 1405-1433* (Upper Saddle River, NJ, 2006).
[4] Vincent Cornell, 'Ibn Battuta's Opportunism: the Networks and Loyalties of a Medieval Muslim Scholar', in M. Cooke and B. Lawrence, ed., *Muslim Networks*, pp. 31-50.

They travelled via transnational networks as agents of religious knowledge, and they added value to the networks they inherited and developed. Today, the cosmopolitan language of Islamic religious discourse continues to cut across frontiers, making a universe of reciprocal benefit to those who master it. This religious exchange is at once flexible and transferable across time as well as space. From Muhammad Shibli Numani (1857-1914) to Abul-Hasan Ali Nadwi (1914-1999) to Yusuf al-Qaradawi (1926-), an Egyptian jurist currently preaching and issuing legal opinions out of Qatar, 20th-century Islamic scholars are bound to their predecessors by a shared commitment that is also evident in a shared practice. They form interpretive communities that may be mobilised against the excesses of outside forces, whether they are 12th-century Crusaders or 21st-century neo-colonialists.

Yet this mobile and enduring juridical authority comes at a price. While their shared discourse has always allowed ulama to communicate easily with each other wherever they happened to be, it has sometimes blocked their ability to communicate even with other Muslims who were not in their social class. The majority of pre-modern Muslims were villagers or rural agriculturalists; they did not concern themselves with the range of juridical values or the custodians of those values, the ulama. Pre-modern networks were expansive but they were travelled by the elite.

During the 14th century, organised Sufism was beginning to take hold. Sufis breathed the same air of reciprocity and hierarchical value that characterised other men of the pen. Brotherhoods supplemented and competed with juridical forms of Islamic loyalty. Muslim adepts travelled from one shaykh to another, acquiring esoteric knowledge and certificates of competency (*ijazas*) as evidence of their growing erudition. The shaykhs generally presided over *zawiya*s that offered accommodation and set no limit to the time visitors might stay. They encouraged a form of horizontal or social trust between believers that presupposed a vertical or spiritual trust between the individual believer and the transcendent One. At its core was hospitality to 'the son of the road' (*ibn al-sabil*). Hospitality was more than a cultural mandate; it was also an act of piety.

Pursuit of spiritual knowledge often motivated travel, and travel itself could be a religious act. A famous hadith or tradition exhorts Muslims to seek knowledge even in China. In most places, Muslim travellers could find lodging in a *madrassa* (religious school) or *zawiya*, a more secular form of hostel. In Anatolia, *fityan* associations (brotherhoods of young artisans) prided themselves on their generosity to learned strangers. Like the *madrassas* and *zawiyas*, they operated on an unspoken and dynamic principle of trust; bonds were formed of idealism rather than the professionalism that bound guilds.

Trust was perhaps the most important factor in Muslim travel because it was at its core the key trait of spirituality. Even when travellers were not in the vicinity of a *zawiya*, *madrassa* or *fityan* association, they could rely on a pervasive code of trust. It translated into hospitality that was religiously underwritten by *zakat* or almsgiving, one of the five pillars of Islam. The basic meaning of Islam is submission to the One who is the Creator, the Guide and the Arbiter of all human existence. Trust in others, hospitality and charity were measures of one's trust in God; they were vital elements of the pervasive social code of Muslim travel, and rulers competed with each other to show foreigners the greatest generosity. Wherever Ibn Battuta travelled, he was with hospitable people who not only shared his beliefs and rituals but also his values, ideals and *adab* or customary manners.

Ibn Battuta's experience was not exceptional for a man of his class and education. By his own admission he was not especially learned, yet he was able to find patronage wherever he went because of his training in Maliki jurisprudence. Even basic instruction in one of the four schools of Sunni jurisprudence qualified adventurers for employment. The further they went beyond the heartlands of Islam, the more appreciated were their talents. The ulama traveled widely, especially to frontier kingdoms that were in need of jurists. Since the ulama were deemed to be the official guardians of Islamic law, practice and morality, there was mutual benefit to be gained from travelling scholarship. The foreign ulama mediated between newly Islamised rulers and their people. As imported scholars, they gave prestige to rulers whose appreciation of the scholars' learning proved their own credentials. Thus empowered, rulers could link themselves to the heartlands of Islam. The scholars, for their part, gained prestige and remuneration from their employment by generous patrons.

So it was with Ibn Battuta. When he left Tangiers in 1325, he was 21 years old. With the exception of a short stint as qadi of the Tunis hajj caravan, Ibn Battuta was constantly on the move. He went wherever he could market his legal skills. He benefited from the largesse of his fellow Muslims until he arrived eight years later in the court of the Delhi Sultan Muhammad ibn Tughluq, who immediately appointed him qadi. By 1334 Ibn Battuta had acquired a profile for which his education alone would not have sufficed. His travels had included several extended visits to Mecca. He became a *mujawir*, that is, someone honoured for having lived for long periods in the precincts of the Kaaba. More than the ordinary pilgrim who came to Mecca for the annual pilgrimage, the *mujawir* was credited with exemplary devotion to God and to His House. In a more practical light, a season or more in Mecca gave him the chance to make friends on whom he might draw for hospitality in the coming years. His titles were proofs of personal piety that added weight to his professional formation and allowed Ibn Battuta to move easily and comfortably throughout *Dar al-Islam*.

Travel demonstrates how Muslim networks have functioned as a medium. Approaching Islamic civilisation from a different angle, it also stresses their function as a method of knowing. Networking through travel is not uniquely Muslim, yet it compels attention to key elements in a Muslim worldview that are otherwise ignored. Travel accents both mobility and place. It gives place or location, an important role in the production of knowledge in a networked civilisation.

Courtly patronage throughout the region eased the travel and residence of writers and artists in a networked civilisation. In other words, royal courts served as more or less secular platforms for the articulation of the larger Muslim network of scholarship and creative production. And so we might follow the travels of the poet al-Mutanabbi (915-965) through sources of livelihood –

now in Cairo praising his patron, now in Baghdad satirizing him – to re-imagine the umma in his day. When we read the poetry of al-Mutanabbi through a networked lens, we can situate his writings in the places where he wrote and also the places between which he travelled. It is only through examining the urban-based networks of writers and artists that we can begin to understand the world they inhabited, and how that world is filtered through their writing and painting.

Medieval history acquires a new life when we put dates, people and places into conversation with each other. Ibn Battuta becomes the product as well as the subject of his far-flung travels. When we think about the materiality of the places he inhabited and their cultural and political climates, we may detect how his travel influenced him; the places he visited shaped his understanding of Islamic norms. We can ask: how did his interaction with patrons and also with Asian scholars affirm and extend the legal knowledge he had brought from Africa? How did he transform bits of information from his urban hosts into his own body of knowledge?

History provides a series of signposts, each pointing to the zigzag process of connection and transition, each offering cultural translations, even if they are necessarily fragmentary and provisional. Individual actors and narrators need to be read in terms of this open-ended process. It is an exchange affecting actor and narrator as much as audience, revealing unpredictable outcomes linked to many strands of Muslim memory and imagination. Networked exchanges reinforce norms and orthodoxies but also expose them to constant scrutiny and challenge.

One aspect that still challenges our imagination is the fresh sequence of journeys that the restless Ibn Battuta undertook after his 20-year sojourn in the east. Not content to stay at home in Morocco, he went first of all to Granada in southern Spain, where he enjoyed the full hospitality of the last Muslim kingdom of al-Andalus. While there he remarked on the presence of Sufi dervishes; they seemed much the same as those he had seen in Persia and India. What he did not remark upon was the naturalised presence of a Muslim culture as part of Europe, something that has been denied by the official guardians of European culture. Ibn Battuta observed as a matter-of-fact reality the continuity of life between Islamicate Spain and the regions of the east where he had spent much of his life. The current opposition between Islam and a Euro-American 'West' would have been incomprehensible to this tireless voyager. After Granada, Ibn Battuta took another trip, this time to West Africa, a rich arena for the exploitation both of gold and slaves. Here he observed the region that within a century would become the chief harvesting ground for the slave trade of North America, where Muslims would constitute one-sixth of the population of enslaved Africans. In other words, he was a witness both to the presence of Islam in Europe and the coming participation of Muslims in America.

Crossing Time

From the 11th to the 16th century, Muslims were at the forefront of global change. Muslim scientists and metaphysicians, such as Ibn Sina, al-Ghazali and Mulla Sadra, were linked across polities and territories to other elites; their ideas and writings influenced not only their own but other networked societies. A figure like al-Ghazali (1058-1111) draws on Aristotle as well as Muhammad, then integrates their legacy with his own insights, which he in turn transmits to European figures like Thomas Aquinas and Raymond Llull. The result is that David Hume's Enlightenment project in 18th-century Scotland uncannily reflects al-Ghazali's ideas on causality in Baghdad half a millennium earlier.

The process of transmission and transformation was materially assisted by the global extent of the umma. Until the 16th century, Islamic empires controlled large expanses of the world. Only with the European discovery and conquest of the New World did the axis of world power shift and networks become reconfigured. However, Muslim networks continued to be an important element of the capitalist world system. Under colonial rule they grew more numerous still from the Indian Ocean to the shores of the Atlantic. Despite the imbalances in political power, the colonial and pre-colonial periods are linked as phases in the networking of Muslim knowledge.

It was during the 18th and 19th centuries, while the Mughal and Safavid empires were experiencing internal revolt and foreign invasion that a new strand of Twelver Shia loyalty surfaced. From Karbala and Najaf in Iraq, and commercial centres in Iran to princely courts in northern India, there emerged a major academic network of Shia elites. The traffic was two-way, providing material as well as spiritual benefit to all. While juridical scholars of Iraq and Iran received large sums from their wealthy Indian co-religionists, the scholars of India benefited from the prestige of their northern neighbours. The scholars who participated in this network pursued the rational sciences, along with the traditional religious sciences. They engaged European science as fellow consumers.

Sunni networks of learning also spread from the Arabian Peninsula to the east coast of Africa and the Asian archipelago. Scholarly groups of Muslim reformers cooperated to expand the textual core of Islamic subjects. Several of these Sunni networks were motivated by loyalty to institutional Sufism, including the most socially active of Sufi orders, the Naqshbandiya. Naqshbandi leaders promoted Islamic revitalisation and mobilised their followers for a double jihad. One form of jihad was directed militarily against European imperialism, the other was directed intellectually against imitative Westernization.

A vivid example of modern Sunni Sufi networking is the Senegalese Murid trade diaspora that Mamadou Diouf and Steven Rendall have analysed in their essay on an indigenous cosmopolitanism.[5] Tracing the history of a West African Sufi brotherhood from its foundation in the 19th century to the present, they note that the network grew 'by offering a new religious form, a new memory and new images to peasant communities that had been disrupted and severely disturbed by colonial military campaigns (and) epidemics connected with the Atlantic slave trade'. Members of the Murid brotherhood were engaged in mystical practices

---

[5] Mamadou Diouf and Steven Rendall, 'The Senegalese Murid Trade Diaspora and the Making of a Vernacular Cosmopolitanism', *Public Culture*, 12 (2000), pp. 679-702.

requiring specific social arrangements, and also the international peanut business highly prized by the French. They were hence able to reconcile Islam with colonial modernity. Theirs was 'a unique cosmopolitanism consisting in participation but not assimilation, thus organizing the local not only to strengthen its position but also to establish the rules governing dialogue with the universal'. A major phase in the spread of the Murid network came in the 1970s when drought drove peasants into the Senegalese cities and later out of the country. Members of the brotherhood wove an immense global network linked to their spiritual capital of Touba, with economic and distributive centres in Sandaga and Dakar. Wherever they went they established order and an unbroken trust. Trust remains the key element not only of the Murid brothers but of all Muslim networks.

What took place in the Senegalese trade and spiritual network provides a model case of the integration of Muslims into the contemporary global economy. Muslims were able to turn to their advantage oppressive structures that colonial powers had put in place. For both African and Asian Muslims, a significant part of their history has been marked by European colonial expansion. In the colonial period nationalist networks involving Muslims first emerged. It was networked Indian Muslims who collaborated in the struggle for independence from the British and on behalf of the new Muslim state of Pakistan. Yet they also faced tensions, especially when the horizontal networks enabling the founding of Pakistan had to come to terms with the hierarchical structure of the new nation-state. More will be said about this below.

Not only in India but everywhere the modern history of Islam became inseparable from both European and local nationalisms that gave platforms to competing identities and to selective images. European colonizers reinforced already negative images of Muslims. Civilisations became symbolic envelopes for group solidarity; their hierarchical rankings, though touted as objective, in fact reinforced the Enlightenment bias that only western Europeans were the standard bearers of modern day reason and progress. The record of humankind was etched on a simple model of primitive-classical-modern. If Africa was primitive, Islam, like India and China, was classical. Its adherents had attained a certain level of reason, enough to move beyond the stage of primitive but no further. Muslims could reach the stage of modernity only with the help of western Europeans. The expansion of European colonial rule was pitched as neither aggressive nor acquisitive; it was the logic of 'progress'.

Progress should have dictated that colonial rule would weaken and undercut Muslim networks. The opposite was the case. While colonial rule broke down connections between specific local Muslim groups (such as Berbers and Arabs), it also fostered the revival of these same groups in resistance to European domination. Ironically, the very networks that opposed European rule also linked Muslims to the metropolitan capitals of France and England. Education, both secular and religious, became crucial in expanding Muslim networks throughout Africa and Asia. Education was about more than curricular content; it also involved usage of European languages in new contexts. During the 19th century, French and English became the dominant regional languages for Muslim communities, sometimes displacing local Muslim languages like Urdu, Persian, Pashto or Bengali. Owing to its religious role, Arabic was the only Muslim language to retain its prestige during the colonial period.

Both anti-colonial and other local networks were organised in secular terms, influenced by Europe's nationalism. Ethnic nationalism became the primary organising principle, despite the use of religious symbols and the mobilisation of religious movements. What had begun as an 'attempt to protect Islam by reinterpreting it tended to end as a discussion of the possibility of creating a secular society with social action', notes Albert Hourani.[6] Ethnic and regional nationalisms provided alternatives not only to existing empires but also, more importantly, to the umma.

During the decade or so after World War II, most Muslim countries achieved political independence, but not under the banner of Islam. Despite their notable role in resistance struggles, Muslim activists and reformers took a back seat to the secular politicians

---

[6] Hourani, *History of the Arab Peoples*, p. 73.

who were building new nation-states. It was the circumstances of the late 1960s and early 1970s that returned Islamic rhetoric to the forefront of domestic, regional and international issues. This was a period when Muslims contended not only with outsiders, primarily those in search of oil fortunes, but also with impure insiders, autocratic secularists. Islam was at once the goal and the method: Muslim networks claiming Islamic authority opposed secular networks that invoked national or republican loyalty. Islam became a slogan for freedom and solidarity. The ideal of the umma may have been invoked, but its reality was filled with ideological claims.

The degree of European influence on Muslim public life remains a subject of fierce debate. Did European occupiers repress Islam throughout the vast realm traversed by Ibn Battuta and his co-religionists? Yes and no. Colonial rule played a crucial mediating role in the emergence of present-day Muslim networks, but state and society experienced different fates. Even though Muslim nation-states were often constructed through conciliar decrees, such as the 1919 Treaty of Versailles and the 1920 Treaty of Sèvres, few Muslim societies fully succumbed to European hegemony. Individual Muslims and collective networks found an alternative space between the past and the future that reflected indigenous norms and values. Nowhere is this clearer than in the case of Muslim Personal Law (MPL). With the approval of colonial powers but on behalf of resistant Muslim elites, MPL thrived as a measure of Muslim collective life. In other words, the advocacy of MPL served patriarchal elites. Women rarely benefited in a context where the policing of their bodies was integral to the system. Since the 1980s, some women have organised in reaction to the imposition of MPL. They have banded together and formed associations like Maghreb Collectif, the Arab Women's Solidarity Association and Women Living Under Muslim Laws (WLMUL).

Exchanges between Europe and the Muslim world were mutual. European colonial powers were themselves shaped by their interface with colonial subjects. Especially in the post-independence period, mass migrations from former colonies flowed into European capitals, which affected the shared economic and political life of the late 20th century. Before 1980 one could still speak of a world economy as though there were stable players who managed the world's resources for their own political ends. Since the end of the Cold War, however, the global economy has seen a rapid growth of exchange and institutions that occur outside the limits of relations between states. Widely variable and adaptable networks reflect new economic conditions, even as they aggravate geo-political imbalances among the different regions and players. A key factor in this new global economy is information technology, which affects most areas of life today.

Information Revolution

Until the mid-1990s three forms of media defined the Information Age: print (newspapers), audio (the radio, telephone, tape cassettes and cell phones), and audio-visual (television and movies). Since then satellite television, after overcoming local censorship barriers, has played the greatest role in Muslim countries. No initiative has succeeded or generated as much impact as has the satellite station Al-Jazeera that was established in the late 1990s. Its creators were BBC-trained reporters sponsored by the Emir of Qatar. During the post-9/11 period, this satellite television station broadcasting from the Arabian Gulf became as familiar to American viewers as CNN. It provided the world with otherwise unavailable coverage; in a virtual theatre it brought together viewers from all over the Arab and the Muslim worlds. Programmes like 'The Opposite Direction' feature conflicting personalities who debate one another, often on subjects of religious interest. These programmes have garnered huge audiences unused to such open expression of controversial views.

The most revolutionary potential of the Information Age, however, rests with the internet. In Saudi Arabia, AwalNet was the first internet service provider in the Kingdom. On 7 November, 1999 it published an article online in which it promised to 'marry the Internet and Islam for the millennium'.[7] Linking people,

---

[7] AwalNet Unlimited, 7 November, 1999.

places and commodities with an immediacy that seems to conquer space, the internet has engendered a new way of being in the world that the French philosopher Paul Virilio calls 'tele-presence', or the technologically enhanced capacity to 'be' in several places at the same time. Consider the pious Muslim who would like to make the annual pilgrimage to Mecca but does not yet have the time or the money. She may content herself with a cyber hajj for the time being.[8] For Muslim immigrants trying to make a home far from home and to participate in communities of shared interests rather than shared place or shared ancestry, the internet offers a lifeline.

Muslims may also form virtual communities at the collective and individual levels that provide safety, companionship, social support and a sense of belonging. Tele-presence enables a new form of association that compels a reconsideration of the meaning of community: what is community when participants do not share place but can communicate as if they did? If shared physical place is not a necessary condition, is the idea of community as embodied contact just a romantic projection of an idealised past?

These questions are not all that new. For some, the world has witnessed only two major revolutions in information: first, Gutenberg and the printing press, and now the World Wide Web and cyberspace. Yet we need to look behind the current rhetoric of globalisation; when we do, we find obvious precedents that suggest limits to the transformative power of the information revolution. Trust in one form or another has always been a cornerstone among dispersed groups that link through common needs and interests. Moreover, the growth of Muslim networks brings not only opportunity but rivalry, which may involve the erosion of trust.

For example, Muslim networks compete with each other in the new and enlarged public sphere of Pakistan, a nation-state that was the product of the colonial period. Pakistan – a country created by Muslim networks – raises a hard question: which networks

---

[8] See http://islamicity.com/mosque/hajj/

defined its meaning? The meaning of Pakistan, says David
Gilmartin, 'was rooted in a vision of community defined not by
the networks of the *ulama*, or by the networks supporting the
colonial state, but by the bonds of devotion and love linking individual Muslims to symbols of Islam popularized through the
networks of the press'.[9] Yet these print communities were far from
uniform. Networks of the press, for instance, 'both enabled and
threatened – at precisely the same time – the effective imagining
of a common Muslim community and a Muslim civilisation (in
Pakistan)'. All too often, the top-down bureaucratic power inherent
in the structure of the nation-state harmed the horizontal networks
that had contributed so much to the formation of the country.

Again, while the internet is socially, politically and spiritually
empowering, it is far from egalitarian. Afro-Asian Muslim students
who came to the United States to be trained as engineers in the
1970s were the first to create Islamic web sites (notably, through
Muslim Student Associations). They became catalysts for digital-
ising Islam. They put scripture online, making available many
renditions of Quran and hadith that, in turn, facilitated the production of new *ijtihad*s or interpretations of foundational texts. But
this initial stage in which individual Muslim engineers made texts
available online has been followed by a stage in which official-
ising strategies have become dominant. National orthodoxies
control resources and project their view of Islam in cyberspace.
What matters is not just who can access the internet but who
controls the webmasters and the websites that claim to speak on
behalf of all Muslims.

In short, authority is more diffuse now than it was 200 or even
10 years ago. *Ijtihad* used to be the responsibility of the *ulama*.
The complex language of their religious discourse had blocked
access to the amateur. However, the migrant engineer theologians
changed all that by distributing authority among Muslim cybernauts. To the extent that e-*ijtihad* has opened up debates in cyberspace that had been previously limited or foreclosed, no student
of contemporary Muslim expression can ignore Islam online. It

[9] Gilmartin, 'A Networked Civilization?', pp. 51-68.

has huge implications for the ways in which interpretations and decisions are made and politics are conducted, particularly in the wake of September 11, 2001. Multiple competing groups offer their analyses and prescriptions for the appropriate response to Afghanistan, Iraq and the 'war on terror', some more militant than others.

Religious-minded 'cybernauts' share the concerns of Muslims worldwide. They foster cyber environments that reinforce Muslim values no matter what dominant cultural or vocational demands individual Muslims face. But there is a hierarchy among these cybernauts themselves. At its peak are Euro-American Muslim immigrants with their heightened sense of diversity, their need for faith-based community, and the human and material resources to link themselves with other, like-minded groups; they project themselves as being on the leading edge for change in the Muslim world. They may exaggerate the impact of their own role, but their imagined scope for potential change is itself noteworthy.

Central to the fostering of Muslim values is the challenge to old notions of authority. The World Wide Web both enhances and threatens individual authority. On the one hand, individual authority is enhanced as more options are available for the exchange of information, to reach wide audiences and to elicit trust. On the other hand, the very proliferation of competing sites and the intrinsic democracy of the World Wide Web can undermine ideas of consensual authority. New religious interpreters and online counsellors have become Muslim netizens, advocating local versions of Islam.

Networks and Globalization

'Globalization draws us simultaneously towards two contrasting results, one welcome and the other not: i.e., universality and uniformity', observes Amin Maalouf. Likewise, Muslims and those who study Islam in the 21st century must seek to steer a path between particularisms and absolutist claims. The term 'Muslim network' offers a more complex and nuanced view of Islam and Islamic civilisation. It poses a challenge to media mavens and zealots who strive to demonise Islam. Muslim networks taken out of context, or restricted to the post-September 11 context, may seem to mean one thing: terror committed in the name of Islam. Yet the idea opens the door to understanding the levels of learning and trust that have motivated so many Muslims across time and space.

Today, the internet is the medium empowering both mainstream Muslim groups and marginalized ones. For example, al-Qaeda is a network of hard-line Muslim guerrillas co-founded by Saudi dissident Osama bin Laden and the Egyptian doctor turned activist, Ayman al-Zawahiri. They have exploited the political and military potential of the internet, yet these dissidents need to be understood on their own terms, not as emblems of Muslim networks. Built around scattered points that talk to one another in non-linear space, al-Qaeda relies neither on a hierarchical chain of command nor the usual rules of engagement. It mobilises nimble, dispersed and elusive units capable of penetrating and disrupting, even destroying, massive structures. Their call for physical violence relies increasingly on electronic jihad. This is what Gary Bunt calls 'a digital sword' with a range of strikes, from the hacking of websites to violence and the sanctioning of bloodshed.

The study of social movements should extend to a vital aspect of contemporary Islamic civilisation: the origins, organisation and actions of the Salafi movement worldwide. Though a minority of all Muslims, these conservative activists believe that Islam as text-bound faith has been eroded from within. It is they who must do something to rectify the situation. Though Salafis are united in their devotion to the Quran, they are divided among themselves between non-militant reformists and those who may sometimes be driven to extremes. Dissent from the current world order and/or from Muslim majority states links Muslim militants from Chechnya, Kosovo, Uzbekistan, Tajikistan and Kashmir to Afghanistan, the Philippines, Indonesia and West China. Disgruntled religious activists are calling for a return to the fundamentals. When they stray, Muslim-majority nations must be purified of the legacy of European colonialism and also the threat of American neo-colonialism. Both the civil war in Algeria and Bin Laden's 1996 declaration of war on the US demonstrate that no cost is too high for those Salafis who condone the use of violence. Despite the Salafi condemnation of *bida* or innovation, there has emerged 'net Salafism'. A contradiction? Logically yes, but practically no. Salafi use of the internet, like the use of modern weapons, is cast as a necessary evil in the fight against infidels.

While the case of al-Qaeda has become obvious, there is a complementary case that demonstrates how dissent can be peacefully channelled through Muslim networks. The women of Afghanistan were subjected to intense scrutiny after the US-led invasion in October 2001. The coverage implied that they had to be saved from the Taliban. Originally, no attention was paid to feminist networks like the Revolutionary Association of the Women of Afghanistan (RAWA). Founded in 1977, two years before the Soviet invasion, its members worked to defeat the Soviets, but also to provide help for Afghan refugees in Pakistan. It was a network of transnational cooperation and multi-tiered resistance throughout the 1980s and 1990s. Since 9/11, its pivotal role on behalf of Afghan women at home and abroad has been dramatised through cyberspace. RAWA demonstrates not just the persistence but also the resilience of Muslim networks. They can be understood in a number of ways: a major form of social and political organisation, a prism through which to read history, and a symbol of hope for those who find themselves on the margins of our current world system.

RAWA has plenty of company. Associations such as Women Living Under Muslim Laws (WLUML) have emerged across the globe, bringing new and previously marginalised people into the mainstream. WLUML was established in 1986 by the Algerian Marie-Aimée Hélie-Lucas. Its network has brought together women from all over the world in a bid to provide information and support, including for women living in places governed by Muslim laws who don't know where to turn for guidance. During the 1990s, WLUML undertook a 'women and law' project, the goal of which was to counter the growing influence of Islamists. Like other women's networks, their platform includes peace, prevention of violence against women, opposition to religious fundamentalism, gender equity, and women's rights. It is especially concerned about the needs of peasant, working class and urban poor women. Such networks highlight women's emergent importance within the umma.

Another kind of Muslim women's network emerged after the 1991 Gulf War, among Shia women driven from their homes in southern Iraq to refugee camps in Saudi Arabia and then to new homes in Holland. In all their dislocations, the collective identity of these twice marginalised women was preserved through vertical and horizontal links. The vertical link was constructed by their relationship to foremothers who had for the past 14 centuries connected themselves to Zaynab, the grand-daughter of the Prophet Muhammad. The horizontal link was constituted by groups of Shia women who connected with each other in Iraq, Saudi Arabia and Holland, mainly through ritual and spiritual observances learned and then carefully controlled by the *mullaya*, or religious leader. The women's linkages, as Tayba Sharif explains, are established at special lamentation sessions to commemorate the heroism of Zaynab.[10] The network fosters the telling of sacred stories that connect history and ritual to their own stories of devastation. Through the remembrance of their great foremother, her grief for her murdered brother Husayn and her defiance of the tyrant Yazid (who may stand in for any contemporary tyrant), they link themselves with peers across distance and time.

These modern women's networks are far more inclusive than their precursors, yet they still resemble those that have characterized the Muslim world in the past. Like Ibn Battuta, they find themselves at home in many places that little resemble each other except that they are marked Muslim. Trust is the moral and social glue holding them together, providing both meaning and direction to their lives. There is, however, a crucial difference. Whereas the ability to savour the benefits of *Dar al-Islam* in the 14th century depended on material means, today's networks are less driven by economic or class indices. Ibn Battuta concerned himself only with those who made up the cosmopolitan class, a class that

---

[10] Tayba Hassan Al Khalifa Sharif, 'Sacred Narratives linking Iraqi Shiite Women across Time and Space', in M. Cooke and B. Lawrence, ed., *Muslim Networks*, pp. 132-154.

considered itself the keeper of high culture within the world of Islam. It was only the elite who could afford the costs of travel and so avail themselves of the hospitality of the 14th-century world.

In contrast, Muslim networks in the 21st century require less physical mobility as they become more diffuse and accessible. Reduced costs make them increasingly available to anyone who has basic literacy, typing skills and a little spare cash. In 2002, the Tunis medina cyber cafe charged US $1 per hour for use of the internet, while a Beijing internet bar charged as little as US 5 cents per hour. In the summer of 2003 in US-occupied Baghdad, young Iraqis were flocking to the growing numbers of cyber cafes to keep in contact with the world, while in 2007 an Egyptian journalist could even claim that 'the Internet is the new mosque'.[11]

From the 14th-century world of Ibn Battuta to the 21st-century world of Muslim female cybernauts and heroic descendants of Zaynab, much has changed, but nothing more so than the speed of communication. Cyber networks challenge how we understand space. They reveal a cosmopolitan realm that trumps old, exclusive divisions between East and West. Cyber networks blur the binary distinctions between *Dar al-harb* (the abode of war) and *Dar al-Islam*. Already in pre-modern times, Muslims had modified that distinction to include two other sub categories: *Dar al-aman* (the abode of safety) and *Dar al-muahada* (the abode of covenant). In cyberspace, even these categories are blurred by countless ties across space and time. Muslims in the Information Age have become new Ibn Battutas journeying to assorted 'ports' in search of information that can be transformed into knowledge. Ideas as well as people have continued to travel since his time. Equity then stressed fairness, but accepted slavery and sexism; equality in the 21st century, a norm for Muslims and non-Muslims alike, affirms that race and gender must be inclusive.

[11] Abdallah al-Tahawy, 'The Internet is the new Mosque', *Arab Insight*, 2 (Winter 2008), pp. 11-19.

Conclusion

Networks are not new. Over the past 1,400 years, societies of Muslims have been constantly networked through bonds of trust in a shared ethos. What is new is the sheer multiplicity of Muslim networks through modern information technology. Knowing that they are potentially in touch all the time provides Muslim cybernauts – and also their non-Muslim counterparts – with a fresh way of knowing and of being in the world, of connecting across time and space. The information revolution comes out of radical shifts in technology and patterns of organisation that are scattered across the world. Yet to understand Muslim networks today, one must ask about their historical antecedents and their adaptation to new aspects of the Information Age that have emerged since the mid-1990s.

To relate the cyber umma to the historical umma is to understand how both function together as pathways of Muslim collective existence along the Straight Path (*sirat al-mustaqim*). If networks are a powerful metaphor, so too is the Straight Path. Indeed, the Straight Path is one of the most fertile and recurrent of Islamic metaphors. It is introduced in the opening chapter of the Quran. 'Guide us on the straight path', Muslims ask of Allah each day, whenever they engage in formal prayer. The Straight Path leads to peace and certainty, to trust and truth, in this world and the next. The borders of digital Islam also reflect the borders of thinking about doctrine, history and scripture. There can be no Islam without limits or guideposts. You can't have a Straight Path unless you know what is beyond, outside or against it. Cyberspace, like social space, is sometimes 'appropriately Muslim' and sometimes not. The open-ended nature of the Internet makes the boundaries of digital Islam at once more porous and more subject to change than those of its predecessors. Still, there are familiar guideposts: the scripture (the Noble Quran), the person (the Last Prophet) and the law (the sharia or broad path, with the ulama or religious specialists as its custodians). Each term – the Book, the Prophet, the Law – has to be defined historically, then redefined in cyberspace in order to reflect the diversity of resources and worldviews within the umma.

There are also questions that merit further exploration about the nature of networks. How do they shape and reshape identities, whether individual or communal? In what ways do they affect authority, both local and beyond? How free are individuals to organise in states where authoritarian orders do not trust independent associations, and will try to co-opt them as part of their claim to support civil society? How may women organise in societies that are dominated by patriarchal kinship ties with their strict hierarchies?

What seems clear is that Muslim networks provide a way of understanding Islam across frontiers, where space both matters and does not. In this perspective, individuals are 'pluralised': they can be situated in multiple contexts where no single identity or single interpretation of Islam is dominant. Muslim networks mark a series of creative responses to global systems, past and present. They sustain and contest the systems of which they are a part. The work of Muslim 'netizens' reveals the hope, and also the limits of hope, available to the 21st-century umma. The umma will persist as a universal community bound by faith and ritual practices, yet networks create tensions and competing points of authority that affirm the diversity and synergy of Islam and Muslim civilisations.

Further Reading

Al-Sayyad, Nezar and Manuel Castells. *Muslim Europe or Euro-Islam: Politics, Culture, and Citizenship in the Age of Globalization.* Lanham, MD, 2002.

Blank, Jonah. *Mullahs on the Mainframe: Islam and Modernity among Daudi Bohras.* Chicago, 2001.

Chatty, Dawn and Annika Rabo, ed. *Organizing Women: Formal and Informal Groups in the Middle East.* Oxford, 1997.

Clark, Janine Astrid. *Faith, Networks, and Charity: Islamic Welfare Activism and the Middle Class in Egypt, Yemen, and Jordan.* Bloomington, IN, 2003.

Cooke, Miriam and Bruce Lawrence, ed. *Muslim Networks: From Hajj to Hip-Hop*. Chapel Hill, NC, 2005.

Denoeux, Guilain. *Urban Unrest in the Middle East: A Comparative Study of Informal Networks in Egypt, Iran, and Lebanon*. Albany, NY, 1993.

Diani, Mario and Doug McAdam. *Social Movements and Networks: Relational Approaches to Collective Action*. Oxford, 2003.

Dunn, Ross. *The Adventures of Ibn Battuta: A Muslim Traveller of the 14th Century*. Berkeley, CA, 1989.

Eickelman, Dale F. and Jon W. Anderson, ed. *New Media in the Muslim World: The Emerging Public Sphere*. 2nd ed. Bloomington, IN, 2003.

Maalouf, Amin. *Leo Africanus*. Chicago, 1998.

Mohammadi, Ali, ed. *Islam Encountering Globalization*. London, 2002.

Nouraie-Simone, Fereshteh, ed. *On Shifting Ground: Muslim Women in the Global Era*. New York, 2005.

Singerman, Diane. *Avenues of Participation: Family, Politics, and Networks in Urban Quarters of Cairo*. Princeton, 1995.

Virilio, Paul. *The Information Bomb*. New York, 2000.

6

Women and Social Change

Azizah Yahia al-Hibri

In this age of information technology that shrank our world into a global village, it is fair to ask how this development has impacted Muslim women's rights across the world. All the more so after the complications that flow from the events of September 11, 2001. As the world slowly disentangles these complications and seeks to return to more peaceful relations among nations, the door has cracked open for a reasoned dialogue among Muslims themselves on issues of modernity, human rights and gender-equitable Islamic laws.

Muslim women are often bewildered by the laws and judicial systems of their societies, which are supposed to be Islamic. It is well understood that social justice (*adl*) is a hallmark of Islam, affirmed as such both in the Quran and the theological literature at large. Yet Muslim societies have long dispensed injustice to women in the name of Islam. Women seeking divorce in Islamic courts have been trapped within the system for years – even as divorce and remarriage have been rendered much easier for Muslim men. Again, various protections for women in the sharia (Islamic law) with regard to unhappy wedlock, divorce or custody have been ignored even by the women's own families.[1]

---

[1] Some of these protections include the right of the woman not to be married without her consent, her right to a reasonable *sadaq* (financial or other gift given by the husband upon marriage), as well as her right to education and work. Other neglected safeguards include protection against abuse and interference by the husband in the wife's financial affairs.

While western feminists focus on such issues as the veil and perceived gender discrimination in the laws of inheritance, Muslim women I have spoken to did not regard these issues as vital. They were more interested in re-examining family law and in the proper application of all Islamic laws, including the laws of inheritance as they stand. In short, Muslim women want a just and equitable understanding of, and adherence to, Islamic principles. They appear to believe that existing laws and practices are not conducive to a happy home life or a just society. Indeed, Muslim women have had the support of leading male jurists who share their concerns.[2]

Several factors have forced Muslims to reassess the status quo. The experience of colonialism, wars and exposure to western education and modes of communication have been primary among these factors. Colonisation laid bare the soft underbelly of indigenous systems of governance, while at the same time challenging and marginalising the Muslim individual's religious beliefs and cultural values. Wars dislodged established social structures, especially those relating to the family. Recent information circulated through the internet and media outlets has thrown into question the commitment of the international community to human rights and the motives that underlie such commitment.

The vast web of information available today forces the user to become more sophisticated and discerning. Thus, while resenting recent political developments, Muslim men and women continue to experience simultaneously the other face of western culture and way of life. Generally, they like a good part of what they see, such as democratic governance, freedom of speech, independent women and comfortable, technologically advanced societies. There are other things which they decidedly do not like, such as sexual permissiveness and the divorce rate, social violence among the youth and the treatment of the elderly.

---

[2] They include Abdul Halim Abu Shuqqah, Sheikh Mahdi Shams al-Din and Seyyed Mohsen Saidzadeh. Earlier, Muhammad Rashid Ridha championed a Quranic interpretation which was more equitable toward women, in his position as head of al-Azhar, the traditional centre of Muslim theology located in Cairo.

Many Muslims, male and female, therefore struggle today with these questions: How should they introduce progress into their societies without weakening traditional social bonds, and at the same time protect their deep-seated spiritual beliefs and cultural identities – two valuable foundations that colonialism tried unsuccessfully to destroy? How can they benefit from the positive aspects of the western experience, including the recognition of the legitimate rights of women, without inadvertently destroying their highly valued familial ties? In this context, the experience of those western Muslims who have successfully integrated their religious beliefs and ethnic heritage with European and North American ways of life becomes very valuable. It is living proof of the fact that Islam is not a mere 'Oriental' religion, but a world religion which is capable of meeting the needs of Muslims in all historical eras and all geographical locations.

There is the risk that western Muslim perspectives may be seen elsewhere as suitable only to the circumstances of European and North American societies. Yet others may find inspiration in those perspectives, as pointing to new ways of organising communities and societies while remaining true to their religious beliefs. This chapter will focus on what I consider to be the most significant issues for Muslims in relation to gender, and address them on the basis of key traditional Islamic sources, including the Quran. We will see that patriarchy and cultural distortions have come in the way of a proper appreciation of the sources.

Culture and Religion

The distinction between (and relationship of) culture and religion is critical for understanding the body of Islamic law or jurisprudence. Most importantly, the Quran is the revealed Word of God, whereas culture is a purely human creation. So, while a Muslim is bound by the Quran as scripture, she is not bound similarly by her cultural values. For example, a Muslim may reject certain cultural customs or values, yet remain part of that culture. She cannot, however, reject what the Quran ordains and still call herself a Muslim. Cultural assumptions and values that mask themselves as religious ones can mislead us into believing that they have divine origins, thus denying Muslims the right to assess them critically or even to reject them. Some of the major misleading cultural assumptions relate to issues of democracy and women's rights. The two issues are, in fact, related.

Cultural assumptions and customs have often been introduced legitimately into the Islamic legal system. The Quran celebrates ethnic, racial and other forms of diversity; and the hadith (reported words of the Prophet) emphasises the equality of all human beings.[3] For this reason, jurists have encouraged various cultures to retain their cultural identity by including their customs in their legal systems. The only condition for such inclusion was that these customs be consistent with the basic tenets of Islam itself. In case of inconsistency, the cultural customs must be rejected. This approach permitted a variety of Muslim civilisations to blossom, each with its own cultural heritage but all sharing the same basic religious law.

However, some customs that conflicted with Islamic tenets increasingly found their way into the laws of various Muslim countries. Even today, many countries that claim to be following Islamic law often use religion to justify repugnant laws that are really based on custom.[4] Because such justification is offered in societies where religious education has most likely suffered in the last century, people are often unable to discern the cultural roots of objectionable laws and their conflict with Islam. As a result, devout Muslims hesitate to criticise any part of the law. In other words, confusion as to the religious character of some laws has effectively resulted in silencing important critical voices and keeping

---

[3] See Quran 4:1, 6:98, 7:189; *Khutbat al-wadaa* of the Prophet, in which he stated: 'O People, all believers are siblings. Your God is one and your father is one. You are all from Adam and Adam is from dust. The most favoured amongst you in the sight of God is the one who is most pious; no Arab is favoured over a non-Arab except on the basis of piety.'

[4] For an excellent discussion of such laws, see Asifa Quraishi, 'Her Honor: An Islamic Critique of the Rape Laws of Pakistan from a Woman-Sensitive Perspective', *Michigan Journal of International Law*, 18 (1997) pp. 287-315.

society bound by repugnant customs that are mistaken for religious norms. It is furthermore important to understand that Islamic laws as they relate to *muamalat* (dealings among people) often reflect differences of legal opinion among major Muslim scholars. The most obvious instance of this fact is reflected in the Muslim family law of the various countries.

These differences have many roots. Allowing custom into the legal system is only one of them. Another root derives from the right to freedom of conscience, which is guaranteed in the Quran itself (2:256). For this reason, it is established in traditional Islamic law that scholars have the right to engage in their own *ijtihad* (interpretation) to develop laws that are best suited to their time and jurisdiction. That *ijtihad* is then reflected in the legal system of the country.

Unfortunately, several factors have combined through history to narrow the scope of *ijtihad* and limit freedom of thought. As a result, many schools of thought disappeared and no new ones replaced them. Furthermore, scholars continued to adhere to established schools of thought even when these were no longer best suited to their societies. Only recently, for example, did Morocco revise its personal status code to eliminate a provision allowing the father to force his *bikr* (virgin) daughter into marriage. The provision derived from the Maliki tradition and represented an obsolete cultural interpretation of the parental relationship, yet it remained part of the law for a very long time. A closer look at the Maliki interpretation would have revealed its inconsistency with the hadith that requires the consent (or permission) of a *bikr* for the validity of her marriage. Such inconsistencies were often overlooked by earlier jurists who were caught up in their own cultural ways of seeing things. As these have become outmoded, it is important to expose and eliminate them.

It is not possible, however, to critically assess Islamic law without a proper Islamic education. Politics, unfortunately, has played a major role in denying the average Muslim a good religious education. This denial, which in part is a legacy of colonial policy, helped political regimes to confuse the masses about what is in the Quran or what the Quran actually says. Such confusion did serious damage in areas of Islamic law relating to issues of governance and democracy. Recognising their responsibility towards God and Muslims, jurists made repeated attempts to clarify Islamic law on these matters, as they struggled to keep political influence out of the mosque. Most significant among such attempts in the recent past was the work of Egypt's Abd al-Razzaq al-Sanhuri (1895-1971), who noted that the essentials of the Islamic system of government have much in common with the system of government in the United States.

Too often, rulers blocked these initiatives and punished the leaders who stood in their way. A famous historical example is that of a founding jurist, Imam Malik (714-796), who was tortured by the ruler for refusing to mislead Muslims about the fact that forced consent was not binding on them. Today, it is governments that often appoint the Grand Mufti (highest ranking Islamic authority in the state), as well as imams of mosques. Some governments even limit or specify the topics imams may address on Fridays, when Muslims congregate to pray. At the same time, there are social forces at play in many Muslim countries that wish to narrow the scope of innovative thinking in these matters. Yet Muslim women have determinedly sought spaces – public and private – in which to seriously discuss their rights.

First Principles in Islam

To understand Islamic law, one must begin with the foundations of Islam itself. The primary source of all Islamic law is the Quran. It is supplemented by the hadith. Other important sources are those of *ijma* (consensus) and *ijtihad* which is based on rules of logic as well as on religious texts. Each individual has direct access to the Quran and hadith, and is in principle entitled to engage in *ijtihad*, so long as she has the requisite knowledge. Thus, not only societies but also individuals are entitled to their own jurisprudential choices.

This basic right of Muslims to freedom of juridical choice and to access to the Quran and hadith, combined with Islam's respect for local custom, means that Muslims are not bound by the cultural preferences or juridical choices of those in other countries. We are free to retain from our ethnic heritage these elements that continue to be viable and useful in our society today. But we are fully bound by our religious commitments. We are entitled, however, to interpret Divine Will in ways that are best suited for our own time and space. Of course, such interpretations do not apply to the *thawabit* of Islam, that is, to matters which are fixed, clear and fundamental, such as the unity of God.

In the matter of Muslim women's rights, the patriarchal assumptions of cultures cannot bind societies that reject them. Furthermore, in discovering what the Quran and hadith say, we are not today bound by the patriarchal aspects of interpretations offered by earlier jurists. These aspects reveal themselves as patriarchal when the jurist incorporates into his logic patriarchal assumptions not present in the Quranic verse itself, such as the assumption that women are emotional and irrational.

The Quranic View of Women

Basic Equality

Reading the Quran, I discover that it has only one creation story. The Quran states repeatedly, for emphasis, that both the male and the female were created from the same soul or *nafs* (4:1, 6:98, 7:189). There is no hierarchy of any kind in gender creation. In the Quran, the fall of Adam is not blamed on Eve. Rather, both were tempted by Satan and sinned in the pursuit of power and eternal life. Moreover, God forgave humanity after the fall. There is no continuing burden of 'original sin'. Men and women are responsible towards God for their own mortal choices. They are both judged by the same standards; they also have the same rights, duties and obligations in matters of *ibadat* (worship). There are some differences between them in the realm of *muamalat* (social dealings), where civil matters are regulated; this will be addressed below. In short, a Muslim woman is as complete a spiritual being as the male. She is as entitled as he is to read and interpret the Quran, and to live a full, devout life.

Legal and Financial Rights

In the realm of *muamalat*, the Muslim woman is an independent legal person before and after marriage. A Muslim woman may retain her own name after marriage. She also retains her financial independence and can own property in her own right, whether she is married or single. No one – not even her husband – may access her funds or property, or demand any form of financial support from her. Any money or property of her own that the wife gives her husband, even if she is richer than he, is regarded as a loan unless she expressly specifies otherwise. However, Islamic law differentiates between the financial rights and obligations of the two genders. The male, while also financially independent has additional financial responsibilities. He must support the women in his family regardless of their financial condition, unless there is a financially able male relative who is closer to them. For example, a father is responsible for the support of his daughter, regardless of her age, but if the woman marries, that responsibility is transferred to her husband. The logic of these differences in obligations may lie in the fact that the Quran is simply providing women with added security in a difficult patriarchal world. Put into today's legal language, the Quran engages in affirmative action with respect to women.

Right to *Sadaq*

The Quran also gives the woman additional opportunities to accumulate wealth. For example, upon marriage she has the right to expect a gift from her husband which could range from teaching her a few verses of the Quran (if she does not know them already) to a few silver coins or an immense fortune, depending on the parties' mutual agreement. This is referred to as the *sadaq* or *mahr* of the woman, sometimes erroneously described as 'bride price'. The *sadaq* signifies the willingness of the man to undertake the responsibilities of marriage. The woman has the option of asking for the full amount of the *sadaq* (or designated property) in advance, or of deferring part of it to become due at a specified later time, or upon such event as death or divorce. In the case of death, *sadaq* becomes a senior debt of the deceased husband's estate to be satisfied ahead of all other debts. Therefore, the *sadaq* is at times more valuable than the wife's inheritance from her husband when the estate is over-burdened by debt.

In the case of divorce, the *sadaq* offers the woman a clearly defined property or amount of money she can rely upon after the divorce, without the need for further negotiation. Whereas some rich women tend to settle for a symbolic *sadaq*, many women view it as their security net in case of death or divorce. Some women may prefer to take the full amount of the *sadaq* at the outset. In that event, these women are free to invest the amount of the *sadaq* in any venture they choose. They may start a business with it or even give it to charity. The husband may not touch it or any profit resulting from it.

Of course, patriarchal reality in Muslim countries is quite different from the Islamic ideal. Today, many fathers negotiate the amount or type of *sadaq* on behalf of their daughters. In some cultures, it is a sign of prestige for the family to settle for a symbolic *sadaq* regardless of the financial interest of the daughter. In these cases, many fathers do not adequately protect their daughters' interests. In other cultures where a substantial *sadaq* is at stake, the father may appropriate the *sadaq* from his daughter to cover wedding expenses (which are customarily his responsibility). If he does not, the husband might 'borrow' it from the wife after marriage. More commonly, some cultures pressure the wife to waive the deferred part of her *sadaq* altogether as a gesture of good will towards the husband. In these cultures, the woman has become highly vulnerable financially and has lost a good measure of her independence.

Right to Work

There are other ways in which the Muslim woman can accumulate wealth. For example, she can work. The Quran states that men and women have a right to their earnings (4:32). Khadija, the first wife of the Prophet, was a businesswoman and continues to serve to this day as a lofty exemplar for Muslim women. Again, until recently patriarchal laws prohibited women from entering the work field under the guise of protecting women's morality or because of women's perceived physical limitations. New economic realities have set in, however, and now many personal status codes in Muslim countries no longer prohibit women from working.

Right to Inheritance

Another source of wealth available to the Muslim woman is her inheritance. Islam guarantees for the woman a share in her relatives' inheritance specified on the basis of her degree of kinship to the deceased. The false view in the West is that Islam gives a female a share in the inheritance equal to half that given to a male. The Quran does specify that a *sister* inherits half of the amount her *brother* inherits, but also specifies that other females of different degrees of kinship may inherit more than other males (4:11).

In view of the Quran's specification, it appears that the male sibling inherits double the amount inherited by his sister; but there is one important difference between her inheritance and his. The amount inherited by the sister is a net amount added to her wealth. This is a consequence of the rules of maintenance mentioned earlier. Women have no duty to maintain themselves or others, while related males are obligated to support them. The amount inherited by the brother is a gross amount from which he will have to deduct the expenses of supporting the various women, elderly men and children in his family, one of whom may be the sister herself. As mentioned earlier, even if the sister is wealthy, she is not required to support herself. Her closest male relative has that obligation, which she may waive only if she so chooses. Consequently, the net increase in the wealth of the brother is often less than that of his sister.

These facts illustrate what Muslim scholars have known all along, namely, that inheritance laws in Islam are quite complicated and cannot be reduced to a single slogan. Patriarchy, however, has simplified the inheritance picture drastically. Many Muslim women receive no share of their inheritance at all. Some are forced by their own families to turn their inheritance over to their brothers. Worse yet, many brothers take the inheritance and disappear from the lives of their sisters who have no closer male relative obligated to support them or capable of doing so. Historically, Muslim courts prosecuted such behaviour and compelled the brother to support the sister. Today, such injustices often go unnoticed, and the balance of rights and obligations in the Muslim family has been severely upset.

The Quranic View of Gender Relationships

First Principles

The Quran states clearly and repeatedly that human beings were all created from the same *nafs* and that God created from our own *nafs* mates with whom we could find tranquility (7:189, 30:21). The marital relationship is characterised as one of tranquillity, mercy and affection. Indeed, the husband and wife are described as each other's 'garments', meant to protect each other's privacy and cover each other's shortcomings (2:187). This view has important consequences in various areas of gender relations which are briefly addressed below. Yet, it is often argued that the superiority of men over women was asserted in the Quran itself. The main verse used in this argument is the one which refers to men as *qawwamun* over women. This is a complicated old word, rich in meaning. One translation of the verse states: 'Men are the protectors and maintainers of women, because God has given the one more (strength) than the other, and because they support them from their means.'[5]

---

[5] Sura 4:34, as rendered in A. Yusuf Ali, *The Qur'an: Text, Translation and Commentary* (Elmhurst, NY, 1987).

Qawwamun is translated here as 'protectors and maintainers', though traditional patriarchal interpreters and the average man understood the word to refer to the superiority of men over women (mostly by virtue of their physical strength, as suggested by the above translation). Ancient Arabic dictionaries, on the other hand, include among the meanings of *qawwamun* those of guiding and advising. These meanings are more consistent with the general Quranic view of gender relations than the ones preferred by male jurists.

Properly translated, the verse recognises a male's *qiwamah* over a woman only if he (1) is supporting her financially, *and* (2) has been favoured by God in certain matters he is advising the woman about (and of which he knows more at that time). Otherwise, the male cannot assert his *qiwamah*, whether it is advisory or otherwise. Alas, that single verse has become the hallmark of patriarchal bias, affirming the categorical superiority at all times of men over women. Patriarchal interpreters reduced the second condition in the verse to the claim that men are always in a more favourable position generally *vis-à-vis* women because of their physical strength. Further, by restricting the woman to the home, society ensured that women will almost always need to be supported and advised by some male. With such interpretations, patriarchy has encouraged oppressive males to move away from the Islamic ideal of marital relations.

Housework

Because of the Quranic view of marital relationships, the founding Muslim jurists viewed marriage as a contract for companionship and not as a service contract. The woman was not required to clean, cook or serve in her home. If she did so, then she was deemed to have acted voluntarily. Otherwise, the husband was obliged to bring her prepared food and take care of the home. Despite these facts, in many Muslim cultures today the home is viewed as the wife's realm, and she is viewed as responsible for taking care of it and for raising the children. In fact, the Moroccan personal status code states explicitly that one of the wife's obligations is to 'supervise' the household and manage it.[6] In many families, this means that the wife is required by law to do the housework since she cannot afford house-help.

Motherhood

The Quran views pregnancy as an arduous experience (46:15). Perhaps in part for this reason, Muslim jurists do not obligate the mother to nurse her baby. Children are raised by both parents who, according to the Quran, are to consult each other on important matters (2:233). This is hardly a surprise in light of the Quranic ideal of marital relations. When the Prophet was asked as to who should be honoured most, he replied, 'Your mother'. The questioner then asked, 'Whom should I honour most next?' 'Your mother', was the answer again. Three times did the Prophet repeat this; only the fourth time did he say 'Your father'. He also said that paradise is under the feet of mothers.

Despite this surprisingly modern view of maternal status, today's Muslim societies oblige women through social pressure, if not by law, to nurse their children and be the primary caretakers. Not only is this contrary to tradition, but it also often affects the human development of mothers, especially with respect to their education and career. Yet many men continue to emphasise the fact that mother's milk has special health benefits and that her care in the early years is crucial to the child's emotional well-being. Assuming that the thesis is correct, it is not clear that either the nurse or the caregiver has to be the mother. A wet nurse would impart similar benefits. Wet nurses are readily available in many countries, but are not commonly used these days. Yet the Prophet himself had a wet nurse, with whom he went from Mecca into the desert. Well-to-do families of Mecca had a tradition of sending their children to live for several years in the desert in order to teach them better Arabic and expose them to cleaner air. Far from being

---

[6] Moroccan Code, Royal Decree no. 343.57.1 (1957), as amended by Royal Decree no. 347.93.1 bk. 1, tit. 6, ch. 36(4) (1993).

critical of this practice, Muhammad is reported to have often mentioned it as part of his identity.

These facts open the door to many scenarios of child rearing that can accommodate the special needs of both the mother and the child without unduly burdening either. Clearly, the problem in Muslim societies is not Islam but the existing cultures. The adherence to cultural values rejected by Islam is perhaps best exemplified in the area of ethnic and racial differences as these relate to marriage.

Marriage and Ethnic Differences

Not only does the Quran teach that all humans were created from the same *nafs*, but also that human ethnic and racial differences were created by God so that we would have an impetus to get to know each other (49:13). The text reads as follows:

> O people, we have created you from a single (pair) of
> male and female, and made you into nations and tribes,
> so that you may know each other (not that you may
> despise each other). Verily, the most honoured of you in
> the sight of God is the one who is the most pious
> among you. God has full knowledge and is well-
> acquainted (with all things).

Hence, diversity is a divine blessing which we should celebrate rather than fear or loathe. God judges us solely by our deeds, not our physical attributes. Still, some schools of thought require that a husband be of the same ethnicity and social status as the wife, and that his profession, financial status and lineage be suitable to hers; otherwise, the father would be able to prevent or void the marriage.

The Structure of the Family

Some personal status codes in Muslim countries designate the husband as the head of the household, or require the wife to obey him, or both. Examples include Algeria, Morocco and, until recently,

Tunisia. In Egypt, it used to be that if the wife left her marital home, the police could return her to 'the house of obedience' by order of the court – in keeping with the now abandoned concept of *bayt al-taah* (house of obedience). While the forced return to the house is now gone, the concept of obedience remains very much alive in the law in some societies. For example, a wife who 'disobeys' may be denied maintenance. This is obviously a serious matter for financially vulnerable individuals.

In sum, patriarchal bias inherited by Muslims from their cultures survived the clear injunctions of the Quran to the contrary. It prevented interpreters from seeing the simple truths of the Quran and its ideals of Muslim family and society. Nevertheless, the Quran recognises the depth of the entrenchment of some cultural beliefs and customs, in regard to which it adopts a philosophy of grad-ualism. An appreciation of this is critical.

The Quranic Philosophy of Change

Rationale

The Quran recognises that fundamental changes in human consciousness do not usually occur overnight. They require a period of individual or even social growth. For this reason, the Quran uses a gradualist approach to change in relation to entrenched customs, beliefs and practices. The exception is for fundamental matters such as the belief in the unicity of God and the prophethood of Muhammad, when the weight of the divine message itself is at stake.

The Quran also flatly prohibits behaviour that violates funda-mental moral principles. For example, it prohibits murder, and more specifically, female infanticide (81:8). The gradualist philos-ophy of change was applied to lesser though still important matters. The best known instance relates to the prohibition against drinking wine in a society that was used to drinking; it was imposed in stages. A less-known example comes from the area of constitu-tional law. The Quran specified in a few verses only the basic constitutional features of an Islamic state, such as *baya* (voting) and *shura* (consultation, deliberation). It left it up to the societies themselves to flesh out this constitutional structure according to their varying levels of social consciousness and political and constitutional maturity. The disparate results are evident across the Muslim world.

But the Quran did not recognise only societal variations in levels of consciousness and development; it also recognised individual differences. Its philosophy of gradual change applied to individuals as well. This is most evident in the area of ethics. The Quran describes various actions and words as 'good' and others as 'better' (7:145, 39:18, 39:55, 46:16). This approach recognises that not all humans are capable of the same understanding or behaviour. In criminal matters, some Muslims may insist on 'an eye for an eye' in deciding on punishment; and the Quran does indeed introduce this standard of justice. But it says over and again that it is better to forgive, asking how we mortals could expect forgiveness in the afterlife if we are unforgiving in the present. One could insist on one's right to punish a perpetrator, but it is better to overcome this kind of thinking and to forgive.

Clearly, there are various levels of being a good Muslim. The better ones require higher consciousness, deeper moral insight and greater tolerance of human frailty. In addressing the patriarchal oppression of women and other groups, the Quran utilises the gradualist approach to change in both the societal and individual arenas.

Addressing the Oppression of Women

The Quran and the Prophet mention slaves and women many times, exhorting Muslims to treat them well (49:13, 24:33, 8:70). In his last sermon, *Khutbat al-wadaa*, Muhammad compared the status of women to that of powerless slaves, beseeching the male audience to treat them kindly. Sadly, with their patriarchal blinders, many Muslims saw such guidance as affirming the social conditions and prejudices of the time. They failed to see that the Quran's gradualism was an appeal to higher consciousness, not an endorsement of the status quo. This sort of reasoning persisted over centuries. It took over a millennium for some Muslim societies to prohibit slavery.

However, it is important to note that while some Muslim societies and individuals misunderstood the full force of the Quranic message, others did not. While some Muslims argued that slavery must be acceptable since it was referred to in the Quran, others grasped the ideal and freed their slaves to gain favour in God's eyes. Equally, while some Muslims continue to engage in polygamy, many male scholars have refused to marry more than one woman for fear of violating express Quranic warnings that polygamous men *will* be guilty of injustice (4:129). Indeed, the issue of polygamy is of major concern for many Muslim women, even in the West, and merits further attention here.

Polygamy and Its Cultural Entrenchment

The Quran was revealed to a culture steeped in polygamy. Men frequently married more than a hundred women at a time. It was therefore unrealistic, given human nature, to prohibit polygamous behaviour abruptly. The Islamic approach to this situation as in other matters was to limit the practice severely, designate avenues for ending it, and provide a description of the ideal state of affairs that excludes the practice.

The Quranic statement on polygamy is more complex than some scholars are willing to admit. For example, the permission to marry up to four wives is premised upon the possibility that orphan women may be oppressed (4:3). If men feared being unjust toward orphans, says the Quran, then these men may marry up to four wives so long as they treat them equitably and fairly. Yet the Quran also states that it is not possible to be equitable and fair in these situations (4:129). Although it is not possible to understand this verse about polygamy in all its complexity without understanding fully the social practice (involving orphans) it was revealed to avoid, one thing is nevertheless clear: the Quran expressly holds that polygamy results in injustice. It is not an optimal way of arranging marital relations. For this reason, some men abandoned polygamy in the hope of reaching a higher state of marital and human relations. Others opted for the minimal standard, despite its questionable application to contexts broader than those referred to in the revelation.

Violence Against Women and its Cultural Entrenchment

Another example of Quranic gradualism appears in the verse most often quoted to justify violence against women (4:34). It may be translated to read: '[a]s to those women on whose part you fear disloyalty and ill conduct, admonish them (first), (next) refuse to share their beds, (and last) beat them (lightly)'. Let us examine this verse next, as well as the circumstances of its revelation.

The pre-Islamic or *jahiliyya* society was a rough desert society plagued by tribal wars. Many men beat their wives. They carried this practice into Islam and were so violent that the women complained to the Prophet about the situation. Acting on his own, the Prophet prohibited the practice by allowing the wife the right to *qisas* (retribution). That very evening, the men complained loudly. They came to the Prophet and revisited the issue, arguing that his ruling allowed their wives to gain the upper hand.

At that point, the Prophet sought and received a revelation which reflected the Quranic philosophy of gradualism. The verse appeared to contradict the Prophet. When he received the revelation, the Prophet stated that 'Muhammad wanted, but God did not want [to order a flat ban on hitting one's wife]'. As we shall see, however, the revelation simply changed the approach prescribed by the Prophet for eradicating wife abuse. It did not authorise wife abuse. It only introduced a transitory stage for change and anger management, while preserving the Quranic view of ideal marital relations.

It is a well-known juridical principle in Islam that verses in the Quran explain each other, that is, the Quran is an integral whole and thus the full and proper meaning of any verse cannot be understood in isolation from other verses in the rest of the Quran. Relying on this principle and on the presumption of the internal consistency of the Quran, I now turn to a popular verse in the Quran that early Muslim women sometimes inserted in their marriage contracts. The verse enjoins spouses to 'live together in kindness or leave each other charitably' (2:231). Based on this and other verses, Muslim jurists asserted the prohibition of harm among spouses (*la dharar wala dhirar*). This prohibition still underlies many provisions in the modern personal status codes in Muslim countries. Further, a Muslim woman has the right to take her husband to court or divorce him for abusing her.

The Prophet himself denounced spousal abuse time and again. On one occasion, he asked, 'How can one of you hit his wife like an animal, then he may embrace her?' On another he asked, 'How can one of you whip his wife like a slave, and he is likely to sleep with her at the end of the day?' The Prophet also echoed various Quranic descriptions of ideal marital relations. He told the men, 'The best among you are those who are best towards their wives', and added, 'and I am the best among you in that respect'. This statement is significant given the emphasis Muslims place on emulating the Prophet. He never raised his voice at home, got angry, or asked another to serve him. He cut meat, took care of children and sewed his own shoes. Yet many Muslim men today forget these important Prophetic statements and examples, and limit their emulation of the Prophet to the style of his dress or his grooming habits.

How do we reconcile all these facts, Quranic and prophetic, with the single Quranic verse that permits husbands to 'hit' their wives? How do we reconcile the verse with the Prophet's continued insistence that husbands abstain from beating their wives? We do that by developing our insights further to gain a deeper understanding of Quranic meaning. This is not a quick process. In this case, I shall take a few steps along the road to illustrate my point.

Gradualism and Violence Against Women

This is how the Quranic gradualist philosophy was applied in the matter of wife abuse. First, the Quran imposed on the husband various limitations before he was permitted to resort to 'hitting'.

He was required to communicate with his wife. The man must advise his wife about what he thinks she did wrong – which gives the wife the chance to respond and explain. If the misunderstanding is not resolved by communication, and the husband remains angry, he can separate himself physically from his wife for a while.

Many jurists viewed these steps as directed against the wife, first to admonish her, then to make her suffer from sexual abandonment. Clearly, they miss the fundamental point. These prescribed stages are steps in anger management for an aggressive patriarchal male who is likely to use force as a first resort. Second, the Quran totally excludes righteous women from the scope of hitting (4:34). It limits the possibility of 'hitting' one's wife to extreme cases in which *nushuz* is feared by the husband. According to major jurists, *nushuz* is a word that in the context of the verse appears to refer to disloyalty towards the husband – in the form of dislike, disobedience or discord. This is a questionable interpretation, because the Prophet himself appears to have interpreted *nushuz* differently in his *Khutbat al-wadaa*. He is reported to have said, 'You [men] have rights against women, and they have rights against you. It is your right that they do not bring someone you dislike into your bed, or that they commit clear adultery (*fahishah mubayyina*). If they do, then God has permitted you to desert them in bed, and [then] hit them lightly. If they stop, you are obliged to maintain them.'

Often, jurists living in patriarchal cultures broadened the definition of *fahishah mubayyina* significantly. By doing so, they widened the scope of instances in which the husband may resort to hitting. This is against the letter and spirit of the Quran, which requires that husbands should live with their wives in kindness or leave them charitably. Nevertheless, even if we were to accept the broader definition of *fahishah mubayyina*, the man still cannot hit his wife as a first resort. He is required to take several prior steps.

But what does 'hitting' mean here? Many scholars have pondered over this, and have interpreted the Quranic text in light of the basic principles governing marital relations as articulated by the

Quran and the Prophet. As a result, these jurists defined hitting with a series of limitations. For example, a man may not strike his wife on the face. Further, any hitting that is injurious or leaves a mark on the woman's body is actionable as a criminal offence. If the husband reaches the unfortunate stage of hitting, he may strike only with something as gentle as a *miswak* (a soft small fibrous twig used as a toothbrush in the Arab Peninsula). Finally, given the Quranic ideal of marital relations, scholars concluded that a woman abused physically or verbally is entitled to divorce from her husband (a view that has found its way into the personal status code of countries such as Jordan and Kuwait). This position was developed in Arabia 1,400 years ago when the world viewed beating one's wife as a right.

An important Quranic precedent on the issue of domestic violence is found in the story of Job (38:44). When Job was being tested, his wife lost her faith and blasphemed. As a result, he took an oath to strike her as punishment. A dilemma was thus created: a prophet should not engage in such violent and unworthy behaviour, but neither should he violate his oath. The solution to this dilemma is offered thus in the Quran: Job is instructed to satisfy his oath to discipline his wife by hitting her with a handful of *digth* (grass or basil). This instruction allowed Job to fulfil his promise without harming his wife. The resolution likewise offers Muslim men a way to vent their frustrations in keeping with *all* of the Quranic verses as well as the Prophetic tradition.

To summarise, the Quranic approach to the problem of wife abuse is two-pronged: first, it provides a harmonious view of marital relationships based on tranquillity, affection and forgiveness. These relations are in turn based on a view of humanity that is characterised by mutual respect, equality and dignity. Second, it develops a graduated approach to the problem of wife abuse, which is aimed at confining the aggressive instincts of the patriarchal male and re-channelling anger into less destructive outlets. In doing so, the Quran takes into account the nature of human beings and the need for a period of growth for them to achieve a higher stage of development and communication. Some jurists have concluded in light of the totality of the Quranic revelation, that it is better for a man not to reach the last stage of hitting at all. If conflict persists, the Quran prescribes mediation (4:35). If that also fails, then the parties should leave each other 'charitably'.

Conclusion

Muslims today are experiencing serious socio-cultural, technological and economic change, both within the Islamic world and the diaspora. The settled *ijtihad* of the past few centuries has become unwieldy and calls for fresh thinking – cognizant of scriptural guidance, properly understood within its worldview and its overall ethical and legal principles. Yet the whole notion of *ijtihad* was instituted especially to address such challenges, whether they originate from strength or weakness. Moreover, jurists have long established that difference in jurisprudence among them is a sign of God's mercy.

In family and gender matters, Muslim countries have significantly revised their legal codes, including with regard to family planning and the status of women. This chapter has shown the distance yet to be travelled, and suggested some of the directions. Karamah, the organization that I have founded (www.karamah.org), aims to help Muslim women along those journeys.

Ijtihad is a necessary process that must be engaged in afresh by every generation – and one in which Muslim societies, communities and individuals are entitled to engage with the proper level of knowledge, piety, and commitment. Islamic law and tradition should not be viewed as chaining us to patriarchal systems, but as pointing to the ideals of equitable and harmonious lives. Ultimately, the hope of the umma lies in the new generation of young Muslim men and women who are experiencing a world very different from that of their forebears – a world that takes as non-negotiable the rights of women as full and active citizens.

Futher Reading

Abou El Fadl, Khaled. *Speaking in God's Name: Islamic Law, Authority and Women.* Oxford, 2001.

Afkhami, Mahnaz, ed. *Faith and Freedom: Women's Human Rights in the Muslim World.* Syracuse, 1995.

Ahmed, Laila. *Women and Gender in Islam: Historical Roots of a Modern Debate.* New Haven, CT, 1993.

Al-Hibri, Azizah. 'An Islamic Perspective on Domestic Violence', *Fordham International Law Journal,* 27 (Dec 2003), pp. 195-224.

Barlas, Asma. *Believing Women in Islam: Unreading Patriarchal Interpretations of the Qur'an.* Austin, TX, 2002.

Haddad, Yvonne Yazbeck. *Islam, Gender and Social Change.* New York, 1998.

Mernissi, Fatima. *Women and Islam : An Historical and Theological Enquiry.*, tr. Mary Jo Lakeland. New Delhi, 2004.

Mir-Hosseini, Ziba. 'Debating Women: Gender and the Public Sphere in Post-Revolutionary Iran', in Amyn B. Sajoo, ed., *Civil Society in the Muslim World.* London, 2002, pp. 95-122.

Kandiyoti, Deniz, ed. *Women, Islam and the State.* Philadelphia, 1991.

Shaikh, Sadiyya. 'Transforming Feminisms: Islam, Women, and Gender Justice', in Omid Safi, ed., *Progressive Muslims: On Justice, Gender and Pluralism.* Oxford, 2003. pp. 147-162.

Stowasser, Barbara. *Women in the Qur'an, Traditions, and Interpretation.* New York, 1997.

Wadud, Amina. *Inside the Gender Jihad: Women's Reform in Islam.* Oxford, 2006.

7

Inclusive Governance:
A Fatimid Illustration

Shainool Jiwa

In establishing their sovereignty across the North African stretch of the Mediterranean, the Fatimids (909-1171) faced an essential challenge: how was a Shii dynasty to enjoy political respect and legitimacy in an overwhelmingly Sunni setting? The Fatimid response was to adopt a model of governance that was broadly inclusive in letter and spirit, beginning with the Egyptian phase of their rule. What ensued was not merely a political compromise driven by the need for co-existence. Rather, the political stability, economic prosperity, intellectual energy and artistic grandeur of their two-century reign is widely regarded as a remarkable epoch in both Egyptian and Muslim history. 'Active engagement' (to recall Amir Hussain's perspective in this volume) marked it out in the vein of pluralist episodes in Muslim Andalusia, the Ottoman empire and Mughal India.[1]

Fatimid governance appealed from the outset to the ideals of equity and social justice that were associated with Islam's founding statesman and prophet, Muhammad. It was from him that they asserted their genealogical pedigree, and succession to the leadership of the umma. Indeed, Muhammad's city state in Medina was as much a minority aspiration in a non-Muslim setting as a Shia-led state was in Sunni and Khariji North Africa. As with the Charter of Medina issued by the Prophet, inclusion and just

---

[1] See generally Abdulaziz Sachedina, *The Islamic Roots of Democratic Pluralism* (Oxford, 2001).

governance were hallmarks of the inaugural *Aman* or 'peace proclamation' which the Fatimids issued on entering Egypt. The *Aman*
provided the foundation for respecting the diversity of religious
outlooks in a shared quest, inspired by the Quranic call, 'O
humanity! Truly We created you from a male and a female, and
made you into nations and tribes that you might know each other.
Truly the most honoured of you in the sight of God is the most
God-conscious of you. Truly God is Knowing, Aware' (49:13). The
Fatimids created and sustained institutions and networks that
enabled the flourishing of Muslims, Christians and Jews within
the realm, mirroring the dynamic pluralism that epitomised
Muslim Andalusia. This chapter will focus on the *Aman* as a critical document in the reign of the Fatimids – and an exemplar of
pluralist governance as a basis for political legitimacy.

The Fatimid invasion of Egypt in 969 during the reign of the
fourth Fatimid Imam-caliph al-Muizz li-Din Allah (r. 953-975)
was a key event in the histories of Egypt, North Africa and the
Mediterranean region. It is symbolised by the city that he founded,
al-Qahira al-Muizziyya (the City Victorious of al-Muizz), a
precursor of modern Cairo. Al-Qahira was to become the axis
from which the ascent of the Fatimids would be projected across
much of the Muslim world.

The *Aman* document, issued by the victorious Fatimid general,
Jawhar al-Siqilli (c. 928-992), guarantees the security and safe-
conduct of the Egyptian populace and sets forth the principles on
which Fatimid policies in Egypt would be based for their subsequent two-hundred-year reign. Its notable features include the
nature of the Fatimid mission, which is articulated in their understanding of a divinely designated duty of care and protection of
the cosmopolitan Egyptian populace. Accordingly, the *Aman* document underscores the Fatimid commitment to establish just governance for all their subjects including members of the *Ahl al-Kitab*
(The People of the Book, meaning Jews and Christians), and their
inclusive and tolerant attitude to all Muslim communities. As this
crucial document has received limited scholarly attention, its
analysis followed by its translation forms the focus of this paper.
The Fatimid quest for authority and legitimacy of their rule are

integrally linked to the principles enshrined in the *Aman*; it is necessary to understand these principles before analysing the document.

Authority and Legitimacy

The Fatimid claim to spiritual and temporal authority was integrally linked to their lineage and status as descendants of the Prophet Muhammad through his daughter Fatima and her husband, the Prophet's paternal cousin, Ali b. Abi Talib. In the Shii tradition, the Fatimids maintained that Muhammad designated Ali and his appointed progeny to succeed him, with the prerogative of leadership of the umma and of seeking their well-being and salvation. The Fatimid state was a practical means for the exercise of this supreme authority and responsibility.

The Fatimid caliphate was established in Ifriqiya (the medieval term for Tunisia and parts of eastern Algeria) in 909, as an expression in particular of Ismaili Shiism. Over the course of a few decades it developed a significant cultural, economic and political presence in the medieval Mediterranean region. Ideologically, the Fatimids had to surmount the challenge of reigning over a populace that was predominantly Sunni and which had an enduring Kharijite presence. Ethnically, the region was populated by ancient Berber tribal confederations with Arab influence mainly limited to towns and cities. Consequently, as Shii imam-caliphs, the Fatimids developed a finely tuned balancing act in representing their status and authority as minority rulers. This experience strengthened them when they began casting their gaze eastwards to Egypt. No sooner had the first Fatimid Imam-caliph al-Mahdi billah established himself in Ifriqiya, a Fatimid expedition was prepared and sent to subdue Egypt in 913 and again in 919. Subsequent Fatimid campaigns were undertaken during the reign of the second Fatimid ruler, al-Qaim bi-Amr Allah (r. 934-946) but resolute opposition by the Abbasids prevented Fatimid success. Although the Abbasids and their clients were able to halt Fatimid military advances until 969, an integral feature of al-Muizz li-din Allah's success in securing Egypt was the effective propagation of the Fatimid cause amongst its inhabitants.

Longstanding Ismaili *dawa* activity in the country led many notables and government officials to support the Fatimid cause in seeking the restoration of stability. The *dawa* also harnessed political insignia to assert Fatimid legitimacy. Examples of this have been recorded, such as coins minted in Egypt and issued in the Fatimid sovereign's name nearly two decades prior to the invasion of Egypt, along with the circulation of banners and *tiraz* fabrics with Fatimid formulaic phrases. All these measures contributed to the largely peaceful conquest of Egypt in al-Muizz's reign, succeeding where previous Fatimid military interventions had failed.

The Invasion of Egypt

The swings in Egyptian politics that facilitated the Fatimid invasion of Egypt in the 10th century came to a head during the time of Kafur al-Labi (905-968), the last of the Ikhshidid rulers of Egypt. Though renowned as a patron of culture and learning, his 22-year rule was rife with dissent and factional squabbling between the supporters of the dynasty in whose name he ruled (al-Ikhshididiya) and those with a personal affinity to Kafur himself (al-Kafuriya), whom he created as a military counterforce to the former to further his political ambitions. During this period, major natural disasters such as famine led to severe droughts and endemic food shortages which were exacerbated by financial mismanagement. All these factors fuelled anti-Ikhshidid sentiment, thus facilitating the Ismaili mission to garner support for their Imam, who claimed supreme authority over the Muslim lands and promised to reverse the Abbasid and Ikhshidid wrongs.

Kafur's death in 968 caused a succession crisis, leading to further divisions within Egypt. Moreover, decades of Fatimid *dawa* activity had paved the ground for the Fatimid claim of authority. Hence, significant elements among the Egyptian populace were amenable to the Fatimid presence (including stakeholders from among the Ikshidids, Kafurids, Abbasids and others); the leading notables of the region invited al-Muizz to establish Fatimid rule over Egypt. He responded by beginning extensive preparations, which included the major mobilisation of men, money and armaments. The financial outlay was particularly expensive because al-Muizz insisted that as this was a momentous event, it had to be funded through legal revenues, even though he was acutely aware of the extraordinary strain on the Fatimid treasury, which he sought to alleviate by contributing 24 million dinars from his own resources.[2]

Moreover, al-Muizz assumed an active role in the strategic planning of the campaign. He selected the veteran general Jawhar al-Siqilli to serve as the commander of the Fatimid campaign in Egypt. A protégé of the third Fatimid Imam-caliph al-Mansur billah, Jawhar's merit as military commander was confirmed when he had earlier led the Fatimid armies in reinstating their control over the North African region, extending it to the shores of the Atlantic. From a Fatimid perspective, the critical nature of the invasion of Egypt is illustrated by the fact that the Fatimid sovereign, accompanied by his entire retinue, personally sent off the army, its commander-in chief entrusted with the sword of the ruler to accomplish this mission. Upon reaching Egypt, in 969, Jawhar began the process of negotiation with the leading notables of Egypt that resulted in the proclamation of the *Aman*, an official document that guaranteed the safety and security of the Egyptian populace.

The *Aman* Document

The *Aman* has been recounted in full by the erudite and prolific Sunni Egyptian historian, Taqi al-din Ahmad al-Maqrizi (1364-

---

[2] As attested by the historians Taqi al-din Ahmad al-Maqrizi and Imad al-din Idris, discussed below. Revenues were often generated by different Muslim dynasties through illegal levies. Despite such precedents in Egypt, al-Muizz was stringent about not resorting to such levies on the general populace.

1442).[3] Despite the fact that al-Maqrizi was a Mamluk historian he sustained a unique interest in the Fatimids and systematically recorded multiple facets of their reign in many of his works. Similarly, the Aman has also been recorded in its entirety by the Tayyibi Ismaili historian Imad al-din Idris (1392-1468).[4] Both these authors are in all likelihood quoting Ibn Zulaq (919-996), a prominent historian and biographer contemporary to the Fatimid invasion of Egypt, who wrote a biography on al-Muizz, which unfortunately is no longer extant.

The full reproduction of the Aman document in these sources is testimony to its authenticity as the two authors composed their works independently of each other and with significantly varied focus and interest in the Fatimids. It also underscores its importance in instituting Fatimid rule in Egypt as it represents the first constitution of the Fatimid state there, and is one of a series of covenants and guarantees issued by the Fatimid imam-caliphs after the accession of al-Mahdi enunciating the principles upon which the Fatimids were to govern their rising empire.

Politically, the Aman document represents the negotiation of authority and transfer of power between the existing Egyptian elite and the incumbent Fatimid sovereign. The backdrop to its proclamation and the events leading up to the meeting between the Egyptian notables and the Fatimid commander were, therefore, integral to this conciliatory handover. Equally, the composition of the leading members of the Egyptian delegation was designed to facilitate this rapprochement. Thus, both al-Maqrizi and Imad al-din Idris report at length on the selection of the five delegates who were to meet with the Fatimid commander Jawhar

---

[3] Taqi al-din Ahmad al-Maqrizi, *Ittiaz al-hunafa bi-akhbar al-aimma al-Fatimiyyin al-khulafa* (Lessons for the Seekers of Truth in the History of the Fatimid Imams and Caliphs), vol. 1, ed. Jamal al-din al-Shayyal (Cairo, 1967-1973), pp. 103-107; as well as his biographical dictionary, *Kitab al-muqaffa al-kabir*, ed. M. al-Yalawi (Beirut, 1987), pp. 332-336

[4] Imad al-din Idris, *Uyun al-akhbar wa funun al-athar*, (The Springs of Knowledge and Varieties of Evidence), ed. M. al-Yalawi as *Tarikh al-khulafa al-Fatimiyyun bi l-Maghrib: al-qism al-khass min Kitab uyun al-akhbar* (Beirut, 1985), pp. 673-678.

al-Siqilli upon his arrival in Egypt. Notably, three of these delegates mirrored the Fatimid claim to descent from the household of the Prophet; the fourth was the Chief Justice and the final one the resident Fatimid *dai*.

The asserted sacredness of the Fatimid mission was rooted in the Shii notion of the imamate, which espoused religious and temporal authority over and responsibility for the umma – mirrored in their self designation as the *Ahl al-Haqq* (People of the Truth), and their *dawa* as being the *Dawat al-Haqq* (the Call to Truth). This is reinforced in the *Aman* document, and is affirmed by the Egyptian notables in the selection of representatives from the Husaynid, Hasanid and Abbasid branches of Prophet Muhammad's family, 'so that the whole spectrum of the Prophet's lineage in Egypt' was symbolically represented in the reception committee of notables that met Jawhar at Taruja, south of Alexandria, where the latter had camped upon his arrival into Egypt.[5]

As the Fatimid armies advanced into Egypt, having taken possession of Alexandria, the Egyptian delegation left Fustat with a conciliatory message from the wazir to the commander Jawhar, seeking the guarantee of safety from him. The *Aman* that was subsequently issued contained the terms of agreement that were negotiated by the delegation, to which Jawhar acceded. The *Aman* document contained the blueprint of Fatimid rule in Egypt over the course of the next couple of centuries. On the one hand, it spelled out all the advantages to be gained from submission – an electoral manifesto of sorts. On the other, it laid out the principles on which the new regime would be founded – a constitutional document, whose key features included establishing just governance, ensuring the socio-economic welfare of all subjects and guaranteeing their freedom of religious practice.

Establishing Just Governance

A salient feature of the *Aman* is the emphasis it places on the restoration of security and promotion of justice. Accordingly, its

---

[5] al-Maqrizi, *Ittiaz al-hunafa*, vol. 1, p. 103.

promise to enforce order by curbing the 'tyrant' heads the list of commitments stipulated in the document. The 'tyrant', as attested to in the document, refers to the Qarmati leader based in Bahrain, al-Hasan al-Asam (891-977), who adopted a particularly aggressive posture during this period. Though the Qaramita and the Fatimids had a shared Ismaili heritage, their interpretation regarding the central doctrine of the imamate, and related issues of succession to authority, had rent them apart. Consequently, the Qaramita proved to be among the most aggressive opponents of the Fatimids, particularly after the latter's arrival in Egypt.

The evocative depiction of the terrified and humiliated populace of the eastern Islamic lands in the *Aman* document challenges Abbasid hegemony over the umma, because this entailed responsibility for safety and security for pilgrims to Mecca, which had been undermined due to Byzantine and Qarmati aggressions. The dire predicament of the eastern Muslims is starkly contrasted to the Fatimid-engendered prosperity of western Muslims in North Africa. The document rhetorically bemoans that their eastern brethren have no saviour to rescue them. Abbasid ineptitude and perceived indifference in restoring security to Egypt is juxtaposed with al-Muizz's competence, concern and prioritisation of this situation:

> His eyes have wept for what has affected them and he has been kept awake because of what has befallen them. He is our lord and master, the Commander of the Faithful, may God's blessing be upon him. He has hoped . . . to rescue those who have been constantly living in humiliation and in painful torture, and to make those who have been overwhelmed by terror feel safe, and to dispel the fear of those who have continually lived in dread. He wishes to restore the pilgrimage which has fallen into abeyance, and whose obligations and rights are neglected by the worshippers because of fear of the one who would seize them, as they could not safeguard themselves or their wealth, for they have been repeatedly vanquished, their blood shed and their wealth confiscated.[6]

---

[6] al-Maqrizi, *Ittiaz al-hunafa*, vol. 1, p. 104

In addition to restoring security, the *Aman* document highlights that the duty of care of the Muslim ruler to his subjects entailed attention to the social and economic needs of the populace. Hence, it promises to 'scrutinise [their] living conditions, to offer protection to the inhabitants day and night so that they can strive freely to earn their living and can manage their affairs such that it would restore them to their feet'. Similarly, it reiterates that:

> As has been his custom, al-Muizz will authorise the repair of roads. He will then prevent the offenders from committing crimes, so that people are able to travel on the roads feeling safe and secure, and will be provided with food and provisions. News has reached him . . . that Egypt's roads have been cut off because of the fear of the travel [caravan] leaders, since there has been neither a restraint nor a defence against the unjust aggressors. Then he will renew the coinage and adjust it to be of the same standard as the blessed, auspicious *mansuri* dinars. He will eliminate their metal impurities. These are the three characteristics that must be addressed by a Muslim ruler. He must exert all his time and effort in their achievement.[7]

Following the guarantee of safety and the alleviation of the socioeconomic concerns of the Egyptians, the *Aman* document delineates the Fatimid sovereign's strikingly tolerant and inclusive approach to the varied religious communities that inhabited Egypt.

Protection of Religious Communities

Over half a century of Fatimid experience in reigning over the religiously and ethnically diverse populace in North Africa enabled them to develop an ideologically grounded and pragmatic religious policy in Egypt. Demographically, in the early 10th century Egypt was on the cusp of Islamisation, with Muslims beginning to form a majority among numerically substantive and well-established Christian and Jewish populations. Furthermore, each

---

[7] al-Maqrizi, *Ittiaz al-hunafa*, vol. 1, p. 104.

of these religious communities had their own demarcated sub-divisions which had formed into defined communal groups. For the Shii Fatimid imam-caliphs to claim sovereignty over such a religiously and ethnically diverse populace required a creative rationale which drew upon the broadest shared religious repertoire of the region. To the Muslims of Egypt, the *Aman* document stressed the common and generic roots of the community by emphasising that 'Islam consists of one sunna and a sharia followed by all'. It then guarantees the freedom to practise the faith to each Muslim according to his/her creed by testifying:

> You shall continue in your *madhhab* (school). You shall be permitted to perform your obligations according to religious scholarship, and to gather for it in your congregational and other mosques, and to remain steadfast in the beliefs of the worthy ancestors from the Companions of the Prophet, may God be pleased with them, and those who succeeded them, the jurists of the cities who have pronounced judgements according to their *madhhab*s and *fatwa*s (formal legal opinions). The call to prayer and its performance, the fasting in the month of Ramadan, the breaking of the fast and the celebration of its nights, the [payment of] the alms tax, [the performance of the] pilgrimage and the undertaking of jihad will be maintained according to the command of God and His Book and in accordance with the instruction of His Prophet . . . in his sunna, and the *dhimmi*s will be treated according to previous custom.[8]

Once the Fatimids had secured control of the official Egyptian legal and ritual frameworks, they proactively promoted an inclusive attitude towards other Muslim communities. A case in point is the official decree issued by the Fatimid Imam-caliph al-Hakim bi-Amr Allah (985-1021) permitting Muslims of different persuasions to use their own preferred method of establishing the beginning of Ramadan and the concomitant celebrations of Id al-Fitr.

---

[8] al-Maqrizi, *Ittiaz al-hunafa*, vol. 1, p. 105.

Basing his edict on the Quranic principle that there is no compulsion in religion (2:256), al-Hakim ensured that in the Fatimid state Sunni and Shii Muslims were able to celebrate this annual Muslim festival in peace and harmony, dispelling the acrimonious wrangling that to this day accompanies these celebrations in many Muslim countries.

Similarly, on the Fatimid legal scene, while Fatimid law prevailed as the official statute, on matters of family law Muslims could seek legal judgement according to their own legal tradition through the state-funded judicial infrastructure which remunerated judges from various Sunni and Shii legal schools. Having affirmed the shared foundational beliefs of all Muslims, regardless of their theological interpretations and legal leanings, and guaranteeing their practice according to their belief and custom, the *Aman* document further pledges to:

> Undertake the repair of your mosques and adorn them with carpets and lighting. I will give those who call to prayers, the administrators [of mosques] and those who lead the prayers their allowance. It will be given abundantly to them and not be withdrawn from them. I will only pay them from the treasury and not by draft on tax collectors.[9]

The Covenant

The Medina Charter issued by Prophet Muhammad provides the bedrock for the constitutional framework articulated in the *Aman* document. Consequently, the Fatimids interpret their role as the legitimate protectors of the *dhimma* of God: as caretakers of Muslims of all persuasions as well as of the *Ahl al-Kitab*. Hence the only direct reference to the *Ahl al-Dhimma* – Egypt's Christian and Jewish communities – may be understood as inclusive in 'accord with custom'. The interpretation of custom here is Fatimid Shii and harkens to the Prophetic example, self-consciously bypassing its various other political and theological expressions

---

[9] al-Maqrizi, *Ittiaz al-hunafa*, vol. 1, p. 105.

over the course of centuries, some of which were less favourable to these communities. In doing so, the Fatimids assert a doctrinal stance which is rooted in the paradigm established by Ali b. Abi Talib of referencing the Quran and the sunna of the Prophet as their foundational sources, followed by the example of his descendents whom they considered to be the *ulil amr*, the legitimate holders of authority as defined by the Quranic verse: 'O you who believe, obey God, and obey the Messenger and holders of authority amongst you' (4:59). Thus, they instituted their own custom and practice which was distinct from the ulama-based Sunni model that had developed over the course of time.

The *Aman* solicited the witnessing of an all-embracing and abiding commitment to 'total and perpetual obedience to the representative of God on earth, who was equally committed to their welfare'.[10] In this context, it was also re-invoking the *ahd* (covenant) which the first Fatimid Imam-caliph al-Mahdi had issued to the people of Ifriqiya upon his accession as the legitimate invoker of the covenant between God and mankind.[11] A range of terms are employed in the *Aman* document to reference this covenant, the one most frequently used being *dhimma* (duty of care and protection). This is inferred in its Quranic sense and is reflected in the Prophetic tradition in what came to be called the Charter of Medina where it refers to divine protection of the community of the faithful and the universalist claim that the '*dhimma* of the Muslims is one and the same'. The *Aman* can therefore be viewed as one of a series of public proclamations issuing from the Fatimid imam-caliphs regarding the nature of their rule and their responsibilities as rulers.

---

[10] Michael Brett, *The Rise of the Fatimids: The World of the Mediterranean and the Middle East in the Tenth Century CE* (Leiden, 2001), p. 301.

[11] The *Ahd* document is preserved in full by al-Qadi al-Numan in his *Daaim al-Islam*, tr. Asas A. A. Fyzee and revised by Ismail K. Poonawala, *The Pillars of Islam* (Oxford and New York, 2002), vol. 1, pp. 436-456; and Wadad al-Qadi, 'An Early Fatimid Political Document', *Studia Islamica*, 48 (1978), pp. 71-108.

The *Aman* (translation)

The premier Fatimid public statement in Egypt begins thus:

'In the name of God, the Most Beneficent, the Most Merciful. This is a letter by Jawhar al-Katib – the servant of the Commander of the Faithful, al-Muizz li-Din Allah, may God's blessings be upon him[12], to all the people living in Misr, Egyptians and others. The delegates whom you had asked to correspond and meet with me have arrived. They are:

Abu Jafar Muslim al-Sharif, may God lengthen his life;
Abu Ismail al-Rassi, may God help him;
Abul-Tayyib al-Hashim, may God help him;
Abu Jafar Ahmad b. Nasr, may God strengthen him; and
the qadi, may God strengthen him.

They have mentioned, on your behalf, that you seek a guarantee of *aman* (safety) for yourselves, your wealth, your lands and all your matters. You are already aware of the magnanimity of our master and lord, the Commander of the Faithful, towards you.

So praise God for what he, the Commander of the Faithful, has bestowed upon you and thank Him for his protection of you. Persevere in adhering to what is incumbent upon you and hasten to the obedience of him who protects you from error and leads you to safety and happiness, for he has sent the victorious troops and triumphant armies only so as to strengthen and protect you, and to wage jihad on your behalf as hands have grabbed you. The tyrant has behaved arrogantly towards you, coveting possession of your lands in this year; [he wants] to conquer it and take prisoners from it and desires the possession of your wealth and property, as he has already done to those like you in the east. His determination has been reinforced and his temerity strengthened,

---

[12] The salutations following the name of God, Prophet Muhammad and the imams are translated here only at their first mention but assumed thereafter.

and so, the Commander of the Faithful, our lord and master, has pre-empted him by sending out his victorious armies, and dispatching his glorious troops to fight him and wage jihad against him, on your behalf and on behalf of all the Muslims in the east who have been disgraced and have been unduly humbled and engulfed by disasters and continuous calamities. The sobbing and yelling of those who have been continually frightened has become progressively louder and they have beseeched succour over and over again.

No one has been able to come to their rescue except for him who has been sickened by their suffering and has suffered from their affliction. His eyes have wept for what has affected them and he has been kept awake because of what has befallen them. He is our lord and master, the Commander of the Faithful. He has hoped, by the grace and benevolence that God has always bestowed upon him, to rescue those who have been constantly living in humiliation and in painful torture, and to make those who have been overwhelmed by terror feel safe, and to dispel the fear of those who have continually lived in dread. He wishes to restore the pilgrimage which has fallen into abeyance, and whose obligations and rights are neglected by the worshippers because of fear of the one who would seize them, as they could not safeguard themselves or their wealth, for they have been repeatedly vanquished, their blood shed and their wealth confiscated. As has been his custom, al-Muizz will authorise the repair of roads. He will then prevent the offenders from committing crimes, so that people are able to travel on the roads feeling safe and secure, and will be provided with food and provisions. News has reached him that Egypt's roads have been cut off because of the fear of the travel [caravan] leaders, since there has been neither a restraint nor a defence against the unjust aggressors.

Then he will renew the coinage and adjust it to be of the same standard as the blessed, auspicious *mansuri* dinars. He will eliminate their metal impurities. These are the three characteristics that must be addressed by a Muslim ruler. He must exert all his time and effort in their achievement.

Our lord and master, the Commander of the Faithful, has advised his servant to extend equity and justice and to dispel injustice, to temper aggression, to eradicate transgression, to increase aid, to uphold what is just and to strengthen the oppressed through compassion and beneficence, to supervise fairly, to be generous in companionship, to be kind in associations, to scrutinise living conditions, to offer protection to the inhabitants day and night so that they can strive freely to earn their living and can manage their affairs such that it would restore them. [He has also advised his servant to] establish support for them so that their minds are assuaged, their hearts are in harmony and their words are in unison in obedience to the *wali* (friend) of God, our lord and master, the Commander of the Faithful. His *mawla* [master] has ordered him to annul the unjust taxes that he disapproves of from being levied upon you.

He has instructed me to administer your inheritance according to the Book of God and the sunna of the Prophet. I will discontinue the deduction of money that used to be withheld from your legacies for the public treasury, and sent there without that being stipulated in your wills, for the treasury does not have a lawful claim over it.

He has instructed me to undertake the repair of your mosques and adorn them with carpets and lighting. I will give those who call to prayers, the administrators [of mosques] and those who lead the prayers their allowance. It will be given abundantly to them and not be withdrawn from them. I will only pay them from the treasury and not by draft on tax collectors.

Apart from what our lord and master, the Commander of the Faithful, has mentioned in this letter of his, there is what the delegates who have been sent on your behalf – may God support them and keep you all safe through your obedience to our lord and master, the Commander of the Faithful – have mentioned concerning the inclusion of matters that you have requested be mentioned in the *Aman*. In response to your request and as an assurance to you, I have included these in the *Aman*.

It would otherwise be meaningless to mention them and of no benefit to announce them, for Islam consists of one sunna and a sharia followed [by all]. You shall continue in your *madhhab*.

You shall be permitted to perform your obligations according to religious scholarship, and to gather for it in your congregational and other mosques, and to remain steadfast in the beliefs of the worthy ancestors from the Companions of the Prophet and those who succeeded them, the jurists of the cities who have pronounced judgements according to their *madhhab*s and *fatwa*s (formal legal opinions). The call to prayer and its performance, the fasting in the month of Ramadan, the breaking of the fast and the celebration of its nights, the [payment of] the alms tax, [the performance of the] pilgrimage and the undertaking of jihad will be maintained according to the command of God and His Book and in accordance with the instruction of His Prophet in his sunna, and the *dhimmi*s will be treated according to previous custom.

I guarantee you God's complete and universal safety, eternal and continuous, inclusive and perfect, renewed and confirmed through the days and recurring through the years, for your lives, your property, your families, your livestock, your estates and your quarters, and whatever you possess, be it modest or significant. There shall be no opponent opposing you, no harasser harassing you and no pursuer pursuing you.

You shall be safeguarded, protected and defended. Your [enemies] will be repelled from you and will be proscribed from [harming] you and you will not be opposed. No one will hasten to attack you or to disdain your mighty ones, let alone your downtrodden ones.

I shall continue to exert effort in whatever extends goodness to you, is beneficial to all of you, brings bounty to you, lets you experience blessings and through which you can rejoice in obeying our lord and master, the Commander of the Faithful.

I promise to fulfil what I have pledged to you, in the name of God's sacred covenant and protection, and by the covenant of His prophets and messengers, and by the covenant of the imams, our masters, the Commanders of the Faithful, and by the covenant of our lord and master, the Commander of the Faithful, al-Muizz li-Din Allah. So proclaim and announce [the covenant] by fulfilling the commitment. Come out to meet and greet me and stand before me when I cross the bridge and camp at the blessed halting place. Persevere in your allegiance and hasten to fulfil its obligations. Do not forsake any friend of our master, the Commander of the Faithful and abide by what you are ordered. May God guide you all on the straight path.'

The commander Jawhar wrote the *Aman* in his own hand in Shaban 358 [June–July 969]. Blessings of God be upon our master Muhammad and his righteous, pure and best progeny.

Implications

The *Aman* was instrumental in proclaiming the Fatimid claim to be the legitimate heirs to the spiritual and temporal authority of Prophet Muhammad. They considered it their prerogative to ensure the wellbeing of the umma which they, following the example of Muhammad, defined broadly to include the *Ahl al-Kitab*. The *Aman* document guaranteed the protection of all communities as well as their land and resources, to be implemented by state officials under the authority of al-Muizz. Importantly, the Fatimids sought a rapprochement among all Muslims by affirming that, while they may follow different *madhhab*s, all share in their common faith and fraternity of Islam.

The inclusive spirit of the *Aman* formed the bedrock upon which the Fatimids founded their institutional network in ethnically and religiously diverse Egypt. In the realm of political governance, competent administrators from varying socio-economic, religious and ethnic backgrounds, ranging from Yaqub b. Killis and Isa b. Nestorius to Badr al-Jamali, rose to the most senior positions within the Fatimid wazirate. As such, they contributed significantly to the enduring socio-economic vitality of the Fatimid empire. Again, as noted, the Fatimid judiciary developed a state-sponsored legal framework through which each segment of the Egyptian populace could seek judgements based on their own legal tradition in matters of family law. Fatimid inheritance law followed the Shii precedent and stipulated women's right to inherit, to own property and estates, as well as to bequeath their possessions to their female descendants. Intellectually, the Fatimids invested in the creation of institutions of learning that fostered an inclusive outlook. This included offering 'sessions of wisdom' for women of the Fatimid court as well as of the *dawa*, enabling leading Fatimid women such as Sitt al-Mulk (970-1023) and the Sulayhid queen, Arwa (1048-1138) to achieve prominent rank within the Fatimid *dawa*. The *Dar al-Hikma* established in 1005 is a case in point. Modelled on the Abbasid *Bayt al-Hikma*, the Fatimid academy of sciences provided a state-funded forum where scholars from a variety of intellectual backgrounds, geographical regions and legal traditions gained access and contributed to the development of the natural and religious sciences.

A pluralist ethos in a multi-ethnic and multi-religious empire was not without its challenges. One example was the recurring conflict between key stakeholders in the Fatimid court, notably the *maghariba* (western Berber troops) and the *mashariqa* (eastern Turkish soldiers). Not surprisingly, this factionalism came in the way of effective governance. It was to contribute to the eventual dissipation of Fatimid sovereignty, which yielded in 1171 to the Ayyubid dynasty, with its less inclusive ways of governance. Yet the cosmopolitan culture that was engendered during the quarter millennial reign of the Fatimids fed a vibrant social and intellectual discourse which echoed long after across the Mediterranean and beyond.

Further Reading

Brett, Michael. *The Rise of the Fatimids: The World of the Mediterranean and the Middle East in the Tenth Century CE.* Leiden, 2001.

Cortese, Delia and Simonetta Calderini, *Women and the Fatimids in the World of Islam.* Edinburgh, 2006.

Daftary, Farhad, ed. *Mediaeval Ismaili History and Thought.* Cambridge, 1996.

Halm, Heinz. *The Fatimids and their Traditions of Learning.* London, 1997.

Hamdani, Sumaiya. *Between Revolution and State: The Path to Fatimid Statehood.* London, 2006.

Lev, Yaacov. *State and Society in Fatimid Egypt.* Leiden, 1991.

Sachedina, Abdulaziz. *The Islamic Roots of Democratic Pluralism.* Oxford, 2001.

Walker, Paul. *Exploring an Islamic Empire: Fatimid History and its Sources.* London, 2002.

8

The Art and Architecture of the Mosque

Hasan-Uddin Khan

Architecture expresses identity and cultural continuity through the act of building, and can give clues about who we are. Skyscrapers have become symbols of corporate power, while religious buildings remind us of more spiritual and social concerns. In the architecture of Islam, the mosque stands as its most emblematic type of building.

There are a number of common experiences that have shaped the architectural landscape of the Muslim world, from colonialism to modernism. It is fair to say that the greatest influence on 20th-century building has been the Modernist movement with its emphasis on function and 'rationalism'. Modernism has been both a liberating and destructive force. It freed architecture from the burden of the past into a more democratic present, and yet it destroyed much of the connection to the roots of indigenous, vernacular architecture and in some ways to the local culture itself.

The terms 'Islamic architecture' and 'Islamic world' are laden with cultural and political overtones. However, I recognise the convenience in the shorthand 'Islamic' and use it here to denote the civilisation – cultures and religious mores – of societies whose people profess adherence to Islam. The 'traditional' Islamic world stretches from West Africa to Indonesia, with a population of over a billion people. Few of the states designate themselves as 'Islamic' – while India, with the third largest Muslim population in the world, is predominantly Hindu. Of these societies, very few escaped

direct colonial rule (Afghanistan, Iran and Oman being exceptions); all were subject to significant western influence. Then there
is the diaspora, notably in western Europe and North America,
where the Muslim population in France and the United Kingdom
exceeds that of some states in the 'traditional' Islamic world.

A broad history of the contemporary architecture of Islam still
needs to be written and the discourse deepened.[1] This chapter will
take up several key themes that characterise architecture in the
contemporary Islamic world, focusing on the mosque – a term that
here broadly covers communal places of worship, though their use
of conventional architectural features may vary significantly. The one
great issue that all emerging nations (and indeed more established
ones with newly diverse populations and cultures) have had to address
is that of identity, an issue that percolated down from the political
realm into that of architecture. The notion that architecture is a
reflection of cultural identity remains strongly relevant today.

Issues and Contributions
of Islam to Architecture

A number of issues are important to the 'art of the mosque'. The
most significant of these are outlined here.

Symbolism

Architecture is not only an expression of culture but also demonstrates the symbolic nature of Muslim thought and ideas that
reflect the teachings of Islam. The notion of meaning being

---

[1] Very little meaningful discourse about the contemporary architecture
of Islam occurred until 1977, when a series of seminars and a major prize
was initiated by the Aga Khan Award for Architecture. The Award continues
examination of architecture in the field and emphasises architecture as a
cultural force that can play a significant role in transforming people's
lives. It has probably become the most important forum for the dissemination of ideas and examples of building for Muslim societies, and also
is a serious contributor to the development of architectural ideas in the
international arena.

expressed through Islamic architecture is especially important in the mosque as the House of God.

Space is considered the symbol of Divine Presence and Light of the Divine Intellect. This is why the internal spaces of the mosque, especially the prayer hall, are carefully conceived. For example, notions of repetitiveness, as in the arches in a prayer hall, create architectural rhythms which turn multiplicity into unity. The idea reflects a diverse umma or community of Muslims, bound together by Islam.

Architectural elements themselves have symbolic associations. For example the dome is often seen as a reflection of the heavens, expressed in the perfection of the circle. The shape of the circle is tied to the Islamic doctrine of *tawhid* or unity of Allah. Of course, the architectural expression of this element has taken many forms depending on the regional style, materials and architecture of the mosque complex itself.

Minarets reach toward the heavens, toward God, and are a reminder of the faith. In this they are more than markers on the landscape; they beckon believers and are the sign of the presence of the mosque. The *mihrab* is not only the spatial organising element of the mosque, orienting the worshiper to the correct direction of Mecca, it also provides the focus for concentration and prayer.

Light

As an architectural device and a spiritual idea, light symbolises wisdom/enlightenment and also hope. In architecture, it creates an atmosphere for the space itself. Every religion is aware of this and employs it in different ways to assist the worshipper in achieving a mindset conducive to prayer. The importance of light is evoked some 49 times in the Quran, and most notably in the Verse of Light (*Aya al-Nur*):

> Allah is the Light of the Heavens and the Earth.
> The similitude of His Light is as a niche,
> Wherein a Lamp is placed; the Lamp enclosed in glass;
> The glass as it were a brilliant star,

Lighted with the oil of a blessed tree,
An olive neither of the east nor of the west,
Whose oil is well nigh luminous though no fire touched it.
Light upon Light! Allah doth guide whom He pleases to His Light.
Allah doth set parables for men
For Allah doth know all things (24:35).

Beauty

Of importance to the design is the notion of beauty, which is not a luxury but intrinsic to artistic expression. In Islamic art and architecture, beauty is considered to be a reflection of a divine quality. One of God's 'names' in the tradition is *al-Jamil*, the Beautiful; a hadith says, 'Allah is beautiful and He loves beauty.' Beauty in art is grounded in the inner dimension of Islamic revelation and spirituality. Seyyed Hossein Nasr, at the end of his book *Islamic Art and Spirituality* (1987), elucidates: 'Islamic art ... is the realisation of the One through the inebriating beauty of those forms, colours, and sounds which ... manifest themselves outwardly as limited forms while opening inwardly onto the Infinite, and serve as vehicles for the attainment of the Truth which is at once Majesty and Beauty.' It is an attitude that is reflected in the best of Islamic architecture.

Connection and Separation

The mosque is both connected to the city and everyday life and is at the same time removed as it signifies entry into a different realm where individuals relate to their Maker. It marks an important 'threshold' for entering this realm. This is even more important today in the rapidity of change and pressures of modern existence. As the Quran states:

> O ye who believe! When the call is proclaimed
> To prayer on Friday,
> Hasten earnestly to the Remembrance
> Of Allah and leave off business (and traffic);
> That is best for you if ye but knew (62:9).

In addition to the above issues, Islamic civilisation has made a number of contributions to the field of architectural design.

Geometry

A major contribution is the use of two and three-dimensional geometry. No other architectural tradition has given so much importance to geometry as a central organisational and decorative scheme. Muslims viewed geometry as an important field of knowledge and, by the 10th century, mathematicians had written about geometry and its relationship to architecture. Although these principles and forms were studied they have been applied and interpreted with great flexibility and were related to building materials, construction methods and symbolism. Geometric forms not only organise space and are used on varying scales, but also give symbolic meaning to buildings.

Geometric patterns, be they in mosaics, stone, ceramics or wood, can transform the tectonic qualities of a structure. Unique to Muslim architecture is the three-dimensional *muqarnas* that reminds one of a honeycomb. This device is usually used as a transitional element between two surfaces, e.g. at a corner. It acts to affect our perception by 'dematerializing' space.

Calligraphy

Calligraphy, part of the tradition where the word of God is expressed in written form, is another important contribution. Such texts on buildings – epigraphy – become a sign of the presence of Islam, and add a sense of beauty and complexity to surfaces. This recalls the noble sentiment that the craft of beautiful writing is 'among the keys to sustenance'.[2]

Depiction of human and animal forms in the arts of Islam has been the subject of debate, but in the mosque it is generally agreed that such forms are out of place. From the earliest times the

---

[2] Mir Sayyid-Ahmad Mashadi, quoted in Wheeler M. Thackston, *A Century of Princes: Sources on Timurid History and Art* (Cambridge, MA, 1989), p. 353.

written word has been used as the major type of mosque ornamentation. The choice and placement of inscriptions of verses from the Quran or hadith are always in some sense appropriate to the locations where they are found, but passages do not consistently appear in any one location. Some verses are associated with Shiism and others more with Sunni Islam.

An exception to the general lack of preference for a specific text to suit a specific location is the *mihrab*. Many *mihrabs* contain one of two Quranic invocations: 'Pray regularly morning and evening; and in the former part of the night,' and '...while he stood praying in the *mihrab*'. The extensive calligraphy on the surfaces of these buildings becomes a sign that they are mosques. In practice, the epigraphy can often only be read by those trained to do so. Knowing what it says may be less important than the fact that it exists and proclaims the building to be a mosque. The choice of the calligraphic form (*kufic, naskhi,* etc.) and inscriptions depend on the community being served and the location.

Gardens

Gardens and landscapes are part of the heritage of Islam, from the Alhambra in Spain to Kashmir in India, and have always been important reminders to Muslims, who are called to be stewards of the earth. Landscapes follow geometric and scientific principles, dealing with sustainability and nature in the recycling of water and so on. Water features are present in almost all gardens. However, gardens are not prominent in most mosques, perhaps because gardens were often seen as places of pleasure and individual contemplation.

It should be remembered that gardens were important to the Prophet Muhammad. For instance in the Masjid al-Nabi between the Prophet's tomb and a free-standing *mihrab* a short distance away is a space called the *rawdah* (garden). It is so named because the Prophet said: 'Between my house and my pulpit is a garden of the gardens of paradise'. The garden and oasis has played an extraordinary role in the development of place and town in the

Islamic world. In the past few decades the use of gardens has been significant in establishing the environment of the mosque.

A Sacred Place?

All mosques are places of worship but they are not sacred or consecrated spaces in the sense of the church being sacred or on hallowed ground. In Islam, the issue of sacred buildings is open to interpretation. The holiest place is the Kaaba in Mecca, the focus of the hajj pilgrimage and the mosque around it. It is, according to the Quran, 'the very first house of prayer established for humanity…The place where Abraham stood…' (2:125). Other places considered blessed are the Dome of the Rock or Qubat al-Sakhra, (built in 692, in Jerusalem with the al-Aqsa Mosque, rebuilt many times since 780) in the Haram al-Sharif or Noble Sanctuary. There is also the mosque and shrine of Imam Husayn some 100 kilometres south of Baghdad, dating from the 10th century and first built in 680 on the site of the grave of the Prophet's grandson, especially important to Shia Muslims. And the Mosque of Quba, just southeast of Medina, built by the Prophet himself around 629.

Let us consider the Mosque of the Prophet – or Masjid al-Quba. Within its development lie several lessons. The mosque, as far as we can tell, started off in the Prophet's house in Medina as a simple courtyard with rooms on two sides. Soon thereafter in 707 the Caliph al-Walid replaced it with a new building to which minarets were added; whether as markers or for the call to prayer, the *azaan*, is uncertain. Over the centuries, because of its symbolic importance, it has grown and expanded. Today the early mosque is unrecognizable.

The Prophet, who is an exemplar *par excellence* for Muslims, led a simple existence. The place of worship was a place of gathering and submission to the will of Allah, not a symbol of the greatness or magnificence of Islam. What we see today is different. The elaborate structure is now much larger to accommodate the multitudes that pray in it. As a point of pilgrimage and as Muslim empires grew, additions were made, especially by the Ottomans who were for centuries the guardians of the Holy Places. What this aggrandisement means is worth considering. It certainly displays the power, the magnificence and the presence of Islam, the recognition of the central role of the Prophet and glorification of Allah. Yet is this an image that reflects the teachings of Islam as submission and humility, and Muslims as stewards of the earth?

For a Muslim the building of a mosque is a pious act. Muhammad is reported to have said, 'Whoever builds for Allah a mosque, seeking by it Allah's grace, Allah will build for him a house in paradise.' The Quran proclaims:

> The mosques of Allah shall be visited and maintained by such
> as believe in Allah and the Last Day, and establish regular
> prayers, and practise regular charity *(zakat)*, and fear none
> except Allah. It is they who are expected to be on true guidance
> (9:18).

When someone commissions a mosque, he or she does not own it. It belongs to the community of users.

Basic Types of Mosque

In broad terms there are five types of mosque (Fig. 2).

The first is the hypostyle mosque that is based upon a series of columns within a space – perhaps the most ancient and traditional construction method. This type occurs in different parts of the world, from Arabia to West Africa, and elsewhere, even though its form and materials of construction can vary. Good examples of this are the Qairawan Great Mosque (836) in Tunisia and the Great Mosque of Djenne (1909) in Mali (PL. 1).

The second is a mosque with four *iwans* or vaulted halls arranged around a central courtyard. This type occurs mainly in Central Asia and Iran. Among the finest examples is the Masjid-i Jami in Isfahan, Iran, begun in the eighth century and expanded and rebuilt through to the 17th century.

The third type is the Indian domed mosque which (almost always) has three domes over the prayer space and the complex set within a colonnaded walled courtyard, often with a pool in its centre. One of the most famous is the Badshahi Mosque (1674) in Lahore, Pakistan.

The fourth, which has become the dominant model for contemporary architecture, is the Ottoman mosque, dating from the 16th century. It is characterised by a large central space without columns. It also has pencil thin minarets at its corners. The 16th-century Suleymaniya complex by the master builder Sinan is one of the most ambitious examples of its kind. The same style occurs in Indonesia and Malaysia, where there is essentially a central space but in a very different style and with timber construction. In Indonesia, mosques did not have minarets; now they do, perhaps to be more 'correct'. The Masjid Agung (1848) in Surakarta, Indonesia, illustrates this well.

The last type is the pavilion complex, which emanates from China. It is also the one mosque type where gardens are prominent. It consists of a series of pavilions, each one having a different function and a different meaning contained within a walled space. The Great Mosque of Xian in China (PL. 2), founded in the eighth century, has an octagonal pagoda as its minaret, a series of pavilions and gardens, and in its prayer hall, dating from the 14th century, a traditional Chinese roof form.

Architectural Elements of a Mosque

The word mosque comes from the Arabic *masjid*, meaning 'place of prostrations'. It is a place for *salat* or ritual collective prayer. It is an expression of the community rather than of the individual, though of course one may pray alone. It is noteworthy that during the hajj men and women pray side by side. This does not apply to the use of mosques themselves – more about this later.

In Houses, which Allah hath permitted to be raised
To honour, for celebration in them, of His name,
In them is He glorified
In the mornings, in the evenings, (again and again) (sura 24:36).

Fig. 2: Sketch of mosque types

What makes a mosque a mosque? The Prophet himself is recorded as saying, 'Wherever you pray, that place is a *masjid*.' Generally, prayer is offered in a mosque facing Mecca, but no kind of structure is mandated. There are several architectural elements that usually constitute a mosque; they are not prescribed by religion, but rather by custom.

Qibla, Mihrab and *Minbar*

The one element that occurs in all mosques is the *qibla* wall, which indicates the direction of prayer. It can be as simple as a line in the sand, or a wall with little decoration, or as complex as the carved wooden wall of the Xian Mosque, or the 16th-century Tillah Kari Mosque of Samarkand.

The *qibla* is marked by the *mihrab*, a niche in the wall (PL. 4). This is the only requirement that a mosque really has. It is noteworthy that the Prophet changed the direction of the *qibla* from Jerusalem to Mecca in 624, to make the mosque distinctive in relation to Jewish and Christian places of worship. In the King Faisal Mosque in Islamabad, the *mihrab* takes the unusual form of the Quran as an open book, while in the historic mosque in Samarkand it uses a *muqarnas* vault.

To the right of the *mihrab* is the *minbar* – the equivalent of a pulpit – usually a free-standing element of a series of steps and a platform, from where the oration or *khutba* is given on Friday. This element too can range from simple to extraordinarily elaborate, made of wood, marble or other material.

Minaret

The minaret has always been a marker in the landscape and today this takes on an even more important function, especially in a city that has both residents and visitors. In many village mosques, there was no need for a minaret as marker as everyone knew where the mosque was. The term itself comes from the Arabic *manarah*, a lighthouse.

As a place to call the *azaan*, the minaret's height was often related to the distance that the voice of the muezzin would have to reach. In the house of the Prophet, the first mosque, the call to prayer was made from the roof and there was no minaret. Diverse cultures have dealt with the call to prayer in different ways; for example, in Indonesia, traditionally the call to prayer used to emanate from a drum.

Today, the minaret is often used for the *azaan* by means of loudspeakers. Electronic communications systems within the mosque itself for broadcasting the prayer or events at the complex are now a part of the modern mosque. In the contemporary city, the *azaan* from various mosques often compete with each other, calling the faithful at slightly different intervals. The resulting cacophony of sound is a very different experience from that of hearing the clear lone voice of a muezzin.

Entrance or Threshold

The entrance to a mosque forms a threshold that marks a symbolic change from one state of mind to another. It often takes the form of an arched gateway, and is usually the point where one formally enters the mosque – an act marked by the removal of one's shoes.

The idea of entrance pertains not only to mosques but also into heaven, as the Quran says:

And the gates thereof shall be ready set open,
And its keepers will say: 'Peace be upon you! Well have you done.
Enter you here, to dwell therein. Praise be to Allah, the Lord of the
Worlds (who hath made us to inherit the earth)' (39:73-75).

Dome

An overt expression of Islam is the dome based on the circle, which symbolises the perfection of heaven. Although found in many historic buildings, from Byzantine to Renaissance architecture, it has now become associated with the mosque. Domes occur in almost all mosques and come in many styles and materials. An historic example is the 16th-century Ottoman mosque complex of Sultan Ahmet in Istanbul. The Turkish Ottoman style serves as the model – in a contemporary abstracted fashion – for the Manhattan Islamic Centre of New York designed in 1991.

Tehran's al-Ghadir Mosque (1987) is an interpretation of the dome, rising from a 12-sided prayer hall, representing the 12 imams. Here the dome incorporates a *muqarnas* and is articulated as a transition from square to octagon to dome. This was done for structural reasons and is not necessary for modern construction, but it can provide a sense of scale and transition of architectural elements.

Prayer Hall

No specific geometric shapes appear historically to have been reserved for mosques. Although mosques are best served for prayer by a rectangular prayer hall, the use of other shapes is not uncommon. But attention to the geometric reconciliation of space is prevalent in Islamic architecture. Most mosques have the *qibla* wall as the longest, to allow for as many people as possible to pray side by side, making the space a lateral one in contrast to the church where the altar is usually on the shortest wall.

Wudu or Ablutions

A significant element is the ablutions facility for cleansing oneself before prayer. Here the importance of cleanliness and the use of water (a precious commodity in the original homelands of Islam) is clearly shown. Some people will have performed the *ghusl* and *wudu* before they come to the mosque, but the great majority use this facility, which is also of symbolic importance. The place of *wudu* is now usually divided into two separate facilities, one for men and the other for women. The area for *wudu* and preparation for prayer is both practical and inspirational, for it marks another threshold in the mosque experience. Perhaps the most elaborate ablutions facilities are in the Hassan II Mosque in Casablanca, where they are conceived in the form of lotus blossoms within a cavernous tiled space.

Themes in Contemporary Islamic architecture

This section puts the contemporary architecture of Islam and its influence on the mosque – and other spaces of worship – into roughly chronological thematic settings. A few countries have been selected to illustrate the dominant trends in architectural thinking and design.

The Modern West

It is in 19th-century colonisation and industrialisation that the roots of the contemporary architecture of Islam are found. Colonisation brought with it the penetration of local institutions, creating confrontational situations between old and new. The colonial attitude towards the Orient was based on the notion that the colonists had an inherent supremacy of knowledge, power and culture. Edward Said identifies this in his *Orientalism* (1978) as a dominant impulse in a relationship where Europeans saw Islam in opposition to their Christian values.

British studies of local Indian or Mughal architecture led to the development of an architecture derived as an assembly of elements and details culled from local building traditions. By the beginning of the 20th century, the so-called Indo-Saracenic style was well established, used not only by the British all over South and Southeast Asia but also by princely rulers and local elites. From the 1920s onwards a more classical treatment was given to buildings, attempting a fusion between Italian Renaissance classicism and selected Indian forms such as the *chatri*, *chajja* and *jali* (the umbrella-shaped pavilion, the cornice or eave, and the perforated screen) that skilfully created a fresh vocabulary and style.

When the Ismaili community built *jamatkhanas* (from the Arabic *jamaa* for gathering and the Persian *khana* for place) in East Africa in the early 20th century, it took the existing British colonial architecture and added features from India, from whence the majority of its population came. Examples of these are *jamatkhanas* in Nairobi, Mombasa and Mwanza.

In the turbulent Ottoman empire at the turn of the 20th century, the western-educated middle classes tended to support westernisation. It was no great surprise that European Neo-Classicism became the preferred style for public buildings in Turkey to express the New Order (*Nizam-i Çedid*). When the Allies forcibly disbanded the empire after World War I, other colonial powers began to wane

due to rising nationalist movements. A new political consciousness arose in Arab and Asian Muslim societies, then in sub-Saharan
Africa. Their political struggles began to relate architectural expression to their own emergent nationalist purposes, giving rise in
some instances to a national style in building. But the link between
local architectures and Europe endured, and European architectural idioms were popularly regarded as more 'progressive' and
desirable than indigenous or regional ones.

At this time, ironically, the incorporation of Islamic architectural styles was a device used by colonisers as a way of recognising
and catering to local interests. But the colonial powers, which
clearly had political, economic and technical superiority, had
usurped local cultures and modes of development by the beginning of the 20th century. The idea of being western was equated
with that of being modern.

The Individual Nation and National Identity

The role of government has been crucial in the expression of a
national identity through architecture in many of the societies in
Asia and Africa. However, the influence of western Modernism
and of individual foreign architects' buildings in these countries
has had a strong impact.

With new states emerging as political entities based on western
models, 'state formation took place during a period when peoples
were being invited to imagine themselves, and often act, as members
of a variety of different communities, some tribal and local, or
narrowly religious, others larger such as pan-Arab, pan-Turkish,
Zionist, or pan-Islamic'.[3] It is not surprising that the Islamic world
began to identify itself not only through political boundaries, but
also in terms of pan-Islamism with reference to the umma. These
forms of identification also found expression in the arts, literature, costume and architecture, where self-definition was based
on the expression of difference from the traditional past.

---

[3] Roger Owen, *State Power and Politics in the Making of the Modern Middle
East* (London, 1992), p. 6.

The idea of nationalism itself was somewhat problematic to many Muslims, though not to the Statists. Nationalism was often used as a tool to get rid of the colonial powers, but it was not easy to build a 'national spirit' when Muslims were accustomed to think of themselves as members of the *Dar al-Islam*. This was true even when they were part of the Ottoman empire. Some of the new nations had been so constructed that there was bound to be tension among their citizens. The southern part of the Sudan, for example, was largely Christian while the north was Muslim: for a people who defined their identity in religious terms, it was hard to establish a shared Sudanese nationalism. The same was true in Lebanon. In another case, when Pakistan and India were carved out of colonial India, ethnic groups like Bengalis and Punjabis were split between the two countries, causing displacement and continued tensions – and eventually leading to the establishment of a new Muslim state, Bangladesh. Kashmir, too, had a predominantly Muslim population; its rule by a Hindu raja and later de facto attachment to predominantly Hindu India has been the source of much strife.

The act of becoming an independent state, be it a republic, dictatorship, monarchy, or socialist regime, brought with it the psychological need to express freedom from a colonial or foreign-dominated past, or even from a past wrapped in the mantle of tradition. In the 1940s many newly independent countries embraced Modernism as the architecture that best reflected not only the new age but also egalitarianism. They saw in Modernism the social desire to serve everyone, rich and poor, a project that was to have been facilitated by the possibilities of mass production.

An important example in the creation of national identity is Turkey, one of the earliest independent Muslim states. The Turkish Republic under Mustafa Kemal Atatürk was the first to achieve a rupture with the symbolic and visual past in the 1920s as it moved to define itself in purely secular terms. The government's proclamation of modern statehood discouraged customary symbols like the fez and veil, and made substantial changes in both ideology and image. It was the first Muslim state to consciously express its new identity through architecture in its search to be Turkish whilst releasing itself from the Ottoman image, and to create a national bourgeoisie with republican ideals. The rich diversity of Ottoman Islamic elements combined with Neo-Classical Greek and Roman forms with symmetrical buildings, tall arched windows, wide eaves and sloping roofs gave rise to what has been termed 'The First National Architectural Movement'. It was so designated after 1912, and coincided with the nationalist political movement. Ottoman modernisation would henceforth be based on overlaying some elements of European civilisation while retaining Turkish identity and Islam. European architects came to the country in the 1920s and helped spread ideas of Modernism that dominated the country's architecture into the 1970s.

In Iran, Turkey's successful refashioning served as an influential model. After a coup d'état in 1921, Reza Shah founded the Pahlavi dynasty and launched a reconstruction and modernisation programme, moving Iran toward secularisation and casting Islam as a force that hindered progress. The traditional Persian Islamic and philosophical thought of the late 19th century gave way to western and 'rationalist' ideas coupled with new economic and political realities. Yet unlike Atatürk, Reza Shah kept the monarchy and, in architecture, revived a consciousness of ancient Achaemenid glory in an interpretation of the newly rediscovered sites of Susa and Persepolis.

The architecture of individual buildings also changed with the influx of foreign architects. The mid-1930s marked the beginning of Modernism in Iran, with its cubic forms, new materials and buildings raised off the ground on columns. After the British deposed Reza Shah in 1941, his son Muhammad Reza, the last Shah of Iran, took over and furthered secular modernism. Under the Pahlavi reign (1925-1979), and especially during the Shah's White Revolution of 1962, many new towns were established. The nation-state, boosted by oil money, embraced Modernism in architecture.

Two individuals who produced fine work are Kamran Diba (1937-) and Nader Ardalan (1939-), both trained in the United States. Diba's work, which includes Shushtar New Town (1980) in

Khuzestan with its modern cubic brick and concrete mosques is spatially and architecturally elegant. Ardalan produced a number of important works including the Iran Centre for Management Studies (1973), now Imam Sadegh University, Tehran. He co-authored with Laleh Bakhtiar an influential publication on Iranian architecture, geometric order and Islam, *Sense of Unity: The Sufi Tradition in Architecture* (1974).

The modernisation of Turkey as a model was powerful throughout the Islamic world, with the success of its built forms and its re-invention as a new state. Even countries such as Libya and Malaysia that styled themselves as Islamic Republics were conscious of the need to be modern in order to be seen as players in the development of an internationalising world. In architecture this was translated into the desire to make new buildings distinct from those of the past.

Pakistan, born out of idealism for an Islamic state, is another example. Led by a secularist, Mohammed Ali Jinnah, the country achieved independence in 1947 in the partition of British India. Soon after, between 1958 and 1969, the military government of Ayub Khan moved to define Pakistan as a modern state. New, modernist concrete buildings were built for offices, homes for the rich and middle-income housing in flats. The city of Karachi expanded rapidly and a new capital, Islamabad, with its modern public buildings (many designed by foreign architects) was developed.

Malaysia with its multi-ethnic mix of Malays, Chinese and Indians poses an interesting counterpoint as a country that styled itself as an Islamic Republic. Various cultural influences, notably Chinese, Indian, Portuguese and the British colonial presence from the 18th century onward, played a major role in forming Malaysia's architecture. A national identity was being shaped in the Federation of Malaysia's capital city, Kuala Lumpur, as expressed in its National Mosque (1965) by Baharuddin Abu Kassim and his colleagues. Designed as a modern building using a folded concrete plate parasol roof, it was as much an emblem of the state as it was a modern form. The search for an expression of a Malaysian Islamic identity was interpreted by and large through the model of the Malay house, with its pitched overhanging roofs.

The Russian Revolution of 1917 inspired some socialist models of development in Muslim societies, influencing concepts of modernisation and equity especially in urban centres. Indeed, the idea of an Islamic Socialism was proffered in the mid 1950s – by Sukarno in Indonesia, Nasser in Egypt and others – in an attempt to reconcile the paternalism and politics of the state with Islamic teaching. A good example of Soviet monumentalism is the Istiqlal Mosque (1955-1984) by Siliban in Jakarta. It is not surprising that the socialist model dedicated to equity was a powerful one adopted by many emerging countries. Besides the progress exemplified by the new social responsibility of the state, progress was also reflected symbolically by modernity.

States often chose to express their independence by creating new administrative cities, responding to their conscious need to express their differences from the colonial settlements. This was the mirror of the French colonisers, who created new cities as an example of modernity, slightly separate from the historic Islamic cities, as in Fez and Marrakesh in Morocco.

Although city building was a very expensive process for the state, post-independence saw the construction of new capitals, such as Ankara (1928), Islamabad (from 1961), Abuja, Nigeria (since 1975), Dodoma, Tanzania (since 1976), and Dhaka (1962-1983), designed as the capital of East Pakistan and now of Bangladesh. The capital city, with its capitol complex, the seat of government, marks the point of transition and signals the change to modern statehood. Power and democracy are expressed through parliamentary buildings, as in Dhaka, Kuala Lumpur and Kuwait City, even in instances where the reality of the latter is an illusion.

In its search for legitimacy, the state required a new set of buildings to serve as symbols expressing a national and collective identity. One of the most important examples of the expression of nationhood and modernity occurred within many of the states with majority Muslim populations in the form of State Mosques. The State Mosques of Malaysia (Kuala Lumpur, 1965), Pakistan (Islamabad, 1966), and Kuwait (Kuwait City, 1976) testify to the desire to express modernity *and* proclaim the importance placed on religion.

In Islamabad, the main mosque was conceived as a national mosque, now called the King Faisal Mosque, mainly because of funding from Saudi Arabia. The Turkish architect Vedat Dalokay (1927-1991) designed it in 1970, using the Ottoman model with its grand open central space and tall thin minarets. The *mihrab* takes on an unusual form of the Quran as an open book, by the Pakistani artist Gulgee. Another unusual element is the raised platform for Quran reading competitions. I know of no other mosque with this element so prominently articulated. The mosque breaks with the past by expressing modernity through its architecture and an identity that proclaims it belongs to the late 20th century.

Fifty years after Turkey became a secular republic with a majority Muslim population, a mosque was built in Ankara in 1989 within the Parliament buildings complex. The mosque fits well into this landscape. It says that there is a place for prayer within government, but it does so with restraint.

The London Ismaili Centre, designed in the 1970s, is situated in the heart of Kensington and was required to blend with the surrounding institutional buildings. It too is a low-key expression of religion in the London urban landscape, but is much more ornate and overtly Islamic in its interior – and on its roof, conceived as a four-part paradise garden.

Pan-Islamism and Historicism

The Modernist movement meshed easily with Islamic sensibilities in the 1960s, as both strove for universality. In the Islamic world, a long period of national consolidation and the search for a new expression of identity began at this time. Professionals and clients began to look at their own histories for 'legitimate' expressions that would echo specific cultural aspirations. Hence, the purer Modernist ideals and forms were soon overlaid by a focus on the once 'glorious past', and a form of historicism came to engulf the building of mosques.

A fine early example is the Washington, DC Islamic Centre. It was commissioned in the early 1950s with donations from different Muslim countries on the instigation of their ambassadors in

Washington, who perceived that Muslims did not have a place to pray or perform the rituals for the dead. The question of what the image for the building should be was raised: it came down to who funded and designed it. In this case it was the architect Mario Rossi, an Italian who lived in Egypt and worked for the Ministry of Awqaf (pious foundations). He used the precedent of 13th-century Mamluk architecture with which he was familiar.

Achieving a modern identity that was at the same time 'Islamic' was the goal in most projects, even when foreign architects were employed. For example, in Saudi Arabia the centrally located mosque at the King Khaled International Airport, Riyadh (1974-1981) and the Sulaiman Mosque (1980) in Jeddah by Abdel Wahid El Wakil, refer to traditional elements.

A similar approach that reinforces this notion of Islamic architecture is taken by a number of Arab architects. In Iraq the 1958 July revolution had a marked influence on architecture due to its nationalist stance. There, in the 1960s, several architects tried to produce and teach a regionally inflected modern architecture. The architect Mohammad Makiya's work tries to reconcile historic architecture based on Islamic ideals with that of contemporary needs. His works include the modernist Khulafa Mosque (1963) in Baghdad that includes a restored 13th-century minaret and the monumental State Mosque (1981) of Kuwait, which is more traditionalist in style.

The architectural models that emanated from the Middle East – with their arches, domes and courtyards – were deemed Islamic, having common features regardless of their location. Pan-Islamism used 'Islamist' ideas rather than those labelled 'fundamentalist' in the West. The term Islamist is used here to describe interpretive and sometimes innovative attempts to reconstruct the social order within the religious traditions of Islam.[4]

---

[4] See Robin Wright, 'Islam, Democracy and the West' in *Foreign Affairs*, 71 (1992), pp. 131-145. Wright points out that various Islamic movements are often called 'fundamentalist' in the West, but most are not fundamentalist in their agendas. Many of them resemble the Catholic Liberation Theology initiatives that urge the active use of religious doctrine to improve living conditions in the modern world.

In Turkey, there was a backlash against Modernism in the 1990s, as conservative and Islamist circles added their voices to the process of development. Not surprisingly, their focus was on questions of mosque design, wherein the preference was to emulate the classic 16th-century Ottoman model.

Continuity with the Past

Indigenous vernacular architecture was often regarded as part of the past and not important to the architecture of most new states. A great deal of building continued to be based on indigenous traditions, materials and practices evolved over the centuries – practices largely ignored by the new elite classes. Nowhere is this more dramatic and beautiful than in West Africa. In Yaama, Niger, a new earth mosque, built by Falké Barmou between 1962 and 1986, continues the regional building tradition, a hybrid of indigenous and Islamic beliefs. There was always, however, a small group of elites that looked to the local or vernacular as the authentic expression of their culture – and a mark of resistance to alien ideas from the West.

The impetus for using the vernacular as a basis for contemporary architecture in Muslim societies came from Egypt, primarily through the work of the architect Hassan Fathy (1900-1989). Fathy's life-long efforts to promote indigenous building in hot dry climates offered a counterbalance to the International Style begun during the formative period of Modernism in the 1920s and 1930s. Fathy attracted a wide following amongst younger architects in the late 1960s; his seminal book, *Architecture for the Poor* (1969) detailed the development of his design for the village of New Gourna (1948), near Luxor, Egypt, with its elegant earth mosque.

Others in Africa and the Middle East have emulated Fathy's poetic use of earth as a building material for vaults and domes. His vernacular stance was seen as 'Islamic'. Several years later in 1981 Fathy designed a residential and religious community complex made of earth. The Dar al-Islam in Abiquiu in New Mexico (PL. 5) is based on his Egyptian model, thus creating what I have called an 'instant Islamic vernacular' architecture in a very different setting.

Saudi Arabia sees itself as the geographic and spiritual centre of the Islamic world, due to the rise of Islam within its borders and the presence of the holy cities of Mecca and Medina. There, the notion of architecture that expresses an Islamic identity assumed great importance and became the centre of its architectural agenda from the mid-1970s. The exploitation of oil made the country extremely wealthy and allowed for the rebuilding of old settlements and the establishment of new ones through five-year plans. The unprecedented architectural activity of that time attracted architects and construction companies from all over the world.

At first, modern International Style architecture took hold as being new, shiny and progressive. This was soon tempered by incorporation of the region's vernacular architecture – especially with reference to Najdi building with its massive crenulated earth walls and deep narrow openings – to reflect a sense of national pride and identity.[5] There are numerous examples of this, including that of the Jordanian architect Rasem Badran's monumental Imam Turki Jami in the Qasr al-Hokm (Justice Palace) complex of 1992 in Riyadh. Architecture that reflected Saudi identity was equated with the expression of an Islamic identity.

Return to the Sources of Islam and Regionalism

In the June 1967 war between Israel and its Arab neighbours, the Israeli victory and the Arab defeat led to a religious revival throughout the Middle East and beyond, as the old secularist policies seemed discredited. Resurgence of confidence in Islam came about in the early 1970s, spurred on by the success of the Organisation of Petroleum-Exporting Countries (OPEC) in remaking the global oil market in its favour. This caused a worldwide fuel crisis, yet as subsequent building activity slowed in the West, it boomed in the Middle East, attracting architects from all over the world. By the mid-1970s many influential western architects were recycling old images of 'Islamic architecture', an easy way to satisfy clients. It was

---

[5] The royal family, which is also a major architectural patron, comes from the Najd region of the country.

an indulgence in kitsch more than a serious inquiry into or expression of Muslim values in contemporary building. As the architectural historian William Curtis expressed it:

> The backlash against modern values implied nothing distinct beyond a greater reverence for traditional moral and aesthetic forms. Once again, the issue of identity was at stake, but pan-Islamic sentiments could even be manipulated to imply a community of cultures between Morocco and Manila; with the wave of a wand, schisms, national boundaries, and centuries of change could all be overlooked.'[6]

In the face of early globalisation in the 1980s, the idea of affirming regional identity had become as important as having a national one. A play between modernity and traditional vocabulary emerged as the focus of the architectural profession. This regionalist architecture, while expressing climatic, geographical and cultural pluralism produced some of the most innovative buildings of the post-colonial period. Ironically, in the 1990s, forms of Islamic post-modernism with their historical references became the counterpoint to the global corporate architecture that had swept the world.

It is worth reminding ourselves that in the nations of the Muslim world, both secular and sacred power have had a role in legitimising government. Governments promoted the idea that state, political party and religion were one, and used this to further their own ends. That Islam is 'a way of life' where religious and everyday existences are intertwined helps serve this purpose. This integration of the sacred and the secular extends to architecture; most activities are permitted in the mosque, from the religious to the social and the political. Indeed, the mosque sometimes takes on a subversive role, though it has also been used as a statement by the state.

There have been leaders who assumed the mantle of political authority through their religious position. For example, the late

---

[6] William J. Curtis, *Modern Architecture since 1900*, 3rd ed. (Oxford, 1996), pp. 584-585.

King of Morocco, Hassan II (1929-1999), belonged to the four-century-old Alaouite dynasty and claimed descent from the Prophet. As such he asserted the right to rule not only as secular head of state but also as religious leader. He appreciated the power of architecture in linking himself to history. In studying the great Moroccan architecture of the 12th-14th centuries, Hassan II decreed in 1981 that new public buildings had to refer to that style and decoration even if they had modern uses. This is now referred to as the Hassanian Style.

The Hassan II Mosque in Casablanca, completed in 1993, is the largest contemporary mosque in the world (PL. 3). It is a huge, indeed kingly gesture, built on the edge of the city, on land reclaimed from the sea. The location was inspired by the verse from the Quran that states: 'the throne of God lies on the water' (11:7). The complex uses forms that come from historic Moroccan architecture, but now scaled up several times in a very ornate structure. Its 210-meter tall minaret projects a laser beam in the direction of Mecca for some 30 kilometres. The prayer hall can accommodate 25,000 worshippers; its centre acts as a courtyard when the roof slides open. There are also some rather fantastic features: a swimming pool and the most elaborate ablutions facilities seen anywhere. The craftsmanship that went into the complex is quite extraordinary.

The building has a huge underground parking space that can also accommodate some 40 large buses, and has television and satellite communication facilities. It is a modern building in the guise of tradition, tying the current regime in Morocco to the historic past through architecture. It is a way of claiming legitimacy through the use of forms that belong to medieval history.

Some of the strongest evocations of Islamic traditionalism in architecture occur in Iran. Opposition to the Shah's regime by Ayatollah Khomeini's followers, beginning in 1977 with the slogan, 'Independence, Freedom, Islamic Republic', led to the Islamic Revolution of 1978-1979. The grievances behind the revolution were as much socio-economic as cultural. There developed amongst the alienated a search for roots and a return to 'authentic Iranian or Islamic values'. Iran questioned the symbols of Modernism, now associated with Pahlavi rule. Yet the alternative style of the 1980s was a pastiche of traditional elements such as the dome, the arch and the courtyard, often poorly interpreted. This architecture paid lip service to traditional Islamic building in formalistic terms, but without any real integration of its intrinsic principles.

Disillusionment with the West and the desire to 'return to Islam' is found in much of the Muslim world. This is not a rejection of modern technology, and it calls for a return to 'Islamic principles' that are interpreted differently by various nations and groups. Even modern leaders who professed to be secularists were by the 1970s using Islam and Islamic rhetoric to bolster their positions. For example, General Zia ul-Haq, who ruled Pakistan from 1977 to 1988, not only restored Islamic penal and commercial codes and reinstated traditional dress, but also supported Islamic architecture that referred to 16th-century models from Mughal India.

The belief persists in the Islamic world that historical (Middle Eastern) models for architecture are more authentic than those provided by the local vernacular. Looking to the sources of Islamic architecture was deemed important in establishing an alternate Islamic identity. Using the cultural anchor of Islam provides an internal strength and counterweight to external, western or global models. It is sometimes very difficult to argue with this approach, as this will usually be interpreted as 'anti-Islamic'.

Two Contemporary Issues related to the Mosque

There are two overarching issues that have to be dealt with in the architecture of the contemporary mosque. The first is the expression of identity and the place of Muslims themselves in a globalising world. The second is the position of women in society and within the mosque itself. In both cases, the Muslim diaspora in Europe and North America has played a vital part: after all, settings with heightened encounters across cultures and faith traditions are sure to bring forth issues of identity and religious expression. As globalisation makes those encounters an everyday matter across societies, the traditional Muslim world must also address those issues.

Expressions of Identity

How identity is expressed and perceived in mosques in the different areas of the world is dependant not only on cultural factors but also on regional building mores and traditions of design, architecture and construction. A number of examples illustrate this well.

The Islamic Society of North America (ISNA) Centre in Plainfield, Indiana, designed by the Canadian-Pakistani architect Gulzar Haider in 1978, speaks of a contemporary Islamic architecture – a modernist concrete and brick structure without obvious traditional elements. It is subtle in its symbolism, dealing with notions of the manifest (*zahir*) and the hidden (*batin*) in its interiority and arrangement of spaces. Twenty years after the mosque was built, Haider said to me that the local community wanted to add a dome, because without 'either a dome or a minaret, it was hard to recognise it as a mosque'. He persuaded them to leave the mosque as it was.

Another example of this is in Chinatown in Jakarta, Indonesia, where Chinese Muslims trying to assimilate into the indigenous population of Indonesia felt that they had to explicitly proclaim they were Muslim. This was achieved by using the ubiquitous dome and minaret applied to the face of a shop-house that was being used as a mosque.

The need to express such physical signs of religion is not new. For example, the insertion of a Catholic church into the Great Mosque of Cordoba in 15th-century Spain, spoke of the domination of Christianity in a country that had been ruled by Muslims for centuries. Physical forms send out symbolic messages.

The use of easily recognised architectural elements to denote a mosque plays its part. The Ottoman influence of the tall pencil-thin minaret has been widely adopted because it fits so well into modern construction technology, and the central dome has a Modernist image. This can be seen in the Islamic Centre in Zagreb

(1987), among the largest in Europe. It again addresses the question of identity, relating to a past when that part of the world was Ottoman. There was a desire to associate with Islam in what was then Socialist Yugoslavia, while at the same time expressing modernity.

A more overt expression of Islam occurs in the Manhattan Islamic Centre of New York, designed in 1991 by Skidmore, Owings and Merrill. It uses the Turkish Ottoman model, in an abstracted contemporary version. It has an Ottoman dome over an open central space and a tall, thin minaret. The prayer hall is bathed in light and the *mihrab*, in luminous shimmering glass, draws attention to itself as being distinct from the rest of the building. It is a carefully crafted work of architecture.

The Ismaili Centre in Burnaby, Canada (1982-1994) by Bruno Freschi also refers elegantly to traditional elements such as the entrance portal (PL. 6) and the shallow Turkish domes over the prayer space, and its elaborate geometric ornamentation in its interior. The courtyard celebrates the classic Persian four-square layout (*chahar bagh*).

More typical is the easy use of the familiar dome in the Islamic Centre of Greater Toledo (1983) in Perrysburg, Ohio, by Talat Itil, as it is in many mosques the world over, from Brunei to Moscow. Indeed, the dome of a mosque built in 2000 in Shanghai, China, is merely symbolic. It has no relationship to the building's interior spaces or structure – it merely sits atop the flat roof as an iconic image. The community was conscious of the need to proclaim the presence of Islam in a newly tolerant atmosphere.

In Indonesia, the indigenous traditional pyramidal roof is being replaced by domes, often by local ready-made pre-fabricated tin domes that are sold along the sides of roads. They signify not only a pan-Islamic approach to architecture, but also stress the historical Middle Eastern model as the legitimate expression of mosque architecture. This is fuelled by Saudi Arabia, which has been greatest funder of mosques in contemporary times all over the world, from Uzbekistan and Indonesia to the USA.

The notion of an umma, to which all Muslims belong and in which all are equal in the eyes of Allah, has given rise to the feeling

PL. 1: Southeast view of the Great Mosque of Djenne, Mali.

PL. 2: The Phoenix Pavilion in the Fourth Court,
       Great Mosque of Xian, China.

PL. 3: The Hassan II Mosque, Casablanca, Morocco.

PL. 4 (*Opposite*): Woman in mihrab at
al-Azhar Mosque, Cairo, Egypt.

PL. 5: Dar al-Islam, Abiquiu, New Mexico.

PL. 6: Ismaili Jamatkhana and Centre, Burnaby, Canada.

PL. 7: The Great Mosque and bridge, Cordoba, Spain.

PL. 8: Bab al-Futuh Cairo, Egypt.

PL. 9 (*Above*): Maydan-i Shah (Maydan-i Imam) complex, Isfahan, Iran.

PL. 10 (*Left*): Aerial view, the dome of the Friday Mosque and view of Old Delhi, India.

PL. 11 (*Over*): Djemaa el-Fna (main square) and Kutubiyya Mosque, Marrakesh, Morocco.

that Muslims should have a shared expression of unity. The dome and the minaret capture this need; they become the 'legitimate' expression of an Islam that seeks to be universal. This may also be interpreted as a sign of uncertainty about complex identities in a globalising world.

A fascinating example of the tensions inherent in the expression of identity is a mosque built in the early 1990s in Christiansburg, Virginia, USA, which eventually became a church. Soon after it was finished, the Muslim community felt uncomfortable with the overt expression of an Islamic presence in a non-Muslim rural area. The mosque was also situated in a place to which people had to drive many miles to reach. It was sold and transformed into a church. The minaret became a steeple while the dome was removed and replaced by a lantern, thus transforming the Islamic architectural symbolism and identity of the mosque to that of Christianity.

Women in Mosques

Another challenging issue in contemporary mosque design is the prayer space for women. In general, about 15 per cent of the prayer space is given over to them; they are frequently housed in a balcony above or to the sides, separated from the men, with their own access, ablutions and prayer areas.

Although there is a separation of prayer spaces, there are a number of functions and spaces that are shared by both men and women. These are generally social events, such as weddings, celebrations of the *Milad al-Nabi* (the Prophet's birthday), children's gatherings, religious education classes for youngsters, administrative functions, funerary rights, and so on.

I know of only one mosque that places women in a central location: it is in Kingston, Ontario in Canada. Perhaps this was due to the fact that women were on the mosque building committee – itself a rare occurrence – and that it serves a liberal university population. The matter of locating women in a mosque was much debated and some hundreds of letters were written to imams all over the world for their opinion. There was no consensus and the community had to make its own decision. They placed women in the centre rear of the prayer space, surrounded by the men on three sides.[7]

Women in many countries go to the mosque to pray and also for educational and social functions. In Europe and the United States, women and children increasingly frequent mosques. Since 2003 some women in the United States have been vocal in their demand for equal treatment in the mosque. One recalls incidents when women prayed in the main hall rather than in a different space. In March 2007 a noted female scholar, Amina Wadud, led mixed male-female Friday prayers in New York, which generated protests by community members but also received support. Also, for the first time in the USA, women have risen to positions of prominence in Muslim organisations; the President of the Islamic Society of North America is Ingrid Mattson. In 2007, the Council on American-Islamic Relations released a brochure for Muslim leaders and imams on how to create 'a sister-friendly environment'.

The use of the mosque complex, especially in the West and in non-Islamic societies, is changing. This may affect the design of mosques, which have traditionally been centres constructed for men.

Conclusion

If there is one idea that preoccupies architects and clients in the Muslim world today, it is the fresh expression in architecture of reference to the past – the presentation to contemporary society of heritage and memory, while using new technologies to construct the built environment. The search continues for a synthesis of architectural expression that reflects cultural and social identities different from global or western architecture (admittedly, terms that are themselves becoming fluid). A kind of eclecticism and sense of uncertainty marks the architecture of Muslim countries

---

[7] It should be noted that in Ismaili *jamatkhanas*, women share equal space with men in a side-by-side division in the prayer hall.

at the beginning of this century. Belief still remains in architecture as an environmental and social moulding force. The architecture of the mosque is not only about design and place making. Its importance lies not just in the forms or architectural language, but also in the collective meanings it transmits to us over time – from its humble beginnings as the house of the Prophet to the pluralistic manifestations we find the world over. It expresses who we are to ourselves and to the community at large. It may not be an overstatement to suggest that to understand the mosque is to understand the architecture of the region and place, and even more significantly, the aspirations and culture to which it belongs.

Further Reading

Ardalan, Nader and Laleh Bakhtiar. *Sense of Unity: Sufi Tradition in Persian Architecture.* Chicago, 1974.

Bianca, Stefano and Philip Jodidio, ed. *Cairo: Revitalising a Historic Metropolis.* Turin, Italy, 2004.

Blair, Sheila and Jonathan Bloom, 'Art and Architecture', in John L. Esposito, ed. *The Oxford History of Islam.* Oxford, 1999.

Bloom, Jonathan. *Arts of the City Victorious: Islamic Art and Architecture in Fatimid North Africa and Egypt.* London, 2007.

Frampton, Kenneth, ed. *Modernity and Community: Architecture in the Islamic World.* London, 2001.

Hattstein, Markus and Peter Delius, ed. *Islam: Art and Architecture.* Cologne, Germany, 2000.

Holod, Renata and Hasan-Uddin Khan. *The Mosque and the Modern World: Architects, Patrons and Designs since the 1950s.* London, 1997.

Frishman, Martin and Hasan-Uddin Khan, ed. *The Mosque: History, Architectural Development and Regional Diversity.* London, 1994.

9

The Umma in the City

Amira K. Bennison

The phrase 'Islamic city' is an evocative one which calls to mind a romantic image of soaring minarets, air redolent with the heavy fragrance of spice, the call to prayer wavering in the air and mysterious veiled figures. However, it is not an innocent term and actually developed out of European distaste for the cities they discovered across the Middle East and North Africa in the 19th and early 20th centuries. Orientalist scholars from Britain, France and the Netherlands were proud of the new cities created by the Industrial Revolution with their long straight streets, elegant boulevards, parks, shops and gas street lighting. Paris, redesigned by Baron Haussmann in the 1850s and 1860s, stood out as a splendid example of the 'modern'.

In contrast, cities like Aleppo, Cairo, Fes or Tehran seemed to be remnants of the medieval past: they were like the bad old towns of Europe, and Orientalists assumed that the reason that they had not changed was Islam. Narrow twisting streets, dead-end lanes, blank almost windowless house walls, and dirty, crowded markets were regarded by such scholars as the inevitable indications of the presence of Islam. This is not to say that Orientalist scholars of the imperial age did not do a great deal of excellent research on cities in the Middle East, North Africa or India. They did, but their preconceptions are not ours, and recent scholars have argued strongly against the notion of an Islamic city in the negative sense, while also seeking to identify what characteristics pre-modern cities in the vast *Dar al-Islam* may actually have shared and why.[1]

This kind of inquiry raises questions not just about religion but also about culture, society and the environment, and how these different things intertwine to create a particular city and way of urban living at a specific time. For a long time, archaeologists, for instance, have stressed that much of the Islamic world is hot and arid and that this encouraged forms of building which fostered a cool interior and circulated air efficiently. It also made people value cool shady gardens and access to water very highly. The environment also dictated the choice of building materials, stone, rammed earth or brick, depending on what was available. Social structures – whether people lived in nuclear families, clans or tribes – also affected how they constructed towns. None of this had much to do with Islam.

On the other hand, Islamic rituals and social conventions, derived from or attached to religion, also shaped the urban environment. The preference for gender segregation, although often more honoured in the breach than the practice, encouraged particular ways of arranging domestic and public spaces; the need to provide flowing water in baths and mosques for ritual ablutions ensured that Muslims paid a great deal of attention to water supply and sewage systems; and the distinctive role of the great mosque as a communal, political and religious space gave it an especially prominent role as a public arena in cities inhabited by Muslims. Moreover rulers of particular sects often wished to imprint their interpretation of Islam on the fabric of cities they founded or modified. In the latter case, rulers also took into consideration the cultural traditions of the existing population which introduced Catholic, Zoroastrian and Hindu strands to urban planning.

It is also crucial to recognise that Muslims themselves have historically believed in the notion of an 'Islamic city', albeit a

---

[1] See Abu Lughod, Janet. 'The Islamic city', *International Journal of Middle Eastern Studies*, 19 (1987), pp. 155-176, and André Raymond, 'Islamic city, Arab city: Orientalist myths and recent views', *British Journal of Middle Eastern Studies*, 21 (1994), pp. 3-18.

rather more positive one than that conjured up by Orientalists. Islam's birthplace was a town, Medina, known in Arabic simply as al-Madina al-Munawwara, the 'Illuminated City' or alternatively, Madinat al-Nabi, the 'City of the Prophet'. Its most holy site is the city of Mecca, which all Muslims aspire to visit on pilgrimage at least once in their lifetime. These two holy sites, the *haramayn*, are joined by another holy site or *haram*, Jerusalem, which connects Islam to the Abrahamic faiths which preceded it, Judaism and Christianity. For early Muslims, the city was thus the place of religion par excellence, and Islam has often been characterised as an urban faith in the sense that its ritual, political and legal requirements are most easily met in cities with their mosques and baths and their cohorts of scholars, jurists and judges.

Muhammad's establishment of his ideal community – umma – in Medina, provided Muslims with an ideal or blueprint which gave them a city of the imagination to be overlaid on numerous real cities across the Islamic world. Time and time again, the myths and legends surrounding the foundation of cities replay the transformation of Medina from a pagan to an Islamic site, the cultivation of a wilderness, and the banishment of the *jahiliyya*, the dark age before the coming of Islam, and the establishment of civilisation (*umran*) in its place. In these stories mosques, palaces and gardens triumphantly replace ruins in the desert, wild animals are driven back, and the power of nature, represented by rivers and springs, is tamed and channelled to serve mankind.

This affection for cities overlapped with Islam's historical sympathy for trade. Empires may be supported in a number of different ways: some rely primarily on agricultural surpluses, others on booty from war, and others on trade. Merchants quickly moved in after the early period of Muslim conquests in the Middle East and North Africa, making the Islamic world a thriving commercial zone which encouraged the flourishing of numerous towns and cities as entrepots, way stations on trade routes, and emporia. Many pre-Islamic cities received a fresh lease of life and several new cities sprung up, sometimes in very inhospitable locations, to service and profit from the trade carried by caravan and sail.

The money generated by trade and taxation enabled Muslims to embellish and beautify their cities with luxurious palaces and mansions, splendid markets and rich mosques. By means of pious endowments (*waqf*) – revenue which people donated in perpetuity for charitable purposes – commercial profits supported an admirable range of public services including education, healthcare and support for the poor. Although pious endowments were private initiatives and no one had to make them, the rich and powerful generally did because such bequests enhanced their reputations in this world and, so they hoped, improved their standing with God. The splendour of Mamluk Cairo, for instance, derived in part from the bad consciences of the Mamluks, military commanders who often drank and had the blood of many on their hands, and sought to expiate at least some of their sins by giving money for the establishment of theological colleges (*madrassas*) with adjacent mausolea where they themselves could be buried and the Quran recited over their biers.

The fine buildings, conspicuous consumption, luxurious living and debauchery which could characterise urban life meant that not all Muslims idealised cities as centres of religion. Some depicted them instead as corrupt in contrast to the clean, simple life of the desert and mystics, in particular, often preferred to live in the less distracting countryside. The celebrated 14th-century North African historian, Ibn Khaldun, certainly viewed city life with ambivalence; but at the same time Muslims remained proud of their cities and in travelogues commented on their religious monuments, markets, water fountains, baths and gardens. They did not lose this sense of achievement until the 19th century when economic difficulties and the rise of new ways of doing things in western Europe began to alter life in the *Dar al-Islam* in myriad ways.

These introductory comments are designed to show that there was certainly a particular religious and cultural ethos behind the establishment of cities in the Muslim world, but that Islam was not the only factor at work in their foundation or development; commerce, society and the environment all played their part. Moreover, the Orientalist critique of such cities rather unfairly analysed them at a time when many were in decline and compared them with modern

European cities, creating a negative and stereotypical image of an Islamic city which conflicts with how Muslim and non-Muslim sources viewed them at an earlier time. We shall now turn to look at a series of such cities across the Islamic world from Spain to India in the different eras when they flourished to present a more varied and positive picture of cities and city life in Islamic civilisation. Some choices are obvious, others less so, and inevitably many great cities have had to be omitted. Yet this selection may evoke the dimensions of city life in the *Dar al-Islam* from the era after its inception in the seventh century up until the early modern period shortly before European colonialism changed the world forever.

We shall begin with the city of Cordoba which the Umayyads took as their capital from the mid-eighth century until their demise in 1031. We shall then move southwards across the Straits of Gibraltar to Marrakesh, a city founded in the 1070s which flourished under the Berber Almoravid and Almohad dynasties in the 11th and 12th centuries, and again under the Sadi sultans in the 16th century. No exploration of Islam's cities would be complete without Cairo, the 'City Victorious', known even today as *Umm al-Dunya*, 'Mother of the World', founded by Muslims shortly after the conquest of Byzantine Egypt in the 640s and rebuilt, extended and embellished ever since. From Cairo we shall move east to Isfahan, an ancient city of pre-Islamic provenance which reached its peak under the Safavids in the 16th and 17th centuries when Jean Chardin considered it equal if not superior to London and Paris of his day. We shall end with the cities of Mughal India, especially Shahjahanabad, better known today as Delhi, from which the British Raj later drew the inspiration for its own Indian imperial architecture.

Cordoba, the capital of al-Andalus

Muslim armies of Berbers and Arabs conquered the kingdoms of Spain, then ruled by the German Visigoths, in a series of campaigns between 711 and 714. The Muslims called their new acquisition al-Andalus, a word whose origin is not entirely clear. These were the days of the Umayyad caliphate of Damascus in far-off Syria, and although al-Andalus was thus an Umayyad province, its governors were generally appointed by the governor of Ifriqiya, modern-day Tunisia. These governors resided in Seville or Cordoba but generally avoided the previous capital of the Visigoths, the turbulent city of Toledo. When Abd al-Rahman I (r. 756-788), the first member of the Umayyad family to rule al-Andalus, fled to avoid death at the hands of the victorious Abbasids who had over-thrown the Umayyads in the east in 750, he chose Cordoba as the seat of his emirate. It remained the Umayyad capital for almost three centuries and became the foremost city in the Islamic west, renowned for its great mosque, its baths, its libraries, and its verdant suburban parks and country estates. Its fame spread as far as the court of the Carolingians where the nun Hroswitha wrote a glowing account of the remarkable Muslim city of which she had heard via the diplomatic network.[2]

What was medieval Cordoba like? When the Muslims arrived it was a small Catholic city whose Roman glory, exemplified by a crumbling bridge over the Guadalquivir river, was fast fading. Just north of the river, the Visigoths had built a palace alongside the Church of St. Vincent and the rest of the city sprawled behind. The Muslim newcomers took over the Visigoth palace and, according to later chroniclers, divided the church into sections for Muslims and for Christians. In 784, however, Abd al-Rahman I demolished the palace and created a new Muslim one; a year later he purchased the church and replaced it with a monumental great mosque, having given permission for the Christians to rebuild elsewhere. Archaeology has shown that there was indeed a Visigoth church where the great mosque of Cordoba later stood, yet the details of the story are very similar to that of the Muslim general al-Walid's appropriation of the Basilica of St. John in Damascus and his replacement of it with a great mosque. Perhaps there was a conscious desire on the part of the Umayyads of Cordoba to evoke their Syrian past in a new land. After all, Abd al-Rahman I had built a country villa called Rusafa after the estate of the same

---

[2] Maria Rosa Menocal offers a colourful account in *The Ornament of the World* (Boston, 2002).

name in Syria where he grew up, and Rusafa became his main residence as well as a nursery for exotic plants from Syria, including date and pomegranate trees, which spread across al-Andalus.

In addition to being distinctively Umayyad and thus appealing to the small Muslim elite, most of whom were Arabs from Syria, Abd al-Rahman's redevelopment of Cordoba also created continuity with the Visigothic past and was thus comprehensible to the Catholic mass of the population. His palace, his mosque and his country estate were all built on Romano-Visigothic foundations or in keeping with Romano-Visigothic precedents. For the majority of the city's inhabitants, life thus went on much as before the conquest with the proviso that advancement in government service now required a mastery of Arabic rather than Latin. The Jewish minority were able to build synagogues and participate fully in Cordoban society like their Christian counterparts.

During the century after Abd al-Rahman's death in 787 Cordoba gradually changed from a majority Christian to a majority Muslim city, and its new role as capital of al-Andalus led to its expansion far beyond the limits of the pre-Islamic city. Its Roman bridge was renovated to become one of the wonders of al-Andalus, numerous suburbs grew up around the original walled city, and its great mosque was expanded several times to cope with the ever-growing number of worshippers pouring into it for the Friday prayer. The Umayyad rulers and members of the elite constructed elegant mansions in town and a series of country estates which enwrapped the city for miles around. While chance references show that scholars often lived close to each other in the city centre, urban quarters were socially mixed and smaller houses would often have clustered around the mansions of the wealthy.

The active building of churches and synagogues created a pluralistic environment in which Islam, Judaism and Christianity co-existed in a largely harmonious way: historians term this interaction *convivencia* or 'living together'. The tensions which existed related mostly to the inexorable conversion of Christians to Islam, a development lamented by some churchmen and also by Muslims who saw their faith as that of the elite, not the masses. Such tensions exploded in the famous Martyr Movement during which 48

Christian men and women courted death by publicly blaspheming against Muhammad or rejecting Islam in the 850s. Efforts by the authorities, Muslim and Christian, to deter such behaviour had mixed success. The amir, Muhammad (r. 852-886), lost his patience and tore down the churches of the city and replaced them with mosques.

The high point of Muslim Cordoba came in the 10th century when Abd al-Rahman III (r. 912-961) declared himself not only amir but *amir al-muminin* (Commander of the Faithful), and constructed a new palatine city outside Cordoba which reflected his aspiration to be caliph of the entire Islamic world and champion of Sunnism. This city, Madinat al-Zahra, was constructed at the foot of a small sierra near Cordoba, beyond the circle of country estates which enwrapped the town. It was a grand creation in the tradition of Baghdad, Samarra and al-Qatai (one of Cairo's many incarnations), but its relationship with Cordoba was unique. Abd al-Rahman withdrew in regal splendour but made sure that his subjects were also part of the spectacle. His visitors usually stayed in one of the other estates outside Cordoba and in order to visit the caliph they had to pass through Cordoba to pay their respects at the gate of the old palace, and possibly the great mosque opposite, before heading down a long boulevard to Madinat al-Zahra, which the geographer Ibn Hawqal described as lined with innumerable shops and houses with belvederes overlooking the street.

At a distance of so many centuries, the ordinary life of the inhabitants of Cordoba is hard to conjure up, but some sense of daily life can be gleaned from the Arabic sources. People either lived in the walled city or in one of the surrounding suburbs in houses which often had internal gardens and sometimes running water. They worked in all manner of trades. Cordoban leather was famous throughout Europe; it was used for binding the books also produced and copied in a city renowned for its libraries, some of which were administered by female librarians. There was a saying that if a musician died in Cordoba, his instruments would be sent to Seville for sale, while if a scholar died in Seville, his books would be sent to Cordoba. Textiles were also produced, as well as a full range of utensils and tools in wood, metal and glass.

The social life of the city revolved around the home and religious buildings. At one end of the scale, the rich gathered in the Umayyad palace itself or in the mansions of the wealthy to enjoy poetry, debates on religious and scientific topics, and entertainment provided by slave musicians and singers of both sexes. Similar gatherings occurred on rural estates which also enabled families to gather away from prying eyes. Religious scholars, judges and intellectuals also gathered in each other's homes and the great mosque to exchange views and learn. At the other end of the social scale, petty traders and craftsmen probably had little leisure time. Most would, however, break to attend the great mosque, church or synagogue and participate in the celebration of rites of passage within their community and in the great festivals of their respective religious calendars. In multicultural Cordoba, Muslims, Jews and Christians also joined in each other's festivals. The poor meanwhile loitered around the mosque hoping for alms in the company of a colourful assortment of quack doctors, story tellers, astrologers and fortune tellers.

In the first decades of the 11th century, the Umayyad state collapsed, Madinat al-Zahra was sacked and fighting frequently took place in the streets of Cordoba. The river slowly silted up and Cordoba became a provincial town, its poets, men of letters and swaggering military commanders scattered throughout al-Andalus to populate the courts of the petty kings of the Taifa period. Its role as capital of al-Andalus was inherited first by Seville and then Granada, but it remained a potent memory for Andalusis and for Muslims more generally. As late as the 17th century, a Moroccan scholar, al-Maqqari, whose family originally came from al-Andalus, wrote a multi-volume eulogy to the peninsula in which Cordoba, its great mosque, its palaces, libraries and parks lived on – as did its scholars, intellectuals and great men.

Marrakesh, Gateway to the South

Unlike Cordoba, Marrakesh was a purely Muslim city. According to legend, the Sanhaja Berbers of the Almoravid movement crossed the High Atlas mountains from their desert home in the mid-11th century. At first they settled in the Masmuda Berber town of Aghmat Warika on the northern slopes of the High Atlas mountains, a thriving market town with a large Jewish population. However, the Sanhaja needed more space to graze their horses and livestock, and the Masmuda of Aghmat disliked having desert nomads in their city. After repeated complaints about the crowding and disruption to the Almoravid leader, Abu Bakr, the Masmuda elders offered the Almoravids a parcel of land about eight miles from Aghmat, inhabited by nothing but gazelles and ostriches according to the sources, to establish a new settlement for their Saharan kinsmen.

Marrakesh was therefore a mixture of garrison town and palatine city at the outset. The sources describe it as a rather dispersed settlement of large clan compounds or mansions with high rammed earth walls inhabited by the Almoravid tribal leaders and their followers, with open spaces between them where date palms and colocynth grew. The only stone building was the residence of the Almoravid amir constructed alongside the great mosque, the fortress-like Qasr al-Hajar. Marrakesh was probably rather like Kufa, Basra or Fustat, some of the garrison towns built by the Arabs during the conquests era with their simple dwellings arranged in tribal units, their wide open streets and gathering spaces for prayer and military mobilisations.

The city became much grander under the second Almoravid ruler, Ali b. Yusuf (r. 1106-1143), who not only commissioned more imposing public buildings, but also opened up the city to non-Sanhaja migrants, including Jewish traders, who helped turn Marrakesh into an important southern emporium for the Saharan trade north, as well as the political seat of the Almoravid amirs. Over the next century and a half, Marrakesh thrived as imperial capital, not only of Morocco but of the entire Islamic west. In the 1090s, a Sevillan visitor to Baghdad proudly informed the Abbasid caliph, al-Mustazhir (r. 1094-1118), that the Almoravids ruled 'from the land of the Franks to Ghana', an area in which there were 2500 great mosques. The Almohads, who overthrew them in the 1140s, ruled an even vaster domain which stretched from al-Andalus to Tunisia.

While Almoravid Marrakesh was shaped by the clan structure of the Sanhaja and their desire to segregate themselves as a ruling elite, Almohad Marrakesh was shaped by the ideology of the Almohad movement. Its founder was Muhammad b. Tumart, a man who believed he was the *mahdi* and that his destiny was to replay the life of Muhammad and found a reformed Muslim community, that of the Muwahhidun, the true monotheists, from which we get the name Almohads. Ibn Tumart died in 1130 before his dream was realised, but his successor and caliph, Abd al-Mumin, had the military ability and political acumen to build an empire and, in the process, reshape Marrakesh which the Almohads captured in 1147 and subsequently made their capital.

Almohad Marrakesh consisted of the Almoravid city and a new royal annex at its southern end, sometimes described as a new town and sometimes as a citadel or fortress (*qasaba*). Medieval descriptions of Marrakesh at this time are hard to decipher because they were mostly written by geographers whose information was second-hand and who thus did not have intimate knowledge of how the elements actually fitted together. Most agree that the Almohad citadel had high walls and several gateways, the most important of which was Bab al-Sada (the Lords' Gate) which led through the Almohads' royal cemetery into a wide plaza known as the *rahba*. At one end, near a gate into the areas of the *qasaba* reserved for the caliph and his family, stood a domed pavilion where he received visitors, plaintiffs, ambassadors and couriers, and from where he was able to watch Almohad military parades and review his troops. The *rahba* was an important meeting place where the people of Marrakesh and the Almohads came together. There were also areas where the different Almohad corps of scholars and troops lived and worked. The Sevillan scholar, Ibn Sahib al-Salah, who joined the Almohads and went to Marrakesh around 1165, describes his own experience of meeting fellow Andalusi shaykhs each day at the gate of the palace, and also of attending scholarly gatherings chaired by the chief Almohad scholar, the *shaykh al-talaba*, at which the rudiments of Almohad Islam were discussed and conveyed to students.

The Almohads also endowed the city with its still-famous Kutubiyya mosque with its soaring minaret, the sister of the Almohad tower minarets of Rabat and Seville which set the style for Maghribi minarets well into the 20th century. Unlike the Umayyads and Almoravids who did not put much stress on the minaret as a symbol of Islam, the Almohads considered their tall square tower minarets veritable beacons of the true faith. They were not just the place from which the call to prayer echoed out but testaments to the Almohad presence in a city. Even today the Kutubiyya dominates the skyline of Marrakesh and can be seen for miles across the southern Moroccan plains, while the Tour Hassan, the minaret of the Almohad great mosque in Rabat, looms over the mouth of the Bou Regreg river from which Almohad fleets once set sail for Spain.

In contrast to many earlier cities in the Islamic west, Marrakesh and other Almohad cities were endowed with impressive circuits of walls and ramparts, punctuated by massive gateways, which spoke to the militancy of the Almohad movement and the Almohads' self-appointed role: to wage jihad against the enemies of their form of Islam, from recalcitrant Berbers to the Castilians in Iberia and the Normans in Tunisia. The style of these walls and gates drew on the architectural heritage of the Berbers and of Islamic Spain, and defined North African urbanism for centuries to come. Most later Moroccan capital cities, and indeed Marrakesh in its later incarnations, exhibited a similar pattern – a civilian city positioned adjacent to a royal quarter within a protective outer wall – right up until the imposition of the French and Spanish protectorates over Morocco in 1912. The Almohads also had a penchant for gardens and created suburban estates outside Marrakesh, of which the best known is the Menara garden which is a popular public park today. In Almohad times this park belonged to the ruler, and its vast central pool is said to have been used to train young Almohads to swim and sail, skills useful given the regular passage of Almohad ships from Rabat and Ceuta to al-Andalus. The Almohads built a similar estate with a large pool outside Seville.

Almohad cities were populated by an eclectic mix of people. The ruling elite was drawn from all the Berber ethnic groups in

North Africa, Arab tribes from Tunisia, Andalusis and African slaves. Although to some extent segregated in the royal annex, the occasional and seasonal nature of medieval military campaigns meant that Almohad soldiers were also civilians much of the time and blended in with local populations, from the Masmuda Berbers of Aghmat to the urbane self-consciously Arab Andalusis of Seville. Many local people joined the movement as scholars, scribes or judges while others continued to pursue their livelihood as before.

The situation of religious minorities under the Almohads was, however, different to that pertaining under the Umayyads of Cordoba. The third Almohad caliph, Abu Yusuf Yaqub (r. 1184-1199), famously announced that Almohadism recognised no *dhimma* or covenant with Jews and Christians. This reflected the movement's aspiration of incorporating all the Abrahamic monotheists into a single community; but its practical effect was to encourage Christian migration north into Castilian territory, and Jewish migration both to Castile and Islamic lands in the east where protection of religious minorities remained the norm. Before long, however, the Almohads realised that they did not have the resources to convert the Muslim, Christian and Jewish inhabitants of their empire, and traditional patterns of interaction reasserted themselves.

With the collapse of the Almohad empire in the 1230s and 1240s, Marrakesh lost its pivotal role, and like Cordoba before it, faded into provincial obscurity. It received a new lease of life in the 16th century under the Sadi sultans, Arab tribal leaders from the southern Dara valley, who succeeded in uniting southern Morocco before capturing Marrakesh in 1525 and turning it into their capital. Although sacked in the late 17th century, the fragments of their palace, the Badi, testify to its splendour. A huge rectangular central courtyard was graced with four sunken gardens overlooked by pavilions flanked by pools at either end. Here the Sadi sultans inaugurated the first state celebrations of the Prophet's birthday in Morocco, which included feasting and poetic recitations at which the noble lineage of the Prophet and his Sadi descendants was eulogised and their achievements praised.

222

A Companion to the Muslim World

Adjacent to the palace stood a walled funerary garden, known today as the Sadi tombs, where the sultans and their relatives were buried alongside the saint, al-Jazuli, who had supported the Sadi movement in its infancy. The Sadi sultans hoped that this opulently decorated shrine, built using the proceeds of sugar production, would become a cult centre to rival the burgeoning Idrisi shrines in Fes and Mawlay Idris, and encourage their subjects to see them not only as monarchs but as *shurafa* (descendants of the Prophet), which entitled them to veneration and respect. They also constructed the famous Yusufiyya Madrassa, a huge theological college designed to give Marrakesh the same higher educational facilities as Fes, which had developed a very strong religious educational infrastructure by this time. With the passing of the dynasty in the early 17th century, Marrakesh settled into a more limited role as the foremost city of southern Morocco and one of a circuit of cities used by the subsequent Alawi dynasty as royal residences. Still, the urban layout of city, royal annex and suburban parks, situated within miles of palm groves established by the Almoravids and Almohads remains to this day.

Cairo, Mother of the World

Cairo is one of the most enduring and successful of the cities founded by the Muslims in the period of conquest, and contemporary Cairo actually consists of several settlements built on the banks of the Nile that have merged into one. The first of these was Fustat, founded in 642 as a garrison town by Amr b. al-As, the conqueror of Egypt, alongside a Byzantine military township known as Babylon, not to be confused with ancient Babylon in Iraq. Fustat was an expansive unwalled settlement in which Arab tribes were allocated plots around a central zone where the great mosque and governor's residence stood, and it developed along much the same lines as Kufa and Basra. Soon, its population of Arab tribesmen lost interest in participating in military campaigns and began to adopt civilian professions. They were joined by a thriving Coptic Christian community and many Jews who together made Fustat into one of the most successful commercial centres in the early Islamic world.

During the Umayyad and Abbasid caliphates, Fustat remained the capital of the rich and populous province of Egypt and as such the seat of its governors, some of whom greatly enhanced the city as an indication of their power and autonomy. The most important of these governors were the Turkish Tulunids who ruled Egypt on behalf of the Abbasids. Ahmad b. Tulun left Samarra for Egypt in 868 when his stepfather became governor and gradually gained effective control of the province. He was succeeded by his son, Khumarawayh (r. 884-896), who adopted a similar posture. In keeping with his power, Ahmad b. Tulun constructed a new city north of Fustat to house the government, the administration and his military forces.

This new settlement was called al-Qatai, a rather inelegant name meaning fiefs. It was nonetheless a grand ensemble modelled on the Abbasid royal city of Samarra in Iraq, with a palace and a large garden watered by ingenious channels and fountains in which rare plants and trees flourished. If the Egyptian historian al-Maqrizi is to be believed, Khumarawayh's taste for the flamboyant stretched to a mercury pool on which his mattress was suspended, a reception hall full of life-size wooden, gilded statutes of himself and his slave-girls and a tame lion who patrolled his bedroom while he slept! Although the palace is long gone, destroyed by the Abbasids as a warning to over-mighty governors, the great mosque of Ibn Tulun which stood across the street from it remains one of the landmarks of Cairo.

This was only the beginning, however. Between the late 10th and the early 16th centuries, Cairo became the most important city in the Middle East and North Africa, inheriting Baghdad's role before finally ceding it to Ottoman Istanbul. This shift occurred as a result of the emergence of a new Ismaili Shii caliphate in North Africa, that of the Fatimids. From their starting point in modern-day Tunisia, the Fatimids sent missionaries and armies west and east and in 969, their general, Jawhar, captured Fustat and built a Fatimid military camp to the north of Tulunid al-Qatai. Called al-Qahira ('the Victorious'), it became their capital city and the location of one of the best-known mosques in the world, al-Azhar.

The Fatimids introduced a new architectural style to Cairo which, among other things, used inscriptions much more extensively than earlier Islamic dynasties which had relied more on motifs to define their identity. This may indicate that literacy had improved making the general population more able to appreciate and understand the Ismaili Shii messages the Fatimids wished to convey. In any case, it distinguished the Fatimids from other regimes and heralded the rise of Arabic calligraphy to centre stage in the decoration of religious buildings.[3]

In essence al-Qahira was rather like Abbasid Samarra in Iraq or Madinat al-Zahra outside Cordoba. It contained palaces, administrative offices and living space for soldiers and their families, while Fustat remained the bustling commercial and manufacturing centre where space was at such a premium that high-rise apartment blocks became common. However, al-Qahira, or Cairo as it came to be called in English, quickly became much more than a governmental enclave. Traders moved in from Fustat and baths, shops and markets began to vie with the royal palaces and parade grounds for space. A serious fire in Fustat in 1168-1169, lit by the Fatimids to deter a Crusader army from the Latin kingdom of Jerusalem, confirmed the shift of the city's economic activity to al-Qahira.

The Ayyubids, the lineage of Saladin, who replaced the Fatimids in the 1170s tried to unite Fustat and al-Qahira within a single wall system whose centrepiece was the citadel on the edge of the Muqattam hills to the east. In a manner similar to contemporary Almohad urbanism further west, Ayyubid developments reflected their commitment to jihad in its military form against the Crusaders. The citadel or Qala is still one of Cairo's most prominent and visited monuments, and the long thoroughfare leading out to it became an important axis for urban development under the dynasty which succeeded the Ayyubids in 1260. The Mamluks remained in power until ousted by the Ottomans in 1516-1517.

---

[3] See Irene Bierman, *Writing Signs: The Fatimid Public Text* (Berkeley, CA, 1998).

The Mamluks were Turkish slaves recruited from Central Asia by the Ayyubids who received a military training, converted to Islam, and were manumitted to form a ruling warrior class from whose number a sultan emerged, usually by fighting or killing his rivals for power and demonstrating the political skills necessary to survive. These archetypal men of the sword legitimised their rule by investing heavily in religion and the city itself. Numerous Mamluk commanders and sultans paid for the construction of mosques, theological colleges, Sufi retreats, hospitals and commercial facilities, and provided revenue endowments in perpetuity to pay for the running of these institutions and the salaries of their staff, from humble cleaners to Quran reciters and eminent theologians. In this way, the Mamluks provided employment for architects, builders, craftsmen and innumerable men of religion, thereby reconciling the population to their rule. They also beautified Cairo and made it a very pleasant place to live. The courtyards of Mamluk theological colleges and mausolea offered cool, restful places to which people could retreat. Many also incorporated schools for children to learn the Quran, and pools and water fountains to cool the hot, dry summer air and slake the thirst of visitors.

Furthermore, by the Mamluk era, the Nile's course had shifted west to create a greenbelt between the river and Fustat and al-Qahira which the Mamluk sultans and amirs were quick to exploit. Mamluk amirs built residences with fine gardens along the river and the nearby lakes, known as Birkat al-Fil and Birkat al-Azbakiyya. They also built on Rawda island where an important Mamluk barracks and the Nilometer, which measured the level of the annual Nile flood, were located. As a result of this new development, the river became a major focus for leisure pursuits. Some sultans had a royal barge, and amirs with riverside residences also had luxury barges where they held feasts and other entertainments such as firework displays. The population joined in the fun by taking to the river on smaller hired boats and by pitching tents on the river banks where numerous taverns could also be found.

The political and ceremonial heart of Mamluk Cairo was the Ayyubid citadel which they greatly embellished, and the Rumayla square below it where a great walled hippodrome stood. Here, the Mamluk sultan presided over races, parades and even royal weddings with great pomp and ceremony. The hippodrome complex also boasted pavilions and gardens and was another desirable area for amirs to build their own mansions and gardens, creating a pleasant suburb which blended into the Northern Cemetery beyond.

This vast cemetery to the northeast of the city and the Qarafa to the southeast were one of Cairo's most distinctive features. They had developed a unique character by the 12th century when the Andalusi pilgrim, Ibn Jubayr, passed through Cairo and commented on the large number of facilities within them. In the Qarafa, for instance, the large domed tomb of the famous jurist, al-Shafii (767-820), was part of a larger ensemble of buildings, including a bath and school. In the Northern Cemetery, developed by the Mamluks in the 14th and 15th centuries, a similar pattern appeared. The foundation of the Mamluk sultan, Faraj b. Barquq (r. 1399-1412), for example, was a substantial *khanqah*, the Sufi equivalent of a residential theological college, which contained tomb chambers for Faraj b. Barquq and his family, and a small school for children, alongside rooms for mystics. Thus, Cairo's so-called 'cities of the dead' were actually lively places bustling with activity, a role they retain today as the poor crowd into them seeking space to live alongside the dead of centuries past. In the words of a couplet quoted by al-Maqrizi, 'While the hermits wander around the tombs and pray/ The revellers let continuous music play'.[4]

Some of the wealth which the Mamluks poured into Cairo, and other cities in Egypt and Syria, came from taxing the land – the rich Nile valley and its delta – which produced enough grain to support not only Egypt but also the holy cities of Mecca and Medina. It also came from the spice trade which was routed from the Indies up the Red Sea to Egyptian ports before being carried to Cairo by caravan or canal, from whence the spices were purchased by local consumers and the Venetians who passed them on to Latin Christendom. Many Mamluks were involved in this trade

---

[4] Doris Behrens-Abouseif, *Cairo of the Mamluks* (London, 2007), p. 63.

and made huge profits on the conveyance of pepper and other spices from the Indian Ocean to the Mediterranean. Without these resources, Cairo would not have flourished as it did. With the Ottoman conquest of Syria and Egypt in 1516-1517, Cairo was relegated to the status of provincial capital and Istanbul became the foremost city in the region. However, the Ottomans also contributed much to the city: many mosques, water fountains and commercial buildings were built and the citadel continued to be the seat of government. The great mosque in the citadel complex which dominates the Cairene skyline today was added in the 19th century by Muhammad Ali Pasha, an Ottoman governor of Egypt who aspired to the same degree of independence as his Tulunid predecessors. In the case of Muhammad Ali and his descendants, their autonomy found material expression in the re-modelling of Cairo according to modern European tastes. New palaces such as the Abidin evoked Versailles rather than Baghdad or Istanbul, and Cairo's modern sector was designed by Baron Haussman, who had already worked his magic in Paris, while the Fatimid and Mamluk cities, models of urban planning in their own day, became relegated to the status of the Orientalists' archetypal 'Islamic city'.

Isfahan

Further east, the early modern period witnessed another remarkable urban experiment, the remodelling of the ancient, pre-Islamic city of Isfahan in Iran which stands out as a synthesis of planning ideals that resonated not only for Muslims but also for Europeans of the day. Along with the Mughal cities in India and Ottoman Istanbul, 17th-century Isfahan speaks of the openness of Muslims to what we might call global trends, and shows how the Orientalist idea of inwardly-focussed Islamic cities without grand vistas, parks or avenues did not apply.

In Sassanian times, Isfahan consisted of two settlements, Shahristan and Yahudiyya, the latter of which was said to have originated as a Jewish town founded by Nebuchadnezzar. Certainly, it had an ancient Jewish population that continued to flourish after the Islamic conquest of Iran in the 640s, alongside Zoroastrians, Nestorian Christians and, of course, Muslims. Medieval Isfahan was an important city and a centre of the textile trade: the 10th-century geographer, al-Muqaddasi, described in glowing terms its covered markets where silks, other textiles, and regional specialities such as almonds were bought and sold. The Buyids, a Shii dynasty from the Caspian region who ruled Iraq and Iran from the mid-10th to mid-11th centuries, added walls and a fortress; in the succeeding century the Saljuq Turks poured money into the great mosque, a new governmental complex, and a grand theological college. Isfahan also had a hospital similar to those in Shiraz, Baghdad and other cities which offered free care and remedies to those who could not afford the services of a doctor at home.

The death of the Saljuq sultan, Malikshah, in 1095 heralded a period of insecurity and unrest that undermined the prosperity of Isfahan. Sectarian strife between Sunni and Shii Muslims in the city, and various sub-divisions of each, further destabilised the situation. The city received another blow with the Mongol conquests and the shifting of the centre of regional power away from southern Iran to Azerbaijan. While Ibn Battuta characterised Isfahan of the 1320s as partially ruined, he also commented on its thriving craft production, suggesting that it was on the path to recovery. Yet further blows were to come. Timur arrived outside the city in 1387 and massacred a large proportion of the population when they attacked his tax gatherers and troops, after which Isfahan was probably half the size it had been in its Saljuq heyday.

Isfahan gained a new lease of life when the Safavid Shah Abbas (r. 1588-1629) decided to transfer the capital and court from Qazvin further north where his predecessor, Shah Tahmasp (r. 1524-1576), had already begun developing Safavid urbanism. This included the construction of a large public square or *maydan*, a palace area consisting of a large entry building, gardens and kiosks, and a garden suburb where the chief officers of state built mansions set in pleasant gardens of Persian quadripartite or *chahar bagh* design. Over a period of a few decades on the cusp between the 16th and 17th centuries, Shah Abbas followed a similar plan in

Isfahan but took it much further, transforming Isfahan from a medieval eastern Islamic city into a model of contemporary urbanism echoed a few decades later in Fathpur Sikri and Shahjahanabad in Mughal India.

Shah Abbas's Isfahan centred on a huge rectangular plaza, the Maydan-i Shah, flanked on all sides by elegant two-story arcades of shops and ateliers with first floor balconies in front of which a line of trees provided shade. Several important public buildings also graced the *maydan*: the Qaysariyya or state market on its north side where it abutted the older part of Isfahan; the Safavid royal palace with its great portal, the Ali Qapu, on the west side; the Safavid great mosque, the Masjid-i Shah, on the south side; and the small Shaykh Lutfallah mosque, dedicated to one of the regime's most prominent Twelver Shii scholars, on the east side. The *maydan* acted as a new centre of gravity for Isfahan, and as an important meeting place for the Safavids and their subjects, rather like the Almohad *rahba* in 12th-century Marrakesh. During the day small traders laid out their wares on mats in the *maydan* while at night jugglers, puppeteers and prostitutes could be found there. It was also used for polo matches and mock battles between inhabitants of the different quarters of the city, and for the performance of some of the first passion plays recounting the martyrdom of Imam Husayn.

The great portal of the palace, the Ali Qapu, was a substantial building of many rooms, including a roofed colonnaded first-floor verandah (*talar*) from which the shah and his guests could view the *maydan* and be viewed by his subjects. The palace area behind it reversed earlier concepts of gardens within a palace by placing kiosks or pavilions at the centre of self-contained rectangular gardens divided into four parts by water channels. Engelbert Kaempfer's 1684-1685 plans of this part of Isfahan clearly show its geometry and strong emphasis on gardens and outdoor space which continued behind the palace along the famous Chahar Bagh Avenue that ran down to the Zayanda river. This avenue was a broad tree-lined promenade with the gardens and mansions of the Safavid elite on either side. While one naturally needed an invitation to enter these homes, the Chahar Bagh Avenue was public and allowed men to stroll down from the city to the river. One day a week, the Chahar Bagh was closed to men to allow the women of the Safavid house to take the air along it. The river was spanned by the Allahvardi Khan bridge, a massive structure which also acted as a barrage facilitating the ingress and egress of water from Isfahan and the irrigation of nearby farmland. Under the bridge were many arches designed for people to sit, relax and take tea in their cool embrasures.

Beyond the walls of Isfahan itself, members of the Safavid family and aristocrats of Turkish, Persian and Georgian extraction built additional mansions within extensive gardens and tomb complexes with mosques, accommodation wings, kitchens and other facilities. Such areas also had markets, caravanserais and theological colleges that made them true suburbs. Within Isfahan itself, the older part of the city was naturally more densely populated and included many lower-class areas where less salubrious forms of entertainment could be found, but even here members of the Safavid elite built mansions and *madrassas*, which avoided a total divide between the old and new parts of the city, or between rich and poor. An interesting feature of poorer housing was its lack of kitchens: most poor Isfahanis purchased food from public kitchens because fuel was very expensive.

The scale of Safavid architecture was grand but still human, and it incorporated many elements which resonated not only with Muslims but also with European visitors, whose number was increasing at this time. Engravings and other illustrations of Safavid buildings show them to be almost neo-classical in their proportions while also thoroughly Islamic, placed at regular intervals and interspersed with trees and gardens. Jean Chardin, a French traveller, commented that Isfahan's beauty lay in 'the great number of magnificent palaces, the agreeable and pleasant houses, the spacious caravanserais, the really fine bazaars, the water channels and the streets of which the sides were covered with tall plane trees'.[5]

---

[5] R. Ferrier, *A Journey to Persia: Jean Chardin's Portrait of a Seventeenth-Century Empire* (London, 1996), p. 44.

Like most major cities in the *Dar al-Islam*, Isfahan's population was culturally and religiously mixed. Although the Jewish, Zoroastrian and Nestorian Christian communities of the early Islamic era had diminished in size, Shah Abbas added to the city's diversity by founding an entirely new Armenian Christian quarter called New Julfa after the hometown of the Armenians, whom he forced to relocate to Isfahan in order to make it the centre of the Iranian silk trade. The greatest change to the religious complexion of the city, however, was the homogenisation of the Muslim population which became steadily more Twelver Shii after centuries in which Sunnis of various persuasions, Ismailis and Twelver Shiis had lived and squabbled side by side. Shah Abbas's city was not simply a grand urban experiment but also a stage on which to promote Twelver Shii beliefs and rituals by means of celebrations and commemorations in the new *maydan*, teaching in the Masjid-i Shah, the Shaykh Lutfallah Mosque and other Safavid religious foundations, and the construction of Shii shrines. Sunni Muslims felt increasingly uncomfortable and either adopted Twelver Shiism or left Safavid Iran, while Shii scholars from the Arab lands, especially Jabal Amil in Lebanon, hastened to serve the new regime.

Isfahan was thus central to the transformation of Iran into a Twelver Shii country. Later Safavid rulers continued to build in the city, but when the dynasty fell to the depredations of the Afghans and the 'protection' of the Turkoman warlord, Nadir Shah Afshar (r. 1736-1747), Isfahan entered another phase of disruption. When a degree of stability returned with the Qajars in the late 18th century, Tehran not Isfahan became their capital, and tentative Qajar urban modernisation focussed on the former.

Shahjahanabad, Mughal Delhi

From early on, Muslim rulers in India took Delhi, located on the Jamuna river, as their seat and, as with Cairo, several settlements built at different times are subsumed within today's metropolis. When Muslim Turkic warriors entered Hindustan in the 12th century, they occupied the riverside Rajput town of Qila Ray

Pithaura, which consisted of a citadel beside the river surrounded on three sides by the town that was enclosed by an outer wall. The first great mosque of the settlement was the Quwwat al-Islam Mosque, which reused materials from Jain and Hindu temples and adopted motifs of Hindu origin, giving early Islamic architecture in India its syncretic style. In the 13th century, Ghiyath al-din Tughluq constructed a new city called Tughluqabad about five miles to the east, complemented by an artificial lake with a central island on which his tomb was constructed in fine red sandstone. His descendants added new settlements, Jahanpanah and Firuzabad, to the motley assortment of royal cities, citadels, suburbs and hunting lodges in the vicinity, this time building with cheaper rubble and plaster techniques which reflected their lack of ready cash.

After its sack by the Timurids, much of the Delhi area fell into disrepair and took on the character of a vast cemetery interspersed with thriving villages in which tombs and shrines seemed to outnumber residences for the living. During this period, Delhi gained a reputation for Muslim sanctity, and mystics and their followers joined the existing population of Muslims and Hindus. When the Mughals conquered northern India in the early 16th century, the area evoked both ancient kingship and more recent piety. It is probably for this reason that the first Mughal building of note was the tomb of Humayun (r.1530–1556), a square red sandstone structure made up of four octagons around a central chamber located in a *chahar bagh* garden of Persian inspiration, to which was attached a *saray* or building where the Quran was recited.

Up until the 1630s, the Mughal emperors preferred to stay in Agra or Lahore but, like the Safavids in Iran, they had a penchant for grand urban experiments. One of the first examples of a Mughal royal city was Akbar's Fathpur Sikri, established in 1571 but more or less abandoned after 1585. This city consisted of a palace-fortress fronted by a large public zone where an audience hall, the *ibadat khanah* ('house of worship') where Muslim and non-Muslim scholars came together, government offices and accommodation for royal employees were located. A wide street flanked by two-story shops led from the palace to the Agra gate at the opposite end of the city; it was bisected by another street and the domed crossroads functioned as a bustling covered bazaar. Outside the roughly rectangular city walls, Akbar's nobles built garden retreats, some overlooking the vast artifical lake on the city's northwestern side. Despite its lively bazaar, Fathpur Sikri was an imperial retreat rather than an inclusive capital. It also marked a transition between the egalitarian Turkic character of early Mughal rule, when the emperor needed to keep his Turkish warlord peers happy, and a later more hierarchical phase characterised by Shah Jahan's new city of Shahjahanabad at Delhi. He chose to found his new city here because it offered an attractive combination of skilled craftsmen, a reputation for sanctity and royal patronage, space to expand and a good water supply. Building started in 1639 at which time Shah Jahan gave out plots to Mughal princes and amirs to build their own *havelis* or mansions. The city's plan combined Hindu and Muslim visions of city planning. On the one hand, the overall plan corresponded to a Hindu 'bow' plan suited to riverside cities; on the other, its constituent parts recalled a Muslim view of the city as an organic entity with a palace-fortress (head), a heart (great mosque) and a spine (an arterial market street) connecting the two.[6]

The red sandstone citadel on the river bank exemplified the mature Mughal sense of hierarchy. The main entrance to the palace led from the city upwards to a large courtyard with a *naqqar khanah* (musicians' gallery) and the main colonnaded audience hall of sandstone, where the emperor received his visitors suspended above them in a marble balcony. The hall itself was divided into concentric sections with those of highest rank and wealth allowed closest to the emperor's balcony. The palace also possessed a second private, more opulent audience hall made of marble with gold domes in which stood the fabulous jewel-encrusted peacock throne. To the east and west side of this central

---

[6] Shama Mitra Chenoy, *Shahjahanabad, A City of Delhi, 1638-1857* (New Delhi, 1998).

area were gardens, divided into sections by water channels in the Persian style. Behind it, the private areas of the palace extended along the river side of the citadel. Finally, a small balcony known as the *jharoka-i darshan* jutted out of the citadel's back wall over-looking the slope down to the river. The emperor appeared at the balcony at dawn to personally dispense justice to all and sundry in a manner which resonated with Hindu and Persian-Islamic traditions of good kingship.

Shah Jahan had heard rumour of Safavid Isfahan, and Persians regularly travelled to Mughal lands; hence it is not surprising that the main streets of his city replayed elements found in Isfahan's bazaar, Maydan-i Shah and Chahar Bagh Avenue. In a bold twist on the Persian plan, the Mughal architects designed extended bazaar thoroughfares lined with two-story buildings containing shops and storage space on the ground floor and an apartment for the shopkeeper and his family above. The main bazaar, stretching from the Lahore gate of the citadel to the Fathpuri Mosque, was lined with trees and a canal ran down its middle. Open squares called *chawks* along the bazaar, sometimes with pools at their centre, broke the monotony.

The great *haveli*s of the Mughal elite took up large areas and were almost cities within a city with their own baths, mosques or temples, offices, gardens and accommodation for retainers set in flower gardens. Some even included small markets. The rest of the city was divided into residential quarters, each inhabited by a separate caste or practitioners of a particular craft, a form of segregation which reflected the cultural norms of Hindu society. Although some homes were little more than hovels there were also many merchant houses, some several stories high, inhabited by Armenians and Hindus among others. Beyond the walls, Shahjahanabad exhibited the same pattern of suburban growth as Isfahan and Mamluk Cairo: elite residences set in large walled gardens, tombs and shrines which bustled with religious and profane activity, and wholesale markets for agricultural produce.

Shahjahanabad is the last city in our survey. Although all have been painted with the broadest of brush strokes, certain colours and themes stand out. Muslim rulers wished to imprint their vision on cities by establishing grand palaces, mosques, gardens and public buildings which at the same time responded to the culture and faiths of their inhabitants. Extensive mosque building only made sense when the population was Muslim. Once cities had numerous mosques, rulers built theological colleges instead; with the development of mysticism, shrines and mausolea became part of the urban landscape. Wherever non-Muslim populations lived alongside Muslims, synagogues, churches and temples could also be found, and architectural styles often blended local pre-Islamic motifs and forms with new Islamic ones, from the Visigoth repertoire in Cordoba to the Hindu tradition in Shahjahanabad. Although streets were often narrow before modern mechanised transport necessitated wider roads, many cities had expansive public areas from the Almohad *rahba* in Marrakesh to the Safavid *maydan* in Isfahan and the *chawk*s of Shahjahanabad. Last but not least, they possessed gardens in abundance – verdant spaces within homes, tree-lined avenues and suburban parks – which were enjoyed primarily by the rich who had time to relax, but were also shared by all who entered the leafy precincts of shrines, caravanserais and public squares.

Until the 17th century at least, European travellers were charmed and impressed by cities in Muslim lands. It was only in the 19th century, when many European cities had been remodelled and many Muslim countries were in economic crisis and their cities impoverished, that negative stereotypes of 'Islamic' cities prevailed in western writing. Britain and France, the foremost colonial powers of the 19th to 20th centuries, either cordoned off traditional cities as museums to a bygone age or destroyed them to build new modern cities. Those cities which were transformed into museums are ghosts of their former selves: shorn of their old economic functions they languish as world heritage sites for tourists, inhabited by poor migrants from the countryside, their social fabric in tatters. Yet it is testimony to their lost splendour that the British empire's final fling was to construct an imperial city at Delhi to rival Shahjahanabad little more than a decade before India achieved independence in 1948.

Further Reading

Abu Lughod, Janet. 'The Islamic city', *International Journal of Middle Eastern Studies*, 19 (1987), pp. 155-176.

Behrens-Abouseif, Doris. *Cairo of the Mamluks: A History of the Architecture and its Culture*. London, 2007.

Bennison, Amira K. and Alison L. Gascoigne. *Cities in the Premodern Islamic World: The Urban Impact of Religion, State and Society*. London, 2007.

Blake, Stephen. *Half the World: The Social Architecture of Safavid Isfahan 1590-1722*. Costa Mesa, CA, 1999.

—— *Shahjahanabad: The Sovereign City in Mughal India, 1639-1739*. Cambridge, 1991.

Bloom, Jonathan. *Arts of the City Victorious: Islamic Art and Architecture in Fatimid North Africa and Egypt*. London, 2008.

Jayyusi, Salma K., ed. *Cities of the Islamic World*. Leiden, 2008.

Menocal, Maria Rosa. *The Ornament of the World: How Muslims, Jews and Christians Created a Culture of Tolerance in Medieval Spain*. Boston, 2002.

Raymond, André. *Cairo*. Cambridge, MA, 2000.

Ruggles, D. Fairchild. *Gardens, Landscape and Vision in the Palaces of Islamic Spain*. Philadelphia, PA, 2000.

Sanders, Paula. *Ritual, Politics and the City in Fatimid Cairo*. Albany, NY, 1994.

10

Cultures of Learning

Anil Khamis

Knowledge and its pursuit have a special place in Islam, beginning with the initial command '*Iqra*!' (Read!), which is part of the first revelation to the Prophet Muhammad in the Quran:

> Read! In the name of thy Lord and Cherisher,
> Who created man out of a clot of congealed blood:
> Proclaim! And thy Lord is Most Bountiful,
> He Who taught (the use of) the pen,
> Taught man that which he knew not (96:1-5).

Indeed, the Quran as well as the hadith literature urge the believer constantly to think, learn, reflect and seek guidance. Words related to learning are the third most prevalent in the Quran after those relating to God and faith; the use of one's senses and intellect (*aql*) in pursuit of knowledge are deemed essential to the human relationship to the Divine. 'We had endowed them with (faculties of) hearing, seeing, heart and intellect: but of no profit to them were their hearing, sight, and heart and intellect, when they went on rejecting the Signs of Allah' (46:26). The spirit of this message is captured in the Prophet's oft-quoted counsel, 'Seek knowledge, even unto China'.

Education and learning assumed importance in early Islam, which led to progress in many fields of activity, particularly politics and governance, as Muslims began to rule over huge territories that had to be administered. This required them to reflect on the human condition, political leadership and governance, and how to improve society. For the course of the next eight centuries from the advent of Islam in the seventh century, Muslim powers, adjacent to contemporary civilisations in the west (Greco-Roman Empire) and the east (India and China), engaged in vibrant learning that contributed to human intellectual history, scientific break-throughs, and the enacting of political-moral principles in the governance of society.

Yet today, Muslim societies – which represent one-quarter of all humanity – are felt to be in a state of 'crisis'. Education and literacy rates are considered to be lowest in Muslim majority countries, and the growth rate of schooling lags far behind the 2015 target of the global 'Education for All' (EFA) movement.[1] What accounts for this state of affairs? Colonial rule over Muslim societies and its legacy form an important part of the picture; literacy was often seen as too dangerous for the colonised, even if it occasionally served the ends of colonial administration. But there is more to the story of decline than colonialism alone.

This chapter is a broad inquiry into the history and development of education in Muslim societies, and a reflection on what might be done in response to the 'crisis' today. We begin with the founding ethos of learning in Islam, in terms of both principles and early Muslim practice. This lays the groundwork for the debates that were to emerge on what education should be about, and why the umma was thought to have fallen short of its ideals. In sketching the situation of Muslim education in the modern period, including the phase of colonial rule, we will look into the causes and effects of the prevailing shortfalls in Muslim-majority as well as minority settings.

Globalisation now frames this situation, linking our responses everywhere to shared concerns about security, poverty, development and effective citizenship. This reality is recognised by the Millennium Development and Education for All goals, signed in 2000 by all the nations of the world in Dakar, Senegal. We conclude

---

[1] The EFA movement began at Jomtien, Thailand, at the meeting of the World Education Forum convened by UNESCO in 1990, with access to education as the primary goal.

with some thoughts about the roadmaps for Muslim institutions – from traditional *madrassas* to the most sophisticated academies.

A Learning Ethic

The first duty of fathers to their sons is to teach them writing, arithmetic and swimming. Teach them arithmetic before writing, it is easier and more useful.

(al-Jahiz, 776-869)

The life and career of al-Jahiz speak to how education had come to be understood in early Islam. He was born into a poor family in Basra and made his illustrious career as historian, poet, philosopher and philologist in Baghdad, writing over 200 books. Al-Jahiz came to enjoy the patronage of the Abbasid caliphate just when the *Bayt al-Hikma* or House of Wisdom was founded in Baghdad. His outlook in the quote above reflects the idea that the duty to educate rests with the parent, who is responsible for the child's upbringing. Education must cover not only literacy and numeracy but also life skills. Practical use is a measure of its value – though the pursuit of knowledge as such is cherished as a sacred calling – and there is an ideal way to educate: the teacher should take into account the learner's need and motivation in guiding progress from simple to more complex matters.

Engaging in instruction was a pre-Islamic activity which found encouragement from basic Islamic precepts. The Quran (literally meaning 'recitation' and thus an oral and aural activity), with its injunctions to pursue learning, came to form an integral part of the education of children as well as adults. This education aimed to provide both practical instruction and moral guidance.

It was appreciated from the earliest times that very young children cannot learn the Quran in an intelligible manner before taking instruction in the language. This comprised letters and word formation, then grammar, syntax and interpretation or application to context. Afterward, or at times concurrently, a child would receive lessons in the Quran for the purposes of religious practice. If it suited the character of the student, who was probably by now a youth, further education was offered. But this was the preserve of the few.

> When it seemed good to the father to train and educate him, he
> made him sit with the men of letters of the age and the virtuous
> of the period till he was educated, able to write a good letter and
> compose verse, being thoroughly cultivated.
>
> (al-Thaalibi, 961-1038)

By the early 10th century, less than 300 years after the advent of Islam, Cordoba established schools for the poor and orphans of the city, which were situated near the mosques and other parts of the city. In Fatimid Egypt, pupils who already had knowledge of the Quran were sent to the *Diwan al-Insha* to learn the art of composition. By the mid-11th century, schools in the Seljuk empire – the Nizamiyya schools – seem to have been relatively wide-spread and well structured. Nizam al-Mulk, the Seljuk wazir, founded the Nizamiyya *madrassa* system in Baghdad in the early 11th century. These schools were established for the purpose of providing secondary or higher education to those who had completed their elementary education. They set a prototype for higher education in Muslim domains from North Africa and the Mediterranean to Central, South and East Asia as far as China.

Learning was not the sole preserve of boys. The hadith actively promoted the education of girls and women: 'Seeking knowledge is the duty of every Muslim, man and woman', and 'The father, if he educates his daughter well, will enter paradise'. Girls also partook in instruction, though the historical sources suggest that this tended to focus on practical skills in societies that were patriarchal. For boys and girls alike, it was parental choice along with their status and aspirations for their children that decided educational matters. There were certainly women who excelled in public life and attained positions of leadership, not least under the Fatimids in Cairo (969-1171).[2]

---

[2] Ruth Roded, ed., *Women in Islam and the Middle East: A Reader* (London, 1999); Delia Cortese and Simonetta Calderini, *Women and the Fatimids in the World of Islam* (Edinburgh, 2006).

We have much historical evidence that education was important, and many anecdotes about learners, teachers and fee payments. Later we learn about problems too: incidents between teachers and pupils, accounts of teachers accused of extortion and charging for instruction brought to court, as well as accusations of bad character and meanness to children. What we do not have from the very early period of Islam, and what we have little direct understanding of, is what exactly was taught and learnt and the extent of learning that is, how widespread this education and schooling was. But we do have insight into the motivations and places of learning, as well as the new principles of education and its scope in early Muslim society.

Motivations and Places

The Prophet Muhammad himself gave instruction in a *halqa* (circle) at the mosque adjoining his home in Medina. His example, in addition to the injunctions in the Quran to pursue learning and the merit attributed to those who acquired it, inspired members of the first umma to learn from each other. This learning is thought to have been informal, mainly involving oral instruction and directed to the formation of character.

Among the most pressing concerns of the early Muslim community were how to govern a large and expanding territory and to resolve disputes. This need gave rise to the sciences of governance and law (*fiqh*). Indeed, learning of all kinds began to flourish, with key contributions from non-Muslims. The sanction to learn with and from non-Muslims, particularly Christians and Jews as 'People of the Book' (*Ahl al-Kitab*) who had received prior guidance from God came from the Quran itself:

> O mankind! We created you from a single (pair) of male and female, and made you into nations and tribes, that you may know each other – not that you may despise. Verily the most honoured of you in the sight of God is (he who is) the most righteous of you. And God has full knowledge and is well acquainted (with all things) (49:13).

Instruction generally took place in mosques or rooms attached to them. In addition, learning also took place in the residences of the ruling cadres, in the homes of teachers or other premises dedicated to teaching: *kuttabs* (places to learn writing) and *madrassas* (places for instruction), among kinfolk in the desert and apprenticeships in the family trade.

Alas, the *kuttab* is understood today as merely a 'Quranic school' where children supposedly only learn verses of scripture by rote. Similarly, the term *madrassa* has been misinterpreted and politicised. Schools all across the Arab world and beyond are today called by that name. As we will see, the caricature of these institutions implies a chasm between educational standards and the educational systems in Muslim communities today.

Principles and Development of Education Systems

> Penmanship is not to be taught with the Quran and religion. There is a certain canon and there are special teachers for teaching reading and writing as all crafts are taught. Reading and writing are not dealt with in the pupils' elementary schools (*kuttab al-sibyan*) and any one who wants to learn them must seek them from the professional teachers.
>
> (Ibn Khaldun, 1332-1406)

Ibn Khaldun, acclaimed as the founder of the discipline of sociology, gives us an account of what had come to pass by the 15th century in education, and its underlying principles. We can be reasonably sure that learning was an important feature in early Islamic societies and that by the 9th-10th century schools were established by the ruling class, or in modern terms, that state-sponsored schools were a feature of Muslim communities. This is evidenced by the Nizamiyya mentioned above. The contribution of the Nizamiyya system was to popularise education, create specialisations within the curriculum and directly involve the state in education.

From this point on, schooling and success in studies began to occupy a central social function linked to celebrations and feasts for children who had learned the Quran or received the commendation of their masters. Schooling offered jobs and better livelihoods for growing numbers of people who aspired to educate their children.

This last point is illustrated by a story from the al-Muwahhid Berber dynasty that ruled North Africa and Spain. The ruler, Abd al-Mumin (c. 1094-1163), used to gather together minor officials who had studied the 3,000 collected writings of the dynasty's founder, Ibn Tumart. Such gatherings took place for al-Mumin's pleasure in the palace after Friday prayers. These officials, maintained by the state, were also taught riding, shooting, swimming and the use of boats. Once they had finished their training, the officials were sent to neighbouring tribes to assume positions of leadership and advise local chiefs.

The Nizamiyya led to a schooling system that offered access to education to all. Students were offered lodging and stipends, and instruction was offered without charge. That is, the principle of free education was evident in Islamic societies as early as the 11th century. As these institutions were under state control, there also arose a system of inspection and control of the curriculum. Hence, teachers in these schools became a specialised cadre with a recognised body of knowledge.

With the systematisation of schooling, thinkers like Ibn Khaldun began to ponder the underlying principles and purposes of education. There was no formal vision for the system at large, or a common curriculum. Rather, education was conducted differently in various places, as it depended on who had access to which knowledge, teachers, thinkers and learning spaces. Instruction within governors' urban palaces was the preserve of the ruling class, while schooling in a room adjoining a rural mosque attracted a different group of learners. The reading of the Quran offered an entry point into various areas of study, which then became specialised subjects in secondary *madrassa* education.

The founding of institutions of higher learning – the Nizamiyya and the *Bayt al-Hikma* in Baghdad, the *Dar al-Ilm* and al-Azhar in Cairo, and the Zaytuna in Tunis – during the 9th-11th centuries, or middle period of Islam, led to major developments. More and more, the founding of libraries and translation activities made virtually the whole body of knowledge available to Muslims, engaging scholars from across the world's civilisations and centres of learning – Indian, Chinese, Greco-Roman and African.

Knowledge of mathematics, astronomy, philosophy and the natural world was collected and expanded. Moreover, these fields were divided into subjects or disciplinary specialisations. Whether in the mechanics of al-Jazari (1136-1206), the optics of Ibn al-Haytham (966-1039) or the encompassing social, political and economic commentary of Ibn Battuta (c. 1304-1368), new vistas opened up. Access to knowledge, opportunity for study, and the incentive of increased social status as well as religious value combined to create an explosion of intellectual activity.

Legacies

As Muslim civilisations reached summits of knowledge that spanned all fields from astronomy to zoology, scholars from across the world were drawn to Muslim institutions by the innovations and intellectual breakthroughs in human, natural and mystical studies. The fruits of this endeavour could be seen in the built environment, law and civic culture, commerce and transportation, the arts and literature, agriculture, navigation and the sciences. Old fields such as philology, semantics, perception and historiography were newly energised, as the learning canon developed through the collaboration of Muslim and non-Muslim scholars.

One example catches the spirit of the times. Moses ben Maimonides (1135-1204) was born in Cordoba at the height of Jewish culture in Spain, and educated by his father and Arab teachers. He became Rabbi Moses, among the greatest theologians of Judaism, trained also as physician and philosopher. One of Maimonides' greatest surviving works, *The Guide to the Perplexed*, is an attempt to reconcile Greek sciences and philosophy with the Jewish faith. A similar movement is mirrored in al-Ghazali's (1058-1111) *Ihya al-Ulum al-Din* or *The Revival of Religious Sciences* that grappled with the seeming tensions of rationality and revelation, a constant theme in the Abrahamic traditions.

A fascinating aspect of Maimonides' work is that it is written in Hebrew using the Arabic alphabet, and shows its intellectual debt to Muslim scholars, notably al-Kindi (801-873), al-Farabi (c. 870-950), Ibn Sina (980-1037) and Ibn Rushd (1126-1198). Maimonides was careful not to be misunderstood or misrepresented. Thus, anyone who wanted to read his work would have to be knowledgeable not only in Hebrew and Arabic but also in classical Greek philosophy, as well as the theology and wisdom developed in the Abrahamic faith traditions – Judaism, Christianity and Islam.

The work of those thinkers is directly linked to the founding of scholastic philosophy, the advent of the Renaissance and ultimately the Enlightenment in Europe. The Christian scholastics in the medieval period (1100-1500) were based in newly-established European centres of learning modelled on higher education institutions in the Muslim world, where the scholastic guild with its licence to teach was developed.[3] It was in these new European centres that the scholastics began translating into Latin the body of knowledge that was available mostly in Arabic and Persian. They used ideas and thinking systems developed under Muslim patronage, acknowledging their own ties to the work of Ibn Rushd, Ibn Sina and numerous others. Ibn Rushd (known as Averroes) was cited as the 'Commentator of Aristotle', and made the sciences of the ancient Greeks intelligible. Ibn Sina (known as Avicenna, 'Prince of Physicians') wrote the *Canon on Medicine* (*Qanun fil-tibb*), an encyclopaedic work that became a text for the study of medicine and the training of physicians in the West until the 17th century.

These Muslim legacies fed into the European Enlightenment that gave birth to modernity. Yet when two of modernity's most vital developments took place – the Age of Science and the Industrial Revolution – the Muslim world was far from the centre of things. On the contrary, it was (and has largely remained) a consumer of their products.

Muslims took particular notice of their 'knowledge-lags' where their societies bordered on Europe. In the Ottoman empire, for

---

[3] George Makdisi, 'Universities: Past and. Present', in Farhad Daftary and Josef W. Meri, ed., *Culture and Memory in Medieval Islam* (London, 2003), pp. 43-63.

instance, the state of technology as well as governance seemed a far cry from that of its once inferior rivals. But it was Europe's most successful colonial powers – Britain, France, Germany and the Netherlands – that brought home the full measure of the 'education-lag' to their subjects in Algeria, Egypt, India, Indonesia, Morocco, Nigeria, Palestine and beyond.

The 19th-century polymath Jamal al-din al-Afghani (1838-1897), theologian, philosopher and self-styled political reformer, was the first person to use 'the West' and 'Islam' as competing paradigms in the understanding of modernity. In what emerged as a raging debate on Muslim civilisational renewal, the philosopher-poet Muhammad Iqbal (1877-1938) along with other activist-intellectuals weighed in. The arguments ranged from whether pre-modern Muslim civilisations were exhausted, to whether the roots of the crisis lay in the cultural, economic, technological, political or even the philosophical bases of these societies.

Certainly the traditional Islamic idea of man as a created being (abd) and vicegerent of God on earth (khalifa), in a quest that was in keeping with that status, came under challenge from secular modernity. For the imperial powers, with the rise of science, man's status found its basic expression in the claim of French philosopher Rene Descartes (1596-1650), 'I think, therefore I am' (cogito ergo sum). This lay at the heart of the Age of Science, in which the self-defining individual was cast as creating/inventing with no recourse to a Creator.

It was an idea of man that became an intellectual model for the new Europe and America. Knowledge and the aims of education shifted to learning for its own sake. This ran counter to the ulitmate goal of education in Muslim societies: to discover the glory, grace and purpose of the Divine in creation. Education in the Islamic tradition was focussed on realities accessible through facts, rather than facts for their own sake; there was an ethical dimension to the pursuit of knowledge.

Above all, however, it was the experience of colonisation that is the legacy for Muslim societies today. The whole of the Islamic world had become dependent on the imperial powers. Even after gaining political independence, Muslim societies found their agendas of development to be dominated by the major powers – the United States of America, Europe and the Soviet Union. In education, the impact of this dominance was felt across the board in countries that grappled anew with questions about who they were and where they were headed.

The Crisis Today

If we are to make a real, speedy and substantial progress we must bring our educational policy and programme on the lines suited to the genius of our people, consonant with our history and culture and having regard to the modern conditions and extensive developments that have taken place all over the world ... There is immediate and urgent need for giving scientific and technical education to our people in order to build up our future economic life and to see that our people take to science, commerce, trade and particularly, well-planned industries. We should not forget that we have to compete with the world which is moving very fast in this direction. At the same time we have to build up the character of our future generations. We should try, by sound education, to instil into them the highest sense of honour, integrity, responsibility and selfless service to the nation. We have to see that they are fully qualified and equipped to play their part in the various branches of national life in a manner which will do honour to Pakistan.

Muhammad Ali Jinnah, 1947

This quote from Jinnah (1876-1948), the founding father and president of Pakistan, sheds light on the number of areas that we must consider if we are to begin to comprehend the nature of the study of 'Muslim Education' a millennium after al-Jahiz. The time span separating the two quotes enables us to appreciate where we are in the study of Muslim education and the education of Muslims, to determine where we may be heading.

Jinnah's remarks came at the first education conference in the birth year of Pakistan, and signal the priority then given to education. At the time, the majority of the population (80 per cent) lived in rural areas with no access to modern schools. And the country did not have the institutional structure to carry out Jinnah's ambitious vision – nor the financial resources. In 1959, a report commissioned by the Ministry of Education noted that only three per cent of central government revenue was allocated to education; today less than two per cent of GDP is devoted to the health and education sectors combined. The indigenous, traditional schools or *madrassas* were not involved in the process of creating a national policy. They offered education in rural communities without state control, supported by donations and endowments (*waqfs*) as well as religious tithes (*zakat*), though the state is often involved in collecting the latter.

As newly-independent Pakistan struggled to educate its people, various providers were labelled 'modern' or 'traditional': there was seen to be an urgent need to catch up with the world. Given the history of the learning ethos in Islam and its accomplishments, the state of education in Pakistan – a country with a 97 per cent Muslim majority – was all the more shocking. While an earlier generation asked 'what went wrong?' the question now seems to be, 'what's to be done?'

This is not just asked with respect to Pakistan, but across the Muslim world. The most populous developing countries of the world, referred to as the E9, have large Muslim populations; five are Muslim majority countries, and four have significant percentages that together number in the hundreds of millions. A key reason put forward by Muslim-majority countries to explain their educational situation is poverty.

Table 1 lists the populations and the percentages of Muslims living in the E9 countries – all former colonies, or under the dominion of imperial powers. The E9 countries are a priority with regard to the goals of the Education For All (EFA) initiative mentioned earlier. The six agreed goals of the EFA are:

- Expanding and improving comprehensive early childhood care and education, especially for the most vulnerable disadvantaged children;

Table 1: E9 Most Populous Countries, by Total Population and Muslim Population

Country	Total Population (in millions)	Percent Muslim	Total Muslims (in millions)
Bangladesh	144.2	88	126.9
Brazil	176.2	2	3.5
China	1294.9	3-5	64.7
Egypt	70.5	90	63.5
India	1103.6	20	220.7
Indonesia	221.9	88	195.3
Mexico	102.0	0.4	0.4
Nigeria	131.6	50	65.8
Pakistan	162.4	97	157.5
TOTAL	**3407.3**		**898.3 (26.4%)**

Sources: World Bank, Islamic Development Bank, United Nations Development Programme.

- Ensuring that by 2015 all children, with special emphasis on girls and children in difficult circumstances, have access to and complete free and compulsory primary education of good quality (with a target of getting 24 million children into school by 2010, toward which new financial pledges were received in 2008);
- Ensuring that the learning needs of all young people and adults are met through equitable access to appropriate learning, life skills and citizenship programmes;
- Achieving a 50 per cent improvement in levels of adult literacy by 2015, especially for women, and equitable access to basic and continuing education for all adults;
- Eliminating gender disparities in primary and secondary education by 2005, and achieving gender equality in education by 2015, with a focus on ensuring girls' full and equal access to and achievement in basic education of good quality;

- Improving all aspects of the quality of education and ensuring excellence so that recognised and measurable learning outcomes are achieved by all, especially in literacy, numeracy and essential life skills.

Table 2 shows the Muslim population among the world's least developed countries; these are also the most unlikely to reach any of the EFA goals. Muslims are a majority (56 per cent) of the least developed countries, the 'bottom billion'. They are also one-quarter of the three billion inhabitants of the 'developing' world, where most countries will fail to achieve any of the three measurable EFA goals: universalisation of primary education, gender equality and adult literacy targets. The picture that emerges is that the vast majority of the estimated 1.5 billion Muslims worldwide find themselves in poverty or live in areas of 'ultra-poverty' (that is, earning less than US 50 cents a day).[4]

Table 2: The World's Poor and Educationally Disenfranchised, by Total Population and Muslim Population

Country	Education Index	GDP Index	Population (in millions)	Percent Muslim	Total Muslims (in millions)
Afghanistan	n/a	n/a	29.9	95	28.41
Angola	0.54	0.53	15.4	2-5	0.31
Bangladesh	0.45	0.48	144.2	88	126.96
Benin	0.41	0.40	8.4	15	1.30
Bhutan	0.48	0.50	1.0	5	0.05
Burkina Faso	0.16	0.41	13.9	50	6.95
Burundi	0.51	0.31	7.8	10	0.78
Cameroon	0.64	0.51	16.4	20	3.28
Central African Republic	0.43	0.40	3.8	15	0.57
Chad	0.60	0.42	9.7	50	4.85

[4] See Akhter U. Ahmed, Ruth V. Hill, et al, 'The World's Most Deprived', *2020 Discussion Paper no. 43*, International Food Policy Research Institute, Washington, DC, 2007 (available at http://www.ifpri.org/2020/dp/vp43/vp43.pdf).

Country	Education Index	GDP Index	Population (in millions)	Percent Muslim	Total Muslims (in millions
Côte d'Ivoire	0.46	0.45	16.4	60	8.20
Democratic Republic of Congo	0.53	0.42	10.8	10	1.08
Djibouti	0.52	0.51	0.8	94	0.75
Equatorial Guinea	0.78	0.88	0.5	n/a	n/a
Eritrea	0.49	0.36	4.7	n/a (< 5)	0.24
Ethiopia	0.40	0.33	77.4	50	38.70
Gambia	0.41	0.49	1.6	90	1.44
Ghana	0.51	0.52	22.0	30	6.60
Guinea	0.41	0.51	9.5	85	8.08
Guinea-Bissau	0.39	0.33	1.6	45	0.72
Kenya	0.66	0.31	33.8	35	11.83
Liberia	n/a	n/a	3.3	20	0.66
Madagascar	0.64	0.35	17.3	7	1.21
Malawi	0.67	0.30	12.3	20	2.46
Maldives	0.90	0.65	0.3	99	0.30
Mali	0.23	0.38	13.5	90	12.30
Mauritania	0.49	0.48	3.1	99	3.07
Mozambique	0.45	0.40	19.4	20	3.88
Myanmar	0.76	0.39	50.5	4	2.02
Nepal	0.53	0.44	25.4	n/a (< 5)	1.27
Niger	0.17	0.35	14.0	80	11.2
Nigeria	0.66	0.39	131.5	50	65.75
Pakistan	0.44	0.51	162.4	97	157.53
Rwanda	0.61	0.42	8.7	n/a	n/a
Senegal	0.39	0.47	11.7	92	10.76
Sierra Leone	0.35	0.28	5.5	60	3.30
Somalia	n/a	n/a	8.6	90	7.74
Sudan	0.52	0.49	40.2	70	28.14
Tanzania	0.60	0.30	36.5	35	12.78
Togo	0.57	0.47	6.1	10	0.61
Uganda	0.71	0.45	26.9	16	4.30
Yemen	0.51	0.36	20.7	95	19.67
Zambia	0.61	0.36	11.2	35	3.92
TOTAL			1083.8		608.30 (56%)

Sources: World Bank, Islamic Development Bank, United Nations Development Programme.

Muslim majority countries have education systems that are deeply divided, variously controlled and significantly diverse. Most of these states were fashioned by colonial powers as new nation states with little regard to ethnic, religious or regional identities. After independence, the local elites tended to foster parallel education systems which kept traditional schools apart – as we saw in the case of Pakistan.

In Indonesia, 33 per cent of all education is provided by the 'traditional' *pesantren* or *madrassa* system. Egypt and parts of West Africa are in a similar situation. Hard data for India and Pakistan are not available. What is interesting here is that many *madrassa*s across the Muslim world teach English, offer coaching and tuition to enable their pupils to access higher education, and provide vocational training and foreign language study to access jobs. Very few graduates wish to pursue religious training (*jamia* or tertiary education) to prepare them as *ulama* to serve the religious needs of their communities.

Table 3 illustrates the interplay of education provision in various Muslim majority countries or those with large Muslim populations.

Table 3: Examples of Muslim Majority States and their Education Systems

State	Education Systems Available
Saudi Arabia, Syria, Xinjiang (China)	• State-controlled formal and religious education
Pakistan, Turkey	• State-controlled formal education • Large and growing private/independent sector • Independent religious education
Indonesia, Nigeria	• State-controlled formal education • Small but growing private/independent sector • Independent religious education

The upshot is that the quality of access as well as of educational content varies greatly in each society. For the vast majority of children and youth, choices about where to get one's education are shaped largely by the degree of poverty, and secondarily by regional location.

A scholarly critique summed up the state of affairs thus:

> There are at present two systems of education. The first, traditional, which has confined itself to classical knowledge, has not shown any keen interest in new branches of knowledge that have emerged in the West nor in new methods of acquiring knowledge important in the Western system of education ... The second system of education imported into Muslim countries, fully subscribed to and supported by all governmental authorities, is one borrowed from the West. At the head of this system is the modern university, which is totally secular and hence nonreligious in its approach to knowledge. Unfortunately, these people educated by this new system of education, known as modern education, are generally unaware of their own tradition and classical heritage. It is also not possible for this group to provide such leadership as we have envisaged.[5]

In response to what were seen as serious challenges to the integrity of heritages as well as postcolonial systems, the first of five Muslim Education Conferences was held in Mecca in 1977, under the auspices of the Organisation of Islamic Conference (OIC).[6] One outcome of the conferences was the concern about a clash of fundamental purposes:

> Education should aim at the balanced growth of the total person-

---

[5] Syed Sajjad Husain and Syed Ali Ashraf, *Crisis in Muslim Education* (Sevenoaks, UK, 1979).

[6] The OIC is an umbrella body of 57 Muslim majority countries and those with significant minority Muslim populations. It was formed in 1971, with its permanent secretariat in Jeddah, Saudi Arabia, and is represented at the United Nations.

ality of man through the training of man's spirit, intellect, the rational self, feelings and bodily senses ... The ultimate aim of Muslim education lies in the realisation of complete submission to Allah on the level of the individual, the community and humanity at large. The Conference recommends that all Muslim countries must necessarily implement Allah's sharia and mould the lives of people upon Islamic principles and values because only then they shall succeed in systematising their education according to the aims above.

The call for 'Islamisation' here is noteworthy: the correct response to the crisis was seen as a revival of Islamic heritage, which the OIC saw as properly done through the medium of Arabic. While this call was hardly new and could be traced at least to the social and political reform movements of the mid-19th century, the timing was significant. Parts of the Middle East were now developing economic muscle with the fresh discovery of petroleum reserves; this gave impetus to the idea that the resources of knowledge could and should be 'Islamised'. The idea came from a project led by Ismail Faruqi, a key proponent of the OIC Education Conferences. Faruqi (1987) saw the idea thus:

Islamisation does not mean subordination of any body of knowledge to dogmatic principles or arbitrary objectives, but liberation from such shackles. Islam regards all knowledge as critical; that is, as universal, necessary and rational. It wants to see every claim pass through the tests of internal coherence, correspondence with reality, and enhancement of human life and morality. Consequently, the Islamised discipline which we hope to reach in the future will turn a new page in the history of the human spirit, and bring it closer to truth.

Not all Muslims shared those views about the concept or its practice, and whether it was a suitable response to the crisis. Yet the conferences did open up debate on critical issues within and across national frontiers – such as the moral implications of poverty and its associated deprivations, as well as the need to see knowledge as both a practical and spiritual asset. Future OIC deliberations were to focus on the need for Muslims to come to terms with their diversity of heritages, social and religious, in public policy. In the wake of the events of September 11, 2001, an OIC gathering in Amman (Jordan) sought to defend freedom of choice and practice in matters of religion. Indeed, the Amman Declaration of 2005 by a historic Shia-Sunni panoply of representatives put pluralism at the core of Muslim theology, law and practice.[7] The message for educators from the OIC took on a more liberal tone than what came out of the 1977 education conference in Mecca. There was greater sensitivity to human rights standards in matters of religion – and to the way that Muslim practice in this regard will be seen by non-Muslims. At the same time, the assertion of pluralism can be seen as a retrieval of the civilisational values of Islam.

New Horizons

Diversity in the values as well as the offerings of Muslim education systems is the reality today. It is the outcome of the introduction of formal schooling in the postcolonial Muslim world, which gave rise to issues of access to state-sponsored 'secular' schools as opposed to 'traditional' *madrassas* – with a variety of private/public options in between. While poverty and location were key factors that shaped access, there was also the matter of values: the place of religion in education, and how this should be handled by providers of education. The advent of globalisation, which has put societies, institutions and individuals in more direct and intense contact than ever before in history, has brought to the fore issues of economic equity and access, as well as of ethical values in education. But it has also enabled fresh and creative approaches to those challenges, not least with regard to the sizeable Muslim diaspora communities in Europe and North

---

[7] Full details are available at: http://ammanmessage.com/index.php?option=com_content&task=view&id=20&Itemid=34. See also 'Coming Together', *The Economist*, July 28, 2005.

America.

One development is the coming together of private and traditional providers to reshape *madrassa*s into 'hybrid' schools, which offer a full complement of modern education with an emphasis on religious studies. While hybrids have been around for some time in the past century, the new forms are becoming especially attractive in the midst of concerns about both cultural identity and competitiveness in a globalised world.

Complementary, non-formal or alternative programmes have spread to many countries, including Afghanistan, Egypt, Guinea and Mali, as well as other parts of sub-Saharan Africa and South Asia. Indonesia's *pesantren* (traditional boarding schools) have even played a vital role in community trust-building.[8] In Turkey, Imam Hatip schools offer a slate of secular as well as religious subjects, and girls as well as boys can now attend, a shift from the time when they first replaced *madrassa*s. Although graduates of Imam Hatips face discrimination in entering university other than to study theology, the schools remain popular among both conservative and poor families, rural and urban. Turkey's current prime minister, Reçep Erdogan, attended an Imam Hatip school.

Tens of thousands of such alternative schools today serve Muslim communities, and their success reveals that formal schools have had limited success with those who need education the most: the rural ultra-poor. Table 4 shows that for the world's very poor and disenfranchised communities, formal schools have become a 'traditional' rather than an effective needs-based response. The alternative schooling model is more focused on 'learning' and less on 'teaching'. It also appears to be more sensitive to parents' and communities' actual needs than is the more rigid structure of formal schooling.

Of late, greater attention has been given to alternatives to formal schools by UNESCO, the United States Agency for International Development (USAID) and the World Bank, building on earlier work by international non-governmental agencies such as Save the

---

[8] Julie Chernov Hwang, 'Education and Social Cohesion in Malaysia and Indonesia', in Bryan S. Turner, ed., *Religious Diversity and Civil Society* (Oxford, 2008), pp. 143-166.

Table 4: Some Features of Formal and Alternative Schooling*

Formal Schooling	Alternative Schooling
Children are compulsorily assembled in a building called 'school'	Children are given the opportunity to participate in active learning
Children are separated from their peers by age regardless of learning needs or ability and work with a single adult	Children study in multi-grade settings that allow continuous learning processes, with the assistance of peer coaching
Children are required to be in school for fixed periods of time normally exclusive of any other community related activities	Children and adults engage in free-flow movements from school to community
Children devote discrete amounts of time to individual subjects	Children can choose to devote time to different activities dependent upon need and interest
Children are required to study a standard curriculum that will be tested to screen or allocate them to predefined places in college or employment opportunities where available	Children are responsible for their own learning and involved with teachers and community to develop self-instructional learning materials
Different health and education agencies are responsible for children's health and education separately	Community is involved in attention to health and nutritional needs of young children
Fixed school year with terms and vacations that are preset	Locally adapted changes to school cycle and school year
The school's focus is on completion of the curriculum and teaching	The school's focus is on the child's learning, and enabling him/her to continue with their education

* Adapted from J.P. Farrell, 'The Aga Khan Foundation Experience Compared with Emerging Alternatives to Formal Schooling', in Stephen E. Anderson, ed., *Improving Schools Through Teacher Development: Case Studies of the Aga Khan Foundation Projects in East Africa* (Lisse, Netherlands, 2002).

Children and the Bangladesh Rural Advance Committee (BRAC). With rising interest in the potential of *madrassas* to serve EFA goals, there is also greater concern for the quality and relevance of the education that is on offer. Civil society has a key role in supporting socio-economic development, which includes education, and the needs and rights of disadvantaged communities.

For Muslims who live in Europe and North America, issues of diversity in social values and in the type of education on offer are hardly less important. Among the oldest and largest of the diaspora communities are those in the United Kingdom,[9] where they number more than two million. The first officially recognised mosque in the country dates from 1889 in Woking, near London. A host of Muslim nationalities and ethnicities have migrated to the UK since the early waves from Pakistan, Bangladesh and India, among them significant numbers of Afghans, Albanians, East Africans, Filipinos, Iranians, Iraqis, Kosovars, Somalis and Turkish Cypriots. Islam is now the second largest religious tradition after Christianity.

Pupils of Pakistani and Bangladeshi heritage may be the second or third generation of learners to live in the UK. But they have reportedly under-achieved in their educational performance – with boys doing worse than girls, as shown in Table 5. Examination results do not, of course, tell the whole story of social and economic disadvantage; parental background and aspirations also matter. It is noteworthy that Indian pupils, whose families did not generally arrive as itinerant labourers but as professionals, performed better than their Pakistani and Bangladeshi colleagues. This state of affairs led to demands by some Muslims for more appropriate education which, it was argued, state schooling failed to provide for their children.

At the same time, a UK government commission found that

---

[9] See Hisham A. Hellyer, 'British Muslims: Past, Present and Future', *The Muslim World*, 97 (2007), pp. 225-258. Among the earliest settlers were sailors from Yemen. See Fred Halliday, *Britain's First Muslims: A Hundred Years of Yemeni Migration* (London, 2009).

Table 5: Pupils Gaining 5+ A-C Grades at GCSE 1998-2003

Ethnic Group	1998 (%)	1999 (%)	2000 (%)	2001 (%)	2002 (%)	2003 (%)	Change 1998-2003 (%)
African Caribbean Boys	13	20	19	17	25	28	+15
African Caribbean Girls	28	30	31	34	39	43	+15
Bangladeshi Boys	28	31	30	27	43	43	+15
Bangladeshi Girls	36	40	42	50	52	58	+22
Indian Boys	40	43	49	49	57	67	+27
Indian Girls	50	55	61	65	69	73	+23
Pakistani Boys	21	26	27	31	33	37	+16
Pakistani Girls	31	32	41	42	44	50	+19
White Boys	34	33	36	39	41	45	+11
White Girls	44	45	45	50	52	54	+10
All Boys	30	32	34	35	39	44	+14
All Girls	42	44	47	48	51	54	+12
Total	36	38	41	41	45	50	+14

Source: Birmingham City Council, 2005

there was a marked 'aggressive hostility towards Islam', that had increased after the events of September 11, 2001, and the start of the Iraq war in March 2003. 'Islamophobia' as well as social factors like high unemployment and the disproportionate number of Muslim youth in detention centres, fuelled the call for Islamic

schools. Of the 500,000 Muslim children in the UK, the vast
majority – some 95 per cent – are enrolled in state schools. A
small minority attend independent Muslim schools, of which
there are just over 100, in addition to seven state-supported Muslim
faith schools.

In the UK as in Muslim societies across the world, civil society
as well as the state have had to evolve fresh responses to long-
standing questions about how the cultural, religious and economic
identities of their citizens fit into 'national systems' of education.
A shared concern here is about educating all citizens for citizenship, and the range of rights and responsibilities that attach to
civic participation, including pluralist ideals. This is of obvious
importance in multicultural societies, where minorities that face
alienation may find themselves further marginalised in systems
of education that are fragmented. But common citizenship is no
less vital in countering divisions of class, gender and social status.
Alternative approaches to schooling must face this challenge as
much as formal systems, perhaps more so in view of the absence
of a uniform national curriculum.

More broadly, the issue across frontiers is inclusion in what
is termed a 'knowledge society'. It is true that knowledge and
learning have long been at the core of all successful human
societies; this chapter has shown Muslim history to be no different.
Yet the forces of globalisation have brought forth levels of mobility
and linkage across frontiers – of people, ideas, technology and
culture – that put exceptional stress on access to knowledge as
a condition of wellbeing, for individuals and communities alike.
The 2005 UNESCO report, *Towards Knowledge Societies*, sees it
thus:

> [T]he 'information age' knowledge societies differ from older
> knowledge societies because of the focus on human rights and the
> inclusive participatory character ... As long as vast swathes of the
> global population lack equal opportunity in terms of access to
> education – in order to master the available information with
> critical judgement and thinking, and to analyse, sort and incorporate
> the items they consider most interesting in a knowledge base –

information will never be anything but a mass of indistinct data. And instead of controlling it, many people will realise that it is controlling them. [pp.18–19]

Inclusion in this broad sense has also shifted the emphasis from the old idea of formal education that ends during an individual's youth, to *lifelong learning* with no such limits. This may today be a functional need, but it recalls the Muslim ethic of knowledge as an endless pursuit, or as 'education for life'. In that vein, an ambitious Muslim initiative, the Aga Khan Academies programme, aims to have schools in Central and South Asia, the Middle East and sub-Saharan Africa by 2013.[10] Although academic excellence is a priority, it is to be consciously framed to foster a sense of civic responsibility and a grasp of local and global issues – in essence, within an 'ethical and public-minded approach'. By marrying traditional values to the latest advances in teaching methods and content, the initiative may well take the idea of 'alternative education' to a new level.

Conclusion

This chapter has sought to provide an overview of Muslim education as it has evolved since the seventh century. The story is one of rich innovation, moral concern and diversity in how Islam as a faith tradition has influenced communities of Muslims the world over. Often the outcomes have led to the excellence of civilisations and societies – whose legacies in turn shaped the success of western civic and technological modernity. The impact of western colonial legacies on Muslim education has been more mixed. But we no longer inhabit a world where 'Western' and 'Muslim' are neatly distinct categories – certainly not when it comes to the hybrid modes of education that prevail today. It turns out that some of the responses involve unexpected returns to old ideas of schooling, such as the use of *madrassas*. In the process, what is 'traditional'

---

[10] See the programme's publication, *Excellence in Education* (2003), also available at http://www.agakhanschools.org/aka.asp

and what is 'modern' is being redefined by realities on the ground. The formal model of schooling with its secular and secularising outlook falls short in far too many contexts. Poverty, cultural identity and the place of religion in public life in our time have challenged old assumptions about what amounts to a fair and effective system of education. In particular, the failure to respond to the needs of poor and disenfranchised Muslim communities may lead to greater numbers of very poor children withdrawing from formal schools, with all that this implies for the social sector.

Globalisation has pointed up the limitations of the old assumptions; the aftermath of September 11, 2001, has made the need for reform more urgent than ever. This is true not only of Muslim societies but also of non-Muslim ones in an interdependent world.

Further Reading

Anderson, Stephen E., ed. *Improving Schools Through Teacher Development: Case Studies of the Aga Khan Foundation Projects in East Africa.* Lisse, Netherlands, 2002.

Hefner, Robert and Muhammad Qasim Zaman, ed. *Schooling Islam: The Culture and Politics of Modern Muslim Education.* Princeton, NJ, 2006.

Lelyveld, David. *Aligarh's First Generation: Muslim Solidarity in British India.* Oxford, 2003.

Makdisi, George. 'Universities: Past and Present', in Farhad Daftary and Josef W. Meri, ed., *Culture and Memory in Medieval Islam.* London, 2003.

Noor, Farish, Yoginder Sikand and Martin van Bruinessen, ed. *The Madrasa in Asia: Political Activism and Transnational Linkages.* Amsterdam, 2008.

Shalaby, Ahmad. *History of Muslim Education.* Beirut, 1964.

Starett, Gregory. *Putting Islam to Work: Education, Politics and Religious Transformation in Egypt.* Berkeley, CA, 1998.

United Nations Education, Scientific & Cultural Organization (UNESCO). *World Education Report 2000: The Right to Education.* Paris, 2000.

—— *Towards Knowledge Societies.* Paris, 2005.

11

A Conference of Bards:
Rumi to Adonis

Raficq Abdulla

The *azaan*, the Islamic call to prayer that unfolds in voice and ear, is among the most intriguing aspects of how poetry is thought of and practised in the Muslim world. Here, lovers of poetry gather together to listen in concert at *mushairas* – the public and semi-public gatherings where poetry is heard – in the recital of verses of, for example, Hafiz or Ghalib which are also sung as *ghazals*. The audience listens, it shares, participants inspire each other. Poetry becomes a communal public act. At the same time the audience is educated, brought out of the sound and fury of daily life into silent engagement with deeper layers of the self where knowledge is not an acquisition but a function of being.

By reading poetry, we learn to consider where we are and where we might be. We move or are moved from the periphery to our core. Poetry moves us by its musicality and its essential silence, to deeper levels of the self. It is here that we encounter love, loss, desire, longing, where we are taken by anger, freed by compassion, moved to ecstasy. It is also here that despair can overwhelm us, tenderness civilise us, where we are invited to imagine the experience of dying and face the fact of death – our knowledge never being complete or total but tentative, alive, changing, challenging, wild and animated, often ambiguous, amorphous, reflective, contemplative, contradictory, mercurial and finally unattainable.

The idea of possession seems out of place in this world of delicacy and violence, of beauty, love, loss and deep perplexity faced with a dazzling array of realities, and corrupting, sometimes ruinous circumstances. From all of this, and more, poetry – this setting out of words that shine a plane of meaning and move us with fleeting insight – is born.

Why Poetry Matters

To speak of what poetry is, is to flirt with definitions attempting to pin down this mysterious art. Poetry may encourage us to ask: *What* am I? What makes this package of words fit – speaking of vision and loss, of rivers and woods singing greenly, the pallor of skies that filter finally ineffable light, of the chain mail of hate and of love with its excessive quota of inevitable loss that dissevers us, of acquiescent senility, of the last things that intrude and heap sorrow on us? What makes a string of sentences, with their apparent wanton play and eccentric breaks, have such potency on the ghost of our imagination? How does their beauty remind us of our own, or at least of our aspiration to beauty?

The word 'poetry' comes from the ancient Greek word *poeisis* which means 'to make'. Poets make meaning and find beauty, they re-present our feelings, our thoughts, our deepest insights, the delicate weave of intuitions that always slip away from the net of words. Poetry is an alchemical act: its black work turns figurative words into sensibility and marks fugitive sensibility into words. It is a delicate, secret, fragile, intelligent, allusive and precise business with a metaphorical end, trailing grains of glory. The writing of poetry is, in a sense, a plebeian act poets make with words, and making implies doing, technique, discipline, expertise, sometimes elaborate virtuosity which requires intellectual rigour and imaginative effort from the reader in order to enter into the semantic, sometimes brusque, energies the poet sculpts from language.

The critic George Steiner in *On Difficulty and Other Essays* (1978), describes the disciplined act of reading difficult poetry beautifully when he says that it slows reading which enables us to reflect and to '…deepen our apprehension by goading to new life the supine energies of word and grammar'. To be a serious reader of poetry, by which I mean reading much and reading actively, at your own pace, if you reflect on what you read, if you allow yourself to be taken over by a poem, to let it dwell in you and feed you as you, in turn, dwell on the words, in the syllables and silences that work in it – you learn both to uncover the poem and recreate yourself, you deliver your mind to the intimacy of an inner life. A good poem teaches us to learn, to place ourselves surely amongst the names and images that fall on us like ash or pollen as we read the poem so that we die to live again by the poem's word and dance. By reading poems seriously and intelligently, we imagine our souls into becoming.

'Genuine poetry', T.S. Eliot reminds us, 'can communicate before it is understood.' However, there are times when poetry is reduced to snobbish expression, or to the exclusive partaking of divine nectar enjoyed by a subtle few and even then inexplicable to themselves. This autism of dislocated language and seeming difficulty then becomes the measure of a poem's apparent worth.

At the same time, just because we feel something deeply – grief, love, desire, loss, disgust, anger – and write about it sincerely does not mean that we have written a poem. Poetry is something tougher than confession. It requires craft: the muse is cool, she comes and goes at will. The relationship between making and the skill it takes to make something memorable, unfamiliar and yet recognisable, is an enigma. I cannot account for it. It happens if you practise and if you have the talent or grace to let words settle like migrating birds returning to roost. In a sense the poet is a seer; it is a dangerous profession, which sometimes makes unbearable psychic demands on the writer. Above all it is not trivial or trivialising even if it is comic and funny.

One of the finest contemporary English poets, Geoffrey Hill, expresses more succinctly what I am trying to say when he comments that a true work of art is a reflection of the 'artist's authentic self', but that 'in the act of making, the artist may become a stranger to himself or herself'. There is a deep bond of sympathy and of doubt – of concord and the possibility of discord when we find ourselves in that no-man's-land where great poetry pulls us apart and out of ourselves. A bond is created between the reader or listener and the poet who, if he communicates successfully with his audience, becomes a cipher or a conduit for intricate, private, contradictory and at times apocalyptic meanings and puzzles that transcend the criss-cross of concepts and argument, that enter the soul through a sort of primeval sensibility and wonder and take us to a new place of understanding.

Good poetry is a journey or an invitation to a journey. The English poet, Ruth Padel (2007), suggests that this journey '…contains many…spirals; interlocking journeys of thoughts, feelings, associations, images'. Poetry is not only a journey out and away from where we are when we start to write or read, but a journey inwards. Whilst we know that poetry does not change the world or necessarily improve the moral worth of individuals, it would be foolish to ignore its transformative power. Music can affect us, literature can change us, art can stop us in our tracks and make us wonder, poetry can make us tremble and weep and see through our everyday lives.

Beauty is another name for God in Islamic mystical terminology. We admire beauty and try to keep it at a distance so that we may continue to admire it and maintain the necessary perspective, but then there are times when it takes us over and we are lost. Sometimes it makes us weep for something we have lost by never attaining the terrifying perfection it suggests.

Like Rumi's reed torn from its riverbed, we weep because we are reminded by beauty of our psychic origins. He sings in his *Mathnavi* :

> Listen oh listen to my plaintive cry
> Listen to my longing or else I die.
> From the sweet home of my bed I was torn
> So my pain and cruel longing was born.
>
> With so many secrets I sing aloud
> But none sees nor hears in this crowd.
> Oh for a friend to know my burning state
> That our souls may mingle and contemplate.

The flame of love discourses in me
The wine of love so enforces me.
Do you wish to know the fire, the flow
Listen my listeners then you shall know.[1]

This is an intense invocation, a private and unsentimental zone of being – beauty can do that. The artefacts of the creative spirit can refine us and draw us to a central place of wisdom, even of ecstasy, at least for a moment; they can stop us in our tracks and we may be left with a residue of grace. As with music, so with poetry which is music transposed into the sounds of words and the images they inspire; we enter here into the realm of the ineffable – another name for the Divine in Islamic mysticism – by way of the all-too-articulate means of language. We are faced with the possibility or hint of perfection, never to be possessed entirely, through the imperfect – even corrupt – medium of words which are symbols, simulacra, condensations, even displacements of reality or the Real (yet another name for God)...of what is.

Poetry is like the multi-faceted glints of a polished diamond that glitters, but to no avail unless there is an eye to perceive it. It needs a heart that colludes with the meaning and beauty it suggests. We may thus be transformed by language, our dissipated lives recollected by metaphor, image, rhythm, metre, by the sometimes absurd logic of poetry. We turn and turn in its incantatory forms so that we reach a zone of unforced understanding and delight. Rather than grasping, we are grasped by meaning; by the creative act of reading or by listening intelligently and well, we attain a state of atonement or oneness for the time we are nourished by the work of art – and I use the word 'work' both in its passive nominal sense and in its active sense. Art is worked by the artist but it works on us, tuning the metabolism of our sense of beauty, of tragedy, of the ultimate strangeness of being alive, the sense of transcendence. These notions may be 'tasted', I don't

---

[1] Jalal al-din Rumi, *Words of Paradise: Selected Poems of Rumi.* tr. Raficq Abdulla (London, 2006), p. 41. All subsequent references to Rumi refer to this translation.

believe they can be tested by evidence or proved by logic, but they are intense and real for all that – a shift into meaning and purpose.

Poetry answers at a deep level, the question: why are we here? It fosters critical intelligence, it encourages us to sound out our own personhood, enriching our language and thus our self-understanding against those who would control us through our thoughts and feelings. We are both amplified and condensed by poetry, drawn up to pay attention to the inner, occult purposes of our precarious and elusive existence in the world about us, if we read slowly, openly, with empathy and intelligence. It provides not only consolation but it revivifies or revives that sense of strangeness we sometimes experience at those moments when we almost see ourselves from the outside, detached from the mediocrity of our daily perceptions and transactions.

Intelligent reading is a combination or a conspiracy of heart and head that leads the reader to a portal of understanding, an anthology of meanings not necessarily clear and upstanding; in fact the more covert and ambiguous it is, the richer it is. The head may call out the names a poem suggests, but only the heart hears the rich silences that reside in its pauses and enriching lacunae; together they set a pattern of words on the page that dance and stay to welcome readers as guests who know how to receive them. Reading poetry well implies reading a lot of poetry so that one learns to discern; it is like exercise, the more you do it the fitter becomes your faculty of understanding and your ability to see the inter-textual echoes of a poem, so that one poem whispers to another in your reading of it.

Great poetry is sown with lacunae and embedded in a temper of prevailing interiority which invites, indeed demands from the reader, an active response calling for interpretation and the search for meaning by him or her. As we are constantly deceived by those near and dear to us both consciously and unconsciously, and in turn we deceive them and ourselves, so does the poem we read and the reading by which we claim to engage with the poem perform an epitome of mutual deception as we claim to explain it. In a sense the process of reading poetry is very private; it is embarked on with modesty and calls for reflection. T.S. Eliot describes reading as requiring a condition of simplicity that at the same time costs the reader not less than everything.

Geoffrey Hill in his book of poems, *The Triumph of Love*, sees poetry as a mode of consolation framed by its form and made explicit by its content. He asks and answers:

> ...what are poems for? They are to console us
> with their own gift, which is like perfect pitch.
> Let us commit that to our dust. What
> ought a poem to be? Answer, *a sad*
> *and angry consolation.*[2]

All serious poetry – including comic poetry that is well conceived and expressed – can be considered as a concentrated form of consolation by which we remember who we are and might become.

Poetry in the 'Muslim World'

The difference between me and a non-Muslim westerner is that I am aware of the 'Otherness' in my reading. I am not only a European but an Asian, an African and, of course, a Muslim – which covers a wide swathe of the planet's literature and cultures. It is a demanding journey but one which I believe we should at least start on. The Other is not the Other but myself, reading with echoes and suggestions coming from the variants of Muslim expression – and in fact, as I suggest above, from an even wider perspective. The influence may be ghostly, but ghosts often have a powerful subterranean effect on the personality and the subconscious.

Jalal al-din Rumi and the Early Masters

My first real experience of 'Muslim poetry' occurred when I was commissioned to furnish fresh interpretations of the poems of

---

[2] Geoffrey Hill, *The Triumph of Love* (London, 1998), p. 84.

the great mystic and poet, Mawlana Rumi (1207-1273). I worked with transliterations or academic translations of this great poet's works. As I read, I seemed to enter into another world which was also my world. The Other was in place in myself, and Rumi reminded me of this Other which is also in my history and my antecedents. I was enticed, entranced and drawn into the intoxication of Rumi's poetry, and I was able to write what I wrote not so much from an intellectual or academic stance but from a sort of inebriation that flowed from his inspiration. I was – to coin a phrase – vintaged by the wine of Rumi's verse, and so the poetry appeared.

Reading Rumi's poetry undoes us, we are caught unawares, we are drawn like the moth he describes in his poetry, to the fire of his verse where we are brought to naught. In one of his poems Geoffrey Hill speaks of '…the decreation of the self which all must move…' It conveys for me the notion of undoing ourselves like Penelope in Homer's Odyssey. She unravelled her daily weaving each night as if her dreams were cleansing her with their surreal presences which are, in essence, absence or presence that cannot be grasped by the conscious mind intent on possession and control. This taking back of creation is a necessary uncoupling of the self from its rampant embodied self-understanding. Then the words of poetry may work on our less tutored yet real perception which becomes lively enough to discover a new expression that gazes into a non-self.

Rumi describes this state of nullity when we are discovered in the vast desert of the Divine – a place of timeless day converging with the great night where stillness is Light – in this way:

> …I am a cipher of your
> moods, when you're filled with joy, so am I;
> when you're dark I become dark as a cave.
> It's always the same, your bitterness is my brine,
> your sorrow is my fatal grief…

But first we must be in touch with, and we must touch, our soul which will then touch us and transform and illuminate. This is a process of purification. It is not the same as the notion of purity when it is politicised and made 'public', when the principle becomes soiled by the sink of cruelty and public acts, by the craving for power and the sweat of self-justification, the self-deceptive presentation of ugly certitudes.

The process I am talking about is very private. It is embarked on with modesty, beset with doubt and surrounded by confusion. We must proceed through the fog aware that we don't know the way, yet trusting that our intention will encourage the way, in turn, to approach us like a bird, like a tiger, and receive us. It is a sort of spiritual serendipity, what Muslims call *baraka* which may be translated as 'grace'. Only when we have opened the door to the spirit lodged in us can we realise what Rumi is talking about. He tells us:

> When your actions and thoughts strike
> that living spark in you, engender your soul,
> you work from that subterranean flow of
> joy that runs like a laughing torrent in you.
> All other origins bring only dried fruit, no
> love, no energy sinews your being quite as well.

For Rumi, to know is to be in free fall in the Beloved. The lover loses his or her sense of selfhood. Love is creative, a seeking after knowledge, an abeyance of self. It is determined and patient, a form of passionate longing for the Beloved to the exclusion of all else including language, definition, even sanity. This Love is not manufactured, one cannot disguise it, one cannot coax it or argue for it. Like the muse who visits a poet, it takes you over or it does not. It is not technique but art which demands technique or craft. To love is to suffer great ordeal, to taste the most delicate of sensations – of delight and wonder, of beauty and attainment. It is to be burnt, annihilated, created again, only to lose oneself and discover, if one is blessed, a new place in the self, a contradictory place of passion and serenity. It is confusion and clarity, it is astonishment, estrangement and suddenly being at home in the place of the soul's birth, a recognition, discovery and remembering. It

is a mirror that merges image with reality, two into one. Rumi
describes this state of grace as:

> ...you and I, the mystery is you and I as we sit
> together in this royal place, yet in this cusp
> of being in the shade of common bliss we are one
> you and I,
> you and I,
> we are at once in Iraq and Khorasan
> you and I.

However, this is description, words, images – Rumi was speaking
of a lived experience. We read Rumi's poetry, we read of longing
and loss, and about ecstasy when the self dissolves and the soul
merges for a time into the Greater – the *Akbar* of being. But how
many of us have had the same experience as Rumi who suffered
to attain and soar with intimations of no-self, absorbed by the
Beloved's Beauty which was to Rumi as food to life? A feasting
place not possessed but perhaps, if we are struck with grace, we
may be enraptured with grains of insight that displace us, as Rumi
was displaced.

As readers we have to take part in this journey of the spirit that
Rumi shows in his poetry. We have to learn, as the great mystic
and poet Ibn Arabi explained in his philosophy, to *imagine* God.
Rumi understood this very well, he tells us:

> Know this, my friend, it's nothing new,
> these words are turned to bliss when you
> read them with your own imagining heart.

Rumi's poetry is rich, accurate yet wild with yearning and ecstatic
expression, spoken with the authority of someone who has suffered
the longing which is the precursor to love. If we read with the
same level of vulnerability and with honesty (about what we really
know and feel), Rumi's poetry is like the perfume of the Beloved
which lingers after the Beloved has withdrawn and we are left with
an absence, a catalyst for memory to teach us longing.

The Beloved is both the condensation of the self into desire and the source of self-transformation as compassion, when the lover is drawn like the moth to the naked flame, into the depths of being, when the 'out-there' is transformed into the 'in-here'. For Rumi love and suffering are connected like fire and water, like light and shadow. Shadow cannot exist without light. Through the debased and seductive medium of language, Rumi calls or recalls us to our psychic origins, to the Beloved who is there even if we do not realise it.

The Muslim poetic tradition boasts so many important poets whose works are still influential today, like Farid al-din Attar (1142-1220), Nizami (1141-1209), Saadi (1184-c. 1292), Hafiz (c. 1320-1388), Rudaki (859-c. 941) and Nasir-i Khusraw (1004-c. 1072), to name a few. Nasir-i Khusraw is highly respected in the Islamic world both for the mystical quality, the devotional and didactic fervour of his poetry, and for profound philosophical learning which underpinned his writings. He is one of those remarkable poets in the Islamic tradition who not only demonstrate great technique but are also mystics and philosophers. He wrote several theses, including the renowned work entitled *Jami al-hikmatayn* (The Union of Two Wisdoms) in which he sought to combine Islamic theology with Greek thought.

If Rumi can be described as a poet of love, a poet's poet, Nasir-i Khusraw deserves to be recognised as a poet of knowledge or reason, a philosopher's poet. His poetry continually emphasises the essential importance of reason and knowledge, joined with submission to the faith of Islam as he understood it which results in wisdom. Both Rumi and Nasir-i Khusraw not only preached the importance of inner knowledge, they experienced it in their respective ways. Nasir-i Khusraw was a master of *tawil* or the esoteric interpretation of the Holy Quran. To the modern western reader he may at first sight appear over-didactic, judgemental and exclusive in that he was steeped in the final rightness of his faith, but he rewards deeper study. His poetry is not ornament but a means to spiritual instruction. Nasir-i Khusraw exhorts his readers to follow the straight path of faith which requires the faithful to develop inner sight. He writes:

With an inner sight look at the World's mystery
The outward sight cannot discover it,
This world is the stair leading to the higher world
And we must mount its steps.

Nasir-i Khusraw mounted the stair to the higher world with faith and knowledge on the steadfast feet of his poetry.

The Urdu Poets

I shall now touch on some fine Urdu poets to point up the difference between classical Muslim poetry and the western art. In traditional Urdu poetry, style, modes of expression, rhetorical conceits, imagery, the variety of rhyme-schemes and unusual metres are very important. There is a certain Homeric quality to poetry in the Islamic world – it is performed in communal gatherings perhaps more than read privately; it is to be heard with expectant familiarity, so that audiences know what is coming. They are not surprised but they crave to be enchanted by the music of the verse which beats a pattern in the primordial sense of the ear; they admire the ingenuity of the artist working within the constraints of conventional forms and tropes.

The word in the Muslim world has a special place. It is consecrated, after all, as the Word of God in the Holy Quran. However, it is more listened to than read. This love or habit of listening to the word which originates in listening to Quranic recitals spills over into listening to poetry which, I suggest, means that Muslims are seduced by sound rather than sobered by content. Thus beauty as form – and this generally applies to music – takes priority over meaning. The participants are invited to take part in ecstasy as opposed to fret over purpose which in any case is a given, as God's will. Thus poetry is to be heard and savoured for its form, for the beauty of its sound, for the technical skill displayed by the poet.

We attend *mushairas* because we seek the pleasure of recognition together with others – even as we cry we enjoy, we are consolidated by this community of feeling, by this reprise of consolation as an antidote to our own contingency and vulnerabilities. We are not concerned about whether the poet is sharing an actual experience so much as creating a finely-crafted verbal construct that we can admire and by which we can be carried away. The content may be conventional and the imagery well-worn, but it is the way the words are put together, their lacquer, that entrances the right audience.

If one learns to read the layered text of a poem closely in the western tradition in order to extract nuances of meaning, then one learns to listen closely in the various Muslim traditions – and listen again in order to enjoy and suffer with pleasure through the subtleties of the sounds of a poem. If these poems that seek to remind their listeners of love hidden in the folds of conformity are truth-saying, then they are truth-saying in an indirect, stylised way, with polished craft and a civilised ear to appreciate them as objects of beauty. Style, the imitation of the style of respected masters, the polish, the conceit, the metaphors and symbols which the audience knows well – such signifiers as the rose, the tulip, Saqi the cup-bearer, wine, the falcon, eglantine, the sky, moon and sun – these tools are essential in the armoury of the Urdu poets.

Poetry here is not so much the expression of the inner thoughts, feelings or perceptions of the poet who speaks for himself in such a way that he speaks to and for us all, so that his despair, his longing, his anguish, his delight become ours. Rather, it becomes a contest in excellence and fineness of conception, and brio of recital. It must look and sound good enough to move its listeners who in turn must listen intently. An untutored and distracted ear will at best only half-capture what is said, and it will not know how to read what it hears.

This courtly poetry is beautifully expressed in the verses of the great 19th-century poet, Ghalib, who could write and mean what he wrote, but of course with sufficient courtly irony and self-mockery, when he says:

> Other poets there may be, whose verse is very fair,
> But all agree that Ghalib's style is quite beyond compare[3].

---

[3] D.J. Matthews, C. Shackle, S. Husain, *Urdu Literature* (London, 1985), p. 88.

Ghalib valued himself not so much by what he said but by how he said it. Wit, cleverness and a sharp intelligence appear to override the depth of personal feeling and perception, but at the same time Ghalib is understandably popular because of his honesty, the fact that even in the stylised form of his poetry his conviction shines through, and his humour. Of course, there are poems written by Ghalib such as an elegy he wrote for a dead lover[4] where true feeling seeps through the conventional tropes and semantic polish, but there is not sufficient space to deal with them here.

Another fine Urdu poet who scarcely hid deep emotions under a patina of exquisite form and framed images, is the marvellous 18th-century poet Mir Taqi Mir whose delicate and introspective writings still touch the hearts of thousands of people. He wrote exquisite ghazals in which the distracted lover weeps because he is forsaken by his beloved. This is not only written for form's sake; Mir Taqi Mir we know, did actually suffer for love. One of the most sensuous and memorable poems that Mir wrote is reminiscent of that wonderful 17th-century English poet, Marvell. Mir's poem reads:

> Made crimson by the betel which she chewed
> Her lips one day aroused me to declare,
> 'Oh I should be the happiest of men
> If only that sweet juice with me you'd share!'
> At first she said, 'No, no!', but I replied,
> 'Come let me drink and taste sweet ecstasy!'
> She laughed and stopped me for a while, but then
> She passed the liquor of her mouth to me.[5]

One feels a little abashed to be with these playful lovers sharing tender moments of being together, this is erotic intimacy of such innocence and love which was to end in grief. Loss is a recurrent theme in Urdu poetry; we see its remembered appearance in the modern poetry of Faiz Ahmed Faiz (1910-1984). He writes:

---

[4] Matthews et al, *Urdu Literature*, p. 92.
[5] Matthews et al, *Urdu Literature*, p. 51.

All hearts are racked by storms, and so, my love, beware!
The torch-glow of your blazing cheeks may pale, beware!

Oh memory of my love, come back to me again,
And let me sense the passing days and months and years![6]

Faiz, who wrote much great political and socially committed poetry with sincerity and conviction, is recognised as one of the greatest 20th-century Urdu poets. He worked with conventional images but his poetry can be extremely poignant, investing new significance and vitality to old tropes. In the extract above, we see he can also write sharply and lyrically about the private moments which form our sense of self. He calls on memory so that he can taste the passage of time which ages us all with the slow but unavoidable decay of the body and the passing of all we love. The moment of ecstatic belonging becomes a dream, and imagination replaces the beloved's bodily presence. Love becomes an imaginary flux of experience that cruelly creates in the lover the very isolation he believes he has transcended by being in love.

An earlier master was Muhammad Iqbal (1877-1938), born in Lahore and a large presence in the Urdu-Persian poetical tradition of the subcontinent. Although he studied philosophy at Cambridge and wrote his doctoral thesis on Persian philosophy at Munich University in Germany, Iqbal remained in essence a poet. He used Persian for his major poetic work, but Urdu is the language of many of his poems that are based on the *ghazal* tradition; they are loved and recited in Pakistan and India to this day.

These poems often use traditional themes and images that appeal to nature and to Quranic figures – tulips, roses and eglantines flower in his verse, light is veiled, blood pulses through stones, rosy-cheeked Saqi serves the intoxicating wine of mystical ecstasy. The influence of Rumi's verse and mystical insights prevail in Iqbal's poetry. Yet they are poems on the cusp of modernity, knocking on the door of the contemporary world. The noted

---

[6] Matthews et al, *Urdu Literature*, p. 131.

orientalist scholar, R.A. Nicholson, described Iqbal as a poet who was a man of his times but also ahead of his times and at odds with his times. This is an apt description of a poet whose work is both beautiful and occasionally disturbing.

Iqbal's is essentially a poetry of *ijtihad* and of the greater jihad, the inner struggle of each individual to understand purpose and meaning. He believed in the dynamic quality of life and strove to improve not only our material world but also our spiritual station, which for Iqbal is centred on reaching out to the Divine source of all existence. He writes:

> Look to the Self, within your own soul hidden.
> Only one is worthy of prostration.
> To bow in front of others is forbidden.[7]

We are bound to seek for Truth but in a world that is by nature impermanent and incomplete. Iqbal's verse is infused with moral invocations and exhortations, it is steeped in faith from which it reaches out to the modern godless world. He believed that we can only live well if we are prepared to change and not be mired in imagined past glories. We are encouraged to seek new ways of seeing, thinking and becoming. The traditional mingles with the modern in Iqbal's poetry, God is central to his thought and poetry, but his approach to Allah is not traditional submission; there is a thorn in his love for the Greater. This is where his poetry engages with the modern world. He wants from God a better response to our predicament. Thus, he can complain to the Beloved that He is fickle. He writes with a hint of independence that may shock:

> The bonds of unquestioned submission no longer hold
> us fast.
> The heart may not beat with the passion and frenzy by
> which it was ruled.
> The lessons of faith are forgotten in which we were

---

[7] Matthews et al, *Urdu Literature*, p. 114. All further quotes from Iqbal refer to this volume.

formerly schooled.
But sometimes You favour our rivals then sometimes
with us You are free.
I am sorry to say it so boldly: You are no less fickle
than we.

Iqbal's poetry both comforts and quickens its readers and listeners
to think again and afresh in a new age.

Poetic Tradition and Modernity

We can see that much Muslim poetry, even that of the modern
poet Faiz, differs from western poetry – which of course also
works with metre, rhythm, rhyme, common tropes and so on.
The content and novelty of expression are essential, the subtlety
and individuality of the poet's intuitions, insights, psychological
depth, the virtuosic power of her imagination, and so on are key
elements in the value placed on her work. Generally, western poetry
is more personally stated even when it is elaborate, obscure and
complex; it claims to uncover new depths of experience, new ways
of seeing, and the experience is of a single private person. In this
case the notion of a person is understood as an essentially modern
western idea, an individual who is alone in this world and wishes
to share through the play of language his singularity with the
reader and, to a lesser extent, the listener.

Great cultural changes are occurring in the Muslim world –
and we will shortly visit contemporary Muslim poetry which is
far from the conventions of traditional Persian or Urdu modes.
Yet in the Persianate world at least, poetry has been more an expression of a communal experience that depends on the expectations
of a culture; the trick for the poet lies in the way he crafts those
expectations into fine language. In a sense, this is to be expected
of classical Urdu poetry, which was an aristocratic pastime associated with royal courts and patronised by emperors and nobles
who sought praise, diversion and pleasure through dalliance of
form and words which were the basis of a civilised existence. This
did not mean these poems were superficial: they could be enter-

taining but also very serious, working within strict conventions. This is poetry as concert, the voluntary coming together of people to listen, where the audience participates with the appropriate responses to show its approbation or displeasure.

These sorts of experiences of poetry depend on a common understanding of what is good and what is bad verse. The poets themselves are performers who train to be good performers, learning from other more renowned poets. They become apprentices in the same way as musicians, submitting themselves to the disciplines of teachers who train them in the technique of writing and performing according to established rules developed from received tradition. We are not talking here of the anguished confessional expression of the individual who may learn by osmosis from his predecessors or even by attending poetry workshops. Rather, we are talking of professional expressions of love, disappointment, pleasure, joy and even of anguish, polished to be admired and to be moved by, as with a musical phrase. This does not mean that great poets with genuine originality did not exist in the Muslim tradition, but that they operated within explicit parameters of what makes poetry work.

So, I argue there is an intriguing difference in the approach to classical poetry – in terms of its creation and its reception – between the West and the Muslim world. To many western readers, say of Hafiz, the poetry may seem predictable, saccharine and ultimately too stylised to be 'genuine'. To a western sensibility, these poems are held together with the safety pins of clichés that represent moods and feelings which the poet flicks on to the page without genuine thought or content. Of course, many western readers deceive themselves by bearing down on this initial scepticism with a reverent orientalist approach towards the perceived exoticism of these works. There is much bad faith here, caused by the failure to communicate with another culture on its own terms, in its own language. Hence much is lost in translation and is replaced by fashionable preconception of the Other, which the source language represents.

There is no sure-fire recipe for carrying across the sensibility of one culture to another. It happens but it happens rarely. For Muslim readers, much of western poetry that bears the marks of modernism, where beauty is seconded by truth-saying, represents the breaking down of a singular self, and this works against the grain of public expectation. To Muslim ears much of this poetry is crudely expressed, indiscreet and ugly. Both the classical eastern and the western ways of reading and listening are looking for different things in this practice of poetry.

I trust that our journey into the poetic imagination at large has been diverting. The limits of this chapter allow only a broad outline of eastern and western poetic questing. For those wishing to venture further, there is an abundance of human creativity to immerse in, and seek the seeds of vision and insight that touches on and speaks from the spirit that dwells in us.

Muslim Poetry Today

I end with some reflections on modern poetry in the Islamic world. There have been profound changes in expression, in form and in content. The classical traditions of Muslim poetry are still alive and continue to be appreciated by millions of people across the Islamic world. However, globalisation has not only touched the material lives of Muslims, it has also affected their cultural lives and their modes of thought and feeling. The process is disturbing: it threatens to break up the traditional legacies of societies, what is known as *turath*. It is subversive and threatening, yet quite inescapable.

The Muslim world is no longer – was it ever? – a safe enclosed universe with fine and captivating artefacts that express well-understood or learned tropes of glinting desire, of enchantment. That refined society of imagined reflections has been ripped apart by the driven brutality of the modern world, by the experience of cataclysmic wars and consequent suffering, by a profound loss of confidence and the dislocation of settled identity which was once secure within an Islamic fold.

A sense of betrayal, of desperate confusion, of social and intellectual turmoil, are caught and expressed in the dangers and attractions of a new, distraught and often challenging poetry. It offers thought and feeling searching for fresh meaning and purpose in (and beyond) the contemporary Muslim world. With modernity we move from the refined stanzas of classical Muslim poetry, of suffering and loss enacted with emblematic images and in strict forms of verse, to a poetry of calamity experienced, inscribed in language aching with despair and bitter anger against the godless charnel house of the modern world. At times, it drives poets like Adonis and Mahmoud Darwish to injured and inward utterance. The Muslim poets of today are by necessity often writing from the margins of what passes for public discourse in Muslim countries. These poets wrestle with the daily reality of a torn and bleeding body politic, filled with troubling notions of clashing identities.

There are several excellent contemporary Muslim poets practising their art, writers from Iraq, Egypt, Iran, North Africa, Pakistan, India, from various African states and many other countries both in the Muslim world and in the West. I shall mention a few who, I believe, represent some of the fundamental changes occurring in Muslim poetry today, starting with Ali Ahmed Said, alias Adonis.

A Space for Questions

This entire article could easily be devoted to the rich, troubled and troubling work of Ali Ahmad Said Asbar, who adopted the pseudonym Adonis. He was born in Syria in 1930 and lived for many years in Lebanon where he co-founded with the poet Yusuf al-Khal the journal *Shir*, which had an important influence on the development of Arabic poetry. In 1980 he emigrated to France. Adonis' poetry cannot extract itself from the politics of his times – nor does it seek to; it is enlivened by struggle, and it witnesses the suffering and complex treacheries of power and those wielding it. Adonis is widely admired in the Arab world for the originality of his poetry and for the bravura of his critique of the Muslim world. He moves out of the conventions of Arab poetry into Modernism and Surrealism whilst continuing to use the mystical imagery of Muslim poetry from the Middle East.

Adonis' poetry combines the revolutionary and anarchic drive – the *becoming* of reality – with the inner, mystical expression which we find in great classical Arabic Sufi poets such as Ibn Farid (1181-1235) and Ibn Arabi (1165-1240) who attempt to express through words, the *being* of reality. This is a difficult idea to grasp and perhaps, as long as it is only an idea, it is not graspable. However, Adonis sees an underlying unity that runs through all of life like a single note of music, which he tries to fuse with the revolutionary aspect of his poetry in a single harmonious vision. It is this aspect of his work with its paradoxes, its lucidity and lightness of tone, its sense of following a quest from the outer to the inner, suggesting a multiplicity of languages, forms and rhythmic structures that draws him to the works of the French symbolists and the surrealists.

His poetry expresses the despair and bewilderment of the present situation in the Arab world; it also flirts with insanity and with erotic bliss. It is poetry about existence, without the numbing language in which academic philosophy speaks of existence. Adonis shares with the 19th-century German philosopher Nietzsche a fascination with the power of creative destruction. He writes: 'We will die if we do not create gods/We will die if we do not kill them.' Gods have to be created so that we may live with meaning; the same gods have to be destroyed if we are to live with purpose.

Poetry, Adonis believes, has more important things to do than serve as a medium of ideology. He does not regard poetry as an envelope of certitude; rather, it is 'a question that begets another question'. He has a well-developed sense of being an outsider. Heresy, to Adonis, seems to be a natural place to work from; he is no friend of the submissive, hagiographic attitude to the past common amongst the more conservative. He is keen to challenge those who claim to be in possession of absolute truths. 'We live in a culture that does not leave space for questions', he laments, 'it knows all the answers in advance. Even God has nothing left to say.'

As I have already intimated, Adonis is a dangerous poet. He calls for a radical shift in the imagination of the Arab world that will free it from the limits of tradition. Until a way out is found, he argues, Arabs (we can safely add the entire Muslim world today) will only know modernity at second hand. They will be consumers of the dross and superficial aspects of modernity, but will not be creators and originators of modern thought.

Still, his critique of the Muslim Arab world does not make him a natural sycophant of the West. In 1971 he wrote a devastating and angry work about New York, which is both heaven and hell to him. I quote an extract from his prose/poem 'A Grave for New York':

> Picture the earth as a pear
> or breast.
> Between such fruits and death
> survives an engineering trick:
> New York,
> Call it a city on four legs
> heading for murder
> while the drowned already moan
> in the distance.
> New York is a woman
> holding, according to history,
> a rag called liberty with one hand
> and strangling the earth with the other.

To some, this poem is too much on the surface, just the sort of poetry Adonis claims to dislike – it is a howl of rage. However, this piece is more complex and witty, which raises it from the level of propaganda; it is in fact a profound indictment of the state of the Arab world, while at the same time it is a critique of the greed and corruption of the West. Adonis is trying to develop and encourage a new type of modern poetry that attempts to live in the present rather than hark back to some perfect past or to claim authenticity in a drive for communal loyalty. He writes in a telling poem entitled, 'Remembering The First Century':

> We blunder through prophecy as if through sand.
> 'Brother show us a sign that shall prevail.' History
> crumbles downhill like a babble of ants that
> choke on their own dust, on the filth of snails, on
> shell after shell....

Prophecy is as shifting and infertile as sand; history, too, is reduced to nullity falling down like a babble of ants that choke. We choke on our histories without reading them with perception and distance. Adonis wants to displace *tarab*, the beauty of the musicality of Arabic poetry, which creates a sort of ecstatic response from its listeners – which we saw earlier with traditional Urdu poetry. He wants to set this in the context of a more analytic, critical and less predictable subject-matter that is relevant to the problems that the Arab world faces today.

He does not deny the importance of form, and has written a remarkable work on *Arab Poetics* (2003). Adonis wants to break with tradition as a static given, rather than as reflexive and dynamic. Breaking with tradition does not necessarily mean adopting western styles of poetry, but developing or evolving new styles of poetry from within the Muslim/Arab tradition.

Displacement and Exile

Soleiman Adel Guémar is an Algerian poet who writes in French. He is a refugee in the UK and has recently published a book of poetry entitled *State of Emergency* (2007). These poems are expressions of alienation, anger and loss suffered by all exiles. They are memorable not because they make fine points of form elegantly crafted into bright and beautiful imagery; they are, instead, bound to the harrowing experience of the brutal civil war that raged for ten years in Algeria during the final decade of the 20th century, and took over 200,000 lives. This vicious war suppressed and negated the individual, making him voiceless. Guémar warns us:

> ...to speak the terror of murderous minutes
> that regulate the silence
>
> to cry into the treacherous night
> the enormous truth and keep quiet
> – keep quiet –
> hand over mouth on remembering

> that the cries are scattered
> as echoes over the rocks... [8]

The silence is regulated harshly, night is treacherous and the echoes of victims' cries are scattered. This is a hard, unforgiving world where power abuses and reduces the weak to voicelessness and leads them '... by the muzzle to the pit'. There is intense passion in this immediate, idiomatic language which unfolds, suggests, shouts about the terrible violence that appears as a strata of insanity and stricken loss, an embedded constant in many societies – and not only Muslim ones – today. Those in power are casually brutal and obscene, they rule by annulling the citizen who has no human rights. Even on formal occasions when the ruler arrives:

> ...the whole troop
> –including the colonel – stood to attention
> he barely saluted us as if
> we didn't exist
> then straight away scratched
> his crotch.

Even the colonel is simply a complicit tool of state violence, an echelon in the hierarchy of terror that incriminates the state. The ruler is so dismissive of all those beneath him that he scratches his crotch in an absented-minded gesture of contempt. Guémar speaks with lyrical, almost sensual intensity of an existence gripped by oppression answered by resistance. He describes with staccato, eager, gasping lines the state violence that accumulates shadowed traumas and threatens to crush private dreams. This is a painful poetry which spills into politics and outrage, it aspires to be the voice of the people; it demands to be read and reflected upon.

The poetry of Guémar and Adonis shows just how all-pervasive

---

[8] Soleiman Adel Guémar, *State of Emergency*, tr. John Goodby. (Todmorden, Lancashire, UK), p. 41. All other quotes from Guémar refer to this translation.

politics has become in Muslim societies. It is no longer a matter of choice – of choosing one's leaders or representatives, and of choosing whether to participate or not. It has become a matter of compulsion, we are compelled to submit and compelled to be political animals. There is no opt-out clause in the Muslim world, there is no area of private reverie or intimacy save for fugitive lyrical interludes that appear almost by oversight, beyond the purview of the state.

The Palestinian Mahmoud Darwish, who was born in 1942 in Palestine, was among the most important contemporary poets in the Arab world – and also gained respect for his public position on the necessity of human rights in the Muslim world. Darwish spent much of his life in exile. However, in 1996 he returned to his native land and settled in Ramallah on the West Bank, where he lived until his death in 2008. His poetry is infused with the politics of loss and suffering, but it is not as directly wounded as Guémar's verse. His imagination was intensely lyrical, textured with the details of daily life, of the beauty of women and landscapes. Darwish's often complex poetry made up of oscillating imagery, dancing with drastic instabilities, brings to life by way of a sympathetic magic, an entire sensibility rich with similarities and competing differences that ferment alternative and necessary realities.

Sometimes Darwish wrote fragments of shifting and transposed dialogues with peers and preceding presences, creating spectral visions of longing, loss and history that richly dissolve into myth. His is the poetry of exile nuanced with love, of desire that reaches out to the lost land or person enriched with the imagined serenity of absence. Yet, he tells us:

> No blood on the plows. A virginity renewing
> itself. There is no name for what life should be
> other than what you've made of my soul and
> what you make...[9]

---

[9] Mahmoud Darwish, *The Butterfly's Burden* (Port Townsend, Washington, DC, 2007), p. 39.

Despite the suffering of his people and of his own exile, Darwish transcended his situation – which was that of millions in the Muslim world – by seeking not for answers and solutions but by working toward redemption through a healing of wounds.

There are an increasing number of women poets in the Muslim world and abroad, who go against the displacement and exile of their gender from the mainstream of poetry. The late Forough Farrokhzhad (1935-1967) is a vital influence on the contemporary Persian scene, captured with perception and elegance in Farzaneh Milani's *Veils and Words* (1992). The Iraqi poet Nazik al-Malaika is associated with the free verse movement in the Arab world that broke with traditional verse forms during the 1940s and 1950s. Amira El-Zein writes both in Arabic and French and has translated the poetry of Mahmoud Darwish; Salma Khadra Jayyusi is another Palestinian poet, critic and literary historian, now working in the United States where she founded the acclaimed Project for Translation from Arabic (PROTA).

These are but some of those – women and men – striving toward a new poetics that is influenced by Muslim as well as western poetry, but also reacting against both traditions as all poetry must if it is to be grounded, relevant and valued. Poetry, like all other art forms, is not static, it changes. It changes not only in form but in the way the content is regarded and spoken about, explored and divided. Our own troubled times summon those changes with a fresh urgency.

Poetry matters because, like music, it removes us from the mundane; it teaches us to sense the unseen influences that mould us and mature us. Like prayer, it opens us to deeper layers of the self. It is a fragment of the greater jihad whereby we struggle to know ourselves more energetically, through the compunctions and chameleon-like compromises of language, to better the soul's imagining.

The lure and enchantment of poetry has a vast history and impact on our psyche, as we are herded into and distracted by the aggressive and consuming images that crowd the surfaces of our lives today. We may ignore poetry, we may forget it, but poetry will not ignore us, nor forget. It is the primordial language of our beginnings and the suggestive resonance of our faith. It enlightens and addresses the spirit in terms of our mortality; it presents us with a way to the middle of meaning and purpose, founded on a hidden and sacred sense of a greater presence that enlarges our lives with selflessness. In this way we may enter a scene of stillness where we learn to reflect on the world in which we find ourselves. In short, if we read poetry intelligently, if we let its alchemy better us, if we choose to attend to it, poetry can mould our identity and change us.

Identity is and will remain a vexed idea in our globalised world. The nostalgic longing for a pure identity is bound to fail, for our sense of identity seeps into the many Others that live amongst us. It does so in a modernity that constantly undermines our sense of self. Amid the confusion, poetry can be a door to a better appreciation of who we are and what we might become. We read not only for pleasure, but because we want to discover and imagine alternate modernities that are potentially rooted in the several cultures that make up the Muslim world to which we are heirs; poetry thus becomes the mirror in which we imagine ourselves anew.

Futher Reading

Adonis, Ali Ahmed Said Asbar. *The Pages of Day and Night.* Evanston, IL, 2000.

—— *A Time between Ashes and Roses.* Syracuse, NY 2004.

—— *Sufism and Surrealism.* London, 2005.

—— *An Introduction to Arab Poetics.* London, 2003.

—— *Qabr min ajl New York,* in *Al-Athar al-kamila 'shir',* 2 (Beirut, 1971). This poem is from the collection *Waqtin ma bayna al-ramad wal ward,* tr. Lena Jayyusi and Alan Brownjohn as 'A Grave for New York', in Salma Jayyusi, ed., *Modern Arabic Poetry: An Anthology.* New York, 1987.

Darwish, Mahmoud. *The Butterfly's Burden.* Port Townsend, Washington, DC, 2007.

Eliot, Thomas Stearns. *Selected Essays.* London, 1958.

Fuller, John. *The Space of Joy.* London, 2006.

Guémar, Soleiman Adel. *State of Emergency*, tr. John Goodby. Todmorden, Lancashire UK, 2007.

Hill, Geoffrey. *The Triumph of Love*. London, 1998.

Matthews, D.J., C. Shackle, S. Husain, *Urdu Literature*. London, 1985.

Milani, Farzaneh. *Veils and Words: The Emerging Voices of Iranian Women Writers*. New York, 1992.

Padel, Ruth. *The Poem and the Journey*. London, 2007.

____*52 Ways of Looking at a Poem*. London, 2002.

Rumi, Jalal al-din. *Words of Paradise: Selected Poems of Rumi*, tr. Raficq Abdulla. London, 2006.

12

The Digital Umma

Gary R. Bunt

The separation of religious activity between the 'cyber' and 'real' worlds is increasingly becoming hard to sustain. It is true that there are many elements of Muslim social space and society which are not online. Yet the internet is now an essential location for communication, the development of identity and the fostering of community networks for growing numbers of Muslims in the 21st century. Exploring elements of the understanding and practice of Islam that are placed online shows how Muslims creatively draw on the resources of the internet. Indeed, 'authorities' often pronounce on the legitimacy (or not) of the internet in terms of what they regard as appropriate Islamic values and concepts. And they do so more often than not on the internet itself.

For those with access to the internet, the umma or global Muslim community extends into cyberspace. As with the physical version, not all the points within a digital umma necessarily wish to link directly with one another. What the internet brings to the picture of Muslim networking and communication are the spaces within and between societies where like-minded individuals exchange ideas and information. This may take place – whether locally or globally – not just as an addition to conventional religious dialogue but as an alternative (and even a challenge) to it. Advocates of traditional modes of networking and exchange have had to rethink their ways of communicating in order to accommodate these new forms of Muslim space and expression online. In doing so, they have also reconsidered the meaning of authority – in part as a challenge to those who bypass previously held conventions or restraints.

Cyber Islamic Environments

In this chapter, the term 'cyber Islamic environments' refers to a variety of online settings and perspectives as well as applications of the media by those who define themselves as Muslims. These may offer specific ways of seeing the world – whether inclusive or exclusive – combined with regional and cultural understandings of the internet and its validity within Islamic contexts. Cyber Islamic environments have transformed aspects of religious understanding and expression among Muslims. In the process, issues of internet access, dialogue, networking and application of the media have become complex. What was originally an online internet space with an Islamic religious orientation, has now evolved to include fresh web tools and web-enabled telephones and televisions. We have online services such as blogs, social networking sites, media distribution channels and interfaces in which the web is integrated into 'traditional' media delivery, like media channels using online delivery in real time and types of storage.

Previously reluctant sectors of the umma recognised the need to go online, to meet the demands of their communities or networks. By creating attractive portals or gateways and services online, various shades of the Muslim spectrum sought to channel their readers and 'manage' knowledge associated with their belief perspectives. Sites include translations of the Quran, commentaries, chat-rooms, free email services, women's and children's spaces and online community services. Ideas of the sacred and what it implies play themselves out richly in cyberspace, reflecting the continuum of Muslim understandings located in the 'real world'. There is no single model.

Mobile phone access is another thriving channel for internet networking and information distribution, as networks expand, access increases and technology gets cheaper. Service providers have moved into the area of content provision, while competition to obtain licences to operate in various territories has grown and the markets are more regulated. All this has implications in relation to internet access in Muslim contexts.

The types of users have also evolved. It is a cliché to consider generational divides among internet users, but it is also true to say that there are generation(s) for whom the internet and technology in general is a 'natural' expectation for communication, obtaining news, commerce, entertainment and knowledge. This can include the development and exchange of 'packets of data' about Islam, although it is recognised that religiously oriented transactions form only a small component of overall net use by web users who define themselves as Muslim. Determining habits of web surfing is usually speculative: internet use is a highly personalised activity, with participants not necessarily willing to publicise what their activities are about. It is not possible to generalise about 'Muslim' internet surfing habits, though some general trends emerge which may also apply outside of Muslim contexts.

The use of technology has itself been a controversial topic in Muslim circles, but was endorsed at least for certain applications by such traditional authorities as Sheikh Mohamed Sayyid Tantawi at al-Azhar university in Cairo, a principal Sunni centre. A significant online database was launched by al-Azhar, containing manuscripts and a searchable Quran resource,[1] and a programme of digitizing a multitude of Islamic manuscripts was undertaken. Such endeavours are not unique. Institutions elsewhere dynamically embraced computer technology and cyberspace to further religious objectives. There is a project at Qom in Iran, for example, which offers a major Shia database that includes historical and contemporary scholarship on religious opinions.[2]

A very broad range of 'authoritative' Islamic opinions is located on the internet. They have a variety of agendas, ranging from tackling issues of everyday life through to providing commentary and inspiring advice in relation to world affairs. The online *fatwa*

[1] Al-Azhar Library, 'Index', 22 May 2005, *http://www.alazharonline.org/*.

[2] Aalulbayt Information Centre, 'Index', *http://www.al-shia.org*; Steffan Smith, 'Iran's clerics, ayatollahs go online', 1 June 2005, *http://www.middle-east-online.com/english* (citing Sayed Ibrahim Lajevardi of the Aalulbayt Information Centre in Qom).

has become commonplace, with petitioners emailing questions on assorted matters of principle and practice to authorities for a scholarly response. Everyday 'Islamic' online activities such as business, shopping, chat and social networking may fall under the radar of international headlines, but are no less important than 'jihadi' sites or online *fatwas*. One illustration is the abundance of 'Islamically approved' sites for arranging marriage and dating, which rank high in priority for individuals and communities alike.

Religious expressions and orientations located online range from the orthodox to the esoteric and the marginalised. They feature in a variety of settings and draw on many aspects of the internet, including 'Web 2.0' in which the internet serves as a platform for networking rather than just for the exchange of information. The world wide web, social networking sites, chat-rooms, video blogs (vblogs), collaborative wiki sites, podcasts and video upload sites such as *YouTube*, are some of the materials that have been used to represent aspects of Islam and Muslim expression. For those with access, computer use is a key part of political-religious-cultural expression, networking and understanding across generations.

The Digital Divide

While telecommunications play a vital role in Muslim contexts, there are serious differences in access to the various technologies among individuals and communities. Reports from the United Nations, governments and independent sources have drawn attention to the disparities in access among countries and also within them – generally referred to as the 'digital divide'. Access can vary in different settings, from the laying down of a telephone line, enabling simple dial-up access, through to the provision of high-speed connectivity, with wireless technology and mobile phone access. In Muslim as in global contexts at large, there are technology-rich urban locations with a multitude of entry points and connections to the internet, as well as rural environments with limited or no telephone facilities, unable to access the most basic of internet services. A United Nations report observes:

By the end of 2005, just over 15 per cent of the world's population were using the internet. However, the proportions are skewed in favour of richer countries. Over half the population in developed regions were using the internet in 2005, compared to 9 per cent in developing regions and 1 per cent in the 50 least developed countries.[3]

In an analysis of the world's internet users in June 2008, it was estimated that 39.3 per cent of users were in Asia; 3.5 per cent were in Africa; 2.9 per cent were in the Middle East; 43.4 per cent were in Europe and North America; 9.5 per cent in South America and the Caribbean; and 1.4 per cent in Oceania and Australia.[4] It was noted that from 2000 to 2008, the growth in internet usage in Africa was 1031.2 per cent, in Asia 401.8 per cent, and in the Middle East 1176.8 per cent. These figures provide some indication of the immense rise in internet access in Muslim contexts, and also of the gaps that still exist among regions.

The International Telecommunications Union (ITU) provides two basic indices for analysis, the Digital Opportunity Index (DOI) and the ICT Opportunity Index. The ITU's *World Information Society Report 2007* contains a classification of 50 Least Developed Countries that represent 11.9 per cent of the world's population, including a number of countries with substantial Muslim populations. Leading the table for access according to the DOI score are Bahrain, United Arab Emirates and Qatar. The DOI does not include social, cultural and gender variations, which can be significant. The United Nations Development Programme (UNDP)

[3] United Nations, 'Millennium Development Goals Report 2007', *http://mdgs.un.org/unsd/mdg/News.aspx?ArticleId=34*.
[4] Internet World Stats, 'World Internet Users and Population Stats, World Internet users by world religions', 30 June 2008, *http://www.internetworldstats.com/stats.htm*.

made telephone access, cellular access and internet access priorities within the Millennium Development Goals for the year 2015, stressing cooperation with the private sector.[5]

When it comes to the cost of internet access, the reach of technological infrastructure is a critical issue. As developers and commercial enterprises seek out new markets, sub-Saharan Africa is one example of an area becoming ripe for developing internet access through a variety of interfaces and innovations, including satellite-based systems that facilitate access in remote areas. This is a pattern that also applies in other locations with Muslim populations. A 2008 report found that high-speed internet users in Arab countries paid significantly more for their internet services than equivalent users in Europe, while the connection speed and download times were substantially slower.[6] Innovations that would enhance access, such as the latest generation of mobile phones, were by no means standard.

In some situations, the expansion of connectivity can be stimulated by political factors and conflict. For instance, there was a major effort to improve links among and within Palestinian communities worldwide, especially in refugee camps and across the jurisdiction of the Palestinian Authority.[7] Likewise, internet cafes became popular in Iraq after the 2003 US-led invasion. These sites offered better quality connections than domestic telephone systems, which had become targets of bombings.[8] A combination

---

[5] The goals stem from the Millennium Summit of 189 countries that was held in September 2000. United Nations Development Programme, 'Millennium Development Goals, Target 8f: In cooperation with the private sector, make available the benefits of new technologies, especially information and communications', 1 September 2008, http://www.undp.org/mdg/goal8.shtml.

[6] The National, 'Internet in Arab world overpriced, study says', 9 June, 2008, http://www.thenational.ae/article/20080609/BUSINESS/59489486/1053/rss.

[7] Laila El-Haddad. 'Intifada spurs Palestine internet boom'. Al-Jazeera, 11 December 2003. http://english.aljazeera.net/NR/exeres/3707F879-1FB0-41BD-AC75-AF49B2F9F87A.htm

[8] USA Today, 'Iraqis making connection to the outside world online', 5 January 2006, http://www.usatoday.com/news/world/iraq/2006-01-05-iraq-internet_x.htm?csp=34.

of poor telecommunications infrastructure and conflict also led to a growth in the use of email and online chat in Somalia, Somaliland and associated diaspora communities.[9]

Many Muslim regions previously poorly served by telecommunications in general, and the internet in particular, are now becoming emerging markets in which telecommunications companies compete to provide a variety of services. As part of this process, it is natural that content providers, including those with Islamist interests and orientations, will enter these information marketplaces. This has added further stimulus to a complex and competitive area of Islamic knowledge development and dissemination.

Not all aspects of Islam and Muslim societies are fully represented online, especially those from Muslim cultural-religious contexts with low levels of internet connectivity. This situation is evolving as access improves. The picture is complicated because of the expansion of alternate points of access, like cell phones, as opposed to conventional 'desk based' interfaces.

Access is also linked to other factors, especially education, general literacy and computer literacy. The use of a computer may require general literacy, although use of online telephone and video conferencing services would only require a basic (or possibly assisted) literacy. User-friendly interfaces and touch-screens have alleviated the need for keyboard skills in some contexts. The placing of computers in cyber cafes, phone shops and public spaces enables not only basic internet functions of e-mailing and net surfing, but also primary communication, especially when other phone systems are poor. Access issues relate to infrastructures, within built environments as much as in virtual contexts. Having public places where the internet is available is important for those for whom cost or logistics are barriers to obtaining a computer and a connection in a home environment. Technology is integrated into new building projects, such as hotels or mosques. Cyber cafes have a place within the fabric of many places with Muslim populations. Yet there may be sectors of populations who for reasons of culture

---

[9] Joseph Winter. 'Telecoms thriving in lawless Somalia'. *BBC News*, 19 November 2004. *http://news.bbc.co.uk/1/hi/world/africa/4020259.stm.*

or religious interpretation are unable to access those public places, such as women in some Muslim settings.

Wireless broadband services have become popular in many cities, and have also been seen as a possible solution to net access issues in other contexts, being cost-effective (compared with cables), in municipal as well as in rural sites. Each area requires solutions specific to its own environment and interests.

As the technology continues to develop, it is likely that the ways in which authority is transmitted will take into account new technical developments. These include social networking sites, podcasting and wider VoIP (Voice Over Internet Protocol) access. The extension of internet technology access – for example, in sub-Saharan Africa – is opening up new markets for specific forms of religious authority, perhaps challenging traditional norms. In part, this may represent a reflection of 'real world' activities, but also to some extent a speeding up of competing processes of propagating one's views.

A further issue that shapes access is how the government and providers of internet and telecommunications services relate to one another. Where this trio of interdependent elements fails to work 'in sync', the consumer pays the price. Governments have generally encouraged the private sector to develop high-speed (ADSL) services. The loss of internet connections or bandwidth can be catastrophic. But the politics of the relationship can be as challenging in Muslim as in global contexts at large.

The internet has not at present trumped the traditional forms of political expression. But it is a means through which to get past conventional boundaries and barriers. Political expression online forms part of the dialogue about Muslim identities. Opposition voices, creating websites outside of the direct influence of governments, have propagated their views through channels that have been difficult for authorities to censor or block. The investment by governments in filtering and censoring technologies has led to an increase in the technical ingenuity of opposition and activist platforms. All of these issues add to the complexity of cyber Islamic environments, at once fragmented, dynamic and spontaneous – all containing an essence of Muslim concerns and identities.

The reduction of a digital divide is also associated with the availability of cheaper and more accessible hardware, software and infrastructures – especially when they become available in local languages. In the early days of the internet, English was the natural language for many early adopters of technology (including Muslims), reflecting the educational backgrounds and aspirations of software and site developers, as well as the available applications. There have been levels of change in this, as the internet market adjusts. There is substantial software content in Turkish, Indonesian, Somali, Malay, Farsi and Arabic, but a relative absence of content in Urdu and Bangla. Other markets, including sub-Saharan Africa and Central Asian republics, are also demonstrating growth in Islamic materials. Associated with this is the availability of web addresses (URLs or uniform resource locators) in non-Roman scripts, such as Arabic, Farsi and Urdu. In 2008, the Internet Corporation for Assigned Names and Numbers (ICANN) sought to change the way in which web addresses could be enabled, to accommodate non-Roman scripts.

Creative Access

What is called 'open source' software – free or low-cost for development, distribution and use – can be adapted to the needs of users in various languages. The Linux operating system is an example of how such a platform can be created and adapted as an alternative to regular commercial software such as Microsoft Windows. The Ubuntu software system, free to download and based on Linux, has been developed collaboratively through forums and the sharing of data. Ubuntu applications include an open source web browser, email package, word processor, spreadsheet and financial software, media players and instant messaging. It is like commercial software, but without the need for paid licenses. Development work on adapting Ubuntu is underway in a number of languages with substantial numbers of Muslim users, including Albanian, Arabic, Bosnian, Farsi, Malay, Swahili and Urdu.

A Muslim edition of Ubuntu has also been developed. This integrated package is designed as open source software with an

Islamic ethos attached. Its website says: 'we think that for Muslim users it would be great to have "out of the box" Islamic software and tools installed as well'.[10] The package offers conventional Ubuntu operating system and software material, typical of all Ubuntu releases, and Arabic support. It also includes a parental control tool for 'safe' internet browsing, however that might be defined. Other components in the package include a Quran study tool (Zekr 0.7.0) that can play recitations of the scripture, a 'Prayer Times' feature (Minbar and Firefox), a display of Islamic prayers (*Monajat*), an encyclopedia (*Thwab*) and Islamic wallpapers.

Conceivably, it is possible to install all its products through an internet search; the advantage with this particular package is that everything is available in a single installation, which would be particularly relevant for anyone with limited knowledge of computers and the internet. Some elements would also be useful to anybody without an internet connection, especially in relation to the pre-packaging of Quran materials (available on CD-Rom).

From this basic platform, given its open source nature, there is potential for this software to be adapted to different forms of Muslim expression. So, for example, packages representing under-standings and interpretations of Islam relating to aspects of Shiism or Sufism could have their own open source software. Hence, it could also allow for differences in daily religious practice and in the interpretation of basic Islamic sources.

The integration of databases, including religious opinions, which could be searchable and limited to one particular religious perspective, could also be a future development within an open source package of this nature. Quranic commentary based on particular worldviews and religious outlooks might be integrated into software packages, together with translations that represent political or religious positions. One scenario could be that all computers sold in specific religious and cultural settings are required to include software that meets local concerns (legitimate or otherwise); one can imagine a dialogue between religious/political authorities and

[10] Ubuntume.com, 'Ubuntu Muslim Edition 8.04.1', 9 September 2008, *http://ubuntume.com/*.

computer developers in which such packages are negotiated. In educational contexts, this could be in conjunction with regular filtering and controls, which are already an issue. There is also the possibility of a Qom or al-Azhar edition of Ubuntu, or similar products.

The relative absence of materials in Muslim languages was previously a constraint for internet access, but now the information *souq* is becoming saturated with products. The use of Web 2.0 interfaces may bring Muslim societies up to speed rapidly, with rapid growth in internet access being a driving factor. Micro-networks associated with specific belief patterns can rely heavily on information and computer technology to facilitate collaboration and networking across and beyond national frontiers.

As software applications diversify and improve in technical quality, they generate new discussions within Islamic communities, representing ongoing struggles to accommodate or interpret the new issues technology presents. Major computer corporations have established themselves in markets with significant Muslim populations, and adapted their products, marketing and technical support accordingly. The computer industries have placed themselves firmly within Muslim contexts.

The commercial sector has also been responsible for the development of search technology for diverse language and regional markets. Major changes in the wider web structure have an impact, such as the establishment of Arabic-language search engines. Google's search engines also developed a strong profile in various Muslim majority regions, with versions in languages including Arabic, Bosnian, Kurdish, Malay, Persian, Turkish, Swahili and Urdu. Enhanced 'searchability' has an impact on the access of Islam-related content in Arabic across the Middle East, and beyond. Search engines like Google, which are already highly adaptable to specific markets, websites and tastes, could be shaped in relation to culturally and religiously specific perspectives and frameworks.

Blogs and Filters

There has been a global surge in recent years in blogs – short for web logs that cover everything from commentary to 'personal' diaries – a trend that Muslims have readily embraced. Dedicated sites for blogging are offered by a wide range of sources, from newspapers and magazines to individual social and political personalities. They draw people from all walks of life into what has come to be known as the 'blogosphere', the actual size of which is hard to measure.

A number of prominent Muslim bloggers have used English as their communication medium in the formative period, but now blogging tools are available in Arabic, Farsi and many other languages. Much has been written about the enthusiasm for blogs among young Iranian women and men, expressing themselves not only on high politics and culture but also personal matters such as dating and dressing preferences. Iraq, too, has a thriving blogosphere that is fed by accounts of the challenges of daily life in the aftermath of the 2003 invasion.[11]

With the growth in internet access and use, especially through blogs, comes the question of censorship. What are seen as breaches of religious norms or attacks against state policy are the main factors that attract forms of censorship. When it comes to matters such as child pornography, the endeavour by authorities and in some cases internet service providers to limit access is fairly universal. However, the 'freedom of speech' issue is a complex one, and not only in the cyber world, especially when it comes to issues of Muslim expression and interpretation. Indeed, this issue indicates a growing awareness and sensitivity about the impact of the internet on social values, and also its usefulness in advancing a variety of political and religious agendas. As the spectrum of web-based resources expands, it becomes harder to monitor their use, no matter how much time and money is invested in filtering, censorship or research.

---

[11] See especially Nasrin Alavi, *We Are Iran: The Persian Blogs* (Vancouver, 2005); Pax Salam, *Salam Pax: The Baghdad Blog* (London, 2003); and Riverbend, *Baghdad Burning: Girl Blog from Iraq* (London, 2006).

Defining what is hostile to the interests of society or a community can be a highly subjective matter. In Saudi Arabia, it may be *fatwas*, sermons, and/or interpretations that deviate from state policy. In Malaysia, it may be blogs that are seen as inciting tensions among ethnic groups. Censorship can take many forms. Closing down or closely controlling a local blog or service provider for carrying hostile content may be easier than filtering content that is hosted abroad. Certain content may require passwords to access, or shift rapidly across different internet locations, making it difficult to censor. In some cases, the original source of dissent may be beyond censorship or control. In other cases, 'dissident' opinions have been circulated through content masquerading as 'mainstream' authoritative sources.

Protests that some governments are indexing and filtering political opposition, using software from international corporations, raises issues related to 'security' at the national and international levels. This is especially so with regard to the information flow from 'jihadi' and other potentially destabilizing forces online, on which more later. Governments have found more sophisticated means to monitor and control such flows of information, including encryption programmes that impinge on exchanges of email. At the same time, abundant advice is made available online on how to evade controls of internet usage.

Complaints have often emerged from diverse Muslim perspectives on what are seen as willfully anti-Islamic materials published online. Not all objectionable materials were necessarily produced and/or published in the complainants' own countries, making censorship and restrictions problematic. One example is the 2005 episode of the Danish cartoons of the Prophet Muhammad, which began in the print media but quickly spread to the internet, and provoked both official and public distress and protest in dozens of countries. Muslim governments have had to adjust to the consequences of the internet as a phenomenon. Many have recognised the importance of going online, and have done so with varying degrees of effectiveness, developing websites both for domestic and international audiences. Censorship can take many forms, in attempts to prevent apparent breaches of societal and religious norms. Many of these issues are in fact universal – as with pornography, which represents a significant portion of internet content – and their impact is of concern in Muslim and global settings alike.

The Online Muslim Spectrum

A variety of Muslim social welfare, educational and charitable organisations have a presence on the web. Muslim-oriented financial and business sectors are engaging fully with the digital age. The internet represents an important window for those outside of these communities to understand more about Muslim issues and concerns. Cyber Islamic environments offer networking opportunities for a complex array of Muslim viewpoints and causes, with the capacity to interact with the mundane and 'real world' issues, whilst generating an evolving sense of online Muslim identity for those with the inclination, time and access opportunities.

Again, the cyber environment has been congenial for forms of affiliation and networking beyond those of the mainstream, or of militants seeking to present themselves as speaking for Islam. Branches of Sufi and Shia Islam find expression online in ways that are as creative as they are varied. Sufism in its multifaceted forms and strands of thought is often an avenue for the expression of popular Islam on the internet. Sufi websites can range from detailed academic resources of Muslim philosophy, through to individual devotional pages, emerging from a variety of social, cultural and religious contexts. As with many other aspects of Islam, sites with information about Sufism may include academic materials and/or content generated by followers of a specific order. Such sites can link members across continents, enhancing networking and a sense of religious affiliation among members – while also reinforcing distinctiveness in practice and culture.

One example is the Khanqah Chishti Nizami Habibi Sufi order based in Pietermaritzburg, South Africa. While networking with member communities across South Africa, the order also highlights its origins in and affinities with the Indian subcontinent. The site was sponsored by a local business. The order's main page features photos of its *khanqah* in Pietermaritzburg, its national headquarters in Durban, and the international headquarters of the order, based in Ajmer, India. The site offers audio material, including lectures and sermons, uploaded on a regular basis, together with guided reading suitable for specific events in the order's calendar.

Lectures cover topics from interpretations of milestone events in Islamic history (including Quranic revelation and compilation) to esoteric understandings of lived faith. The order's roots and founders are also emphasised in these lectures. Other site content includes an extensive *shajrah* (tree) of the order and its affiliates, linking the South African order with its predecessors in India, Iraq and Pakistan, going back to Mecca and the Prophet Muhammad. The *shajrah* is recited after prayers and an explanation is provided. This certainly provides valuable insight into a specific expression of Sufism and its antecedents. In this way their online presence facilitates unity within the order, while expressing its distinctiveness in the larger Muslim setting.

There are other examples of approaches toward the expression of Sufism in the cyber world. Some present a more globalised perspective, focusing on dissemination of key concepts and tracts through publications. The Nimatullahi order provides content in nine languages on its website, focusing on the teachings of its late Master, Javad Nurbakhsh (d. 2008). Detailed 'discourse' seeks to explain this interpretation of Sufism to a westernised audience, with short pieces on key elements of belief. As well as offering subscriptions to its magazine, the site links to the online vendor Amazon for purchase of books by Nurbakhsh (the books themselves do not appear in electronic versions on the website).

The Association of Islamic Charitable Projects (AICP) or al-Ahbash *tariqa* of Lebanon has an extensive website. It mounts a challenge to aspects of political Islamism, notably those that are hostile to Sufism – though after negotiations it has had good relations with Hizbullah and also enjoys close ties with a number of Arab governments. AICP's pages contain Quranic recitations, English and Arabic audio lessons, and a large archive of Islamic photographs, ranging from conventional images of Mecca and

Medina to the shrines of Sufi shaykhs. The audio archive has recordings of chants and devotional music, indicative of the 'popular' expression of Islam, available in a variety of formats. There are numerous other examples of Sufi expression online, allowing followers to express their fealty to an order, and allowing spiritual guides to communicate with their followers across the globe.

Diversity online is also represented among branches of Shia Islam, such as the Dawoodi Bohras. Indeed, their *Mumineen.org* site includes technical discussions within a blog about Java script, databases, streaming and software issues. Members of the network collaborate on aspects of this at various levels, which can be seen as a religious duty. The World Federation of Khoja Shia Ithna-asharis developed a sophisticated framework linking members and businesses from different regions. To some extent these present an integrated Khoja Shia Ithna-ashari perspective online. However, they also demonstrate specific aspects of regional diversity, such as in the presentation of issues with local implications.

A further relevant example would be the long-standing development of Ismaili content online. Communities have been producing materials online from the early days of the web browser, with a growing focus on social development and education resources relating to the Aga Khan Development Network (AKDN). There are also websites, official and unofficial, that are more specific to community affairs, in which the activities of the Imam, presently Aga Khan IV, are central. In addition, blogging pages and social networking sites can easily be found expressing aspects of Ismaili identity online. A proportion of this content is hosted on generic blogging services such as Wordpress or Friendster; as such, they are integrated into the overall structure of the internet.

A quick search on Google will display the ways in which Ismaili teachings are presented online. This occurs in an ever-changing and fluid manner, which is organic in the way it responds to trends and issues. It certainly shows the diversity of Ismaili traditions, not only among regions in terms of language and outlook, but within regions as well (indeed, the community has a large diaspora in North America and Europe); this is also evident from the resources provided by the website of The Institute of Ismaili Studies (IIS), available in five languages. Many sites that discuss aspects of Ismaili traditions form part of the larger cyber world that includes open source information pages such as Wikipedia. In secular matters, a range of services is offered by Ismaili individuals and enterprises that may be adaptations of conventional web services and products. The sites demonstrate networking among affiliations associated with Ismaili communities on many levels. In many ways, they are an extension of historical patterns of networking, especially within communities of the Indian subcontinent.

Any discussion relating to Islam in the cyber world is no longer tenable without attending to 'jihadi' discourse, which now commonly refers to an orientation marked by militancy. Particularly after the events of September 11, 2001, jihadi activities in cyberspace have generated heated discussion in both community and academic contexts. Such activities represent an interface between virtual and 'real' conflict. By far the most prominent focus of attention is the use of internet technology by entities and networks that share an al-Qaeda ethos, for which the net has acted as a logistical tool, a propagation outlet and a reinforcement weapon for global brand(s) under many names. Some key aspects of this development are discussed in Bruce Lawrence's chapter in this volume.

As much as any sector in cyberspace, those applying militaristic approaches to the term 'jihad' have benefited from improvements in internet access, a reduction of the digital divide and increased web literacy. Media campaigns have been shaped by applying the internet as an effective method to corner support, intimidate opponents, develop logistical planning and in some cases facilitate the raising of funds to support military campaigns.

The influential jihadi strategist and writer, Abu Musab al-Suri (Mustafa bin Abd al-Qadir Setmariam Nasar) wrote about this in his many works and lectures, many of which have been published online. There is an emphasis on the importance of computer science, not only as a logistical tool but as a propagation outlet. This was part of a recognition that strategies must adapt to the contemporary age, while also acknowledging that limited public literacy and education was a constraint on the success of some jihadi organisations. Not only have email and the internet become primary outlets for al-Suri's publications and statements, online communication represents the focus of his strategic outlook. Al-Suri's major work, *The Global Islamist Resistance Call*, was widely distributed online, offering analyses of the successes and failures of jihadi movements and ideas.[12]

Similarly, the statements of key figures in al-Qaeda, including Osama bin Laden and Ayman al-Zawahiri, have regularly been distributed online, including through audiovisual materials. Many other campaigns, including those unconnected with al-Qaeda, have used the internet to promote their objectives. They tend to assert an 'Islamic' ethos, both in terms of their beliefs and campaigns, even if their claims may seem abhorrent to most Muslims. Such a phenomenon is not unique to the Muslim world of course, nor to the contemporary age.

Conclusion

Whether presenting the Quran or other forms of 'knowledge', devotion and community life, there is a plurality of ways in which digital platforms compete for attention in the cyber world. Whether they succeed or not has much to do with the digital divide in the Muslim world (as elsewhere). This will not only influence access in the first instance, but also perceptions of Islamic issues by Muslims as well as non-Muslims. This includes how specific interpretations are disseminated and responded to, and networks are created and reinforced. In an era of globalisation, enabling access allows opportunities for greater awareness of, and engagement in, the numerous dialogues about what it means to be Muslim.

For those with access, the internet provides rich opportunities for dialogue about Islam, and for accessing information on interpretation, history and diversity associated with it. This is especially relevant for societies and individuals who, prior to being able to access the internet, felt disconnected from aspects

---

[12] Brynjar Lia, *Architect of Global Jihad: the Life of Al-Qaeda Strategist Abu Musab Al-Suri* (London, 2007).

of Islam such as sources of knowledge and religious authority. The internet presents opportunities for religious discussion and access to data that can be enabling – not least where they bypass more traditional sources of knowledge and authority. Women and minorities are often among the key beneficiaries. In turn, the traditional sources respond by establishing their own resources online, often in competition with other media-literate players and sources.

The internet has also encouraged greater attention to communities and perspectives within the Muslim diaspora. North American and western European Muslims are conspicuous in every form of cyber expression, from blogs and websites to electronic databases on history and religious practice. Old ways of seeing the Muslim world – or for that matter the world at large – in the terms of 'centre' and 'periphery' were already being altered by globalisation; cyberspace routinely overturns such assumptions. At the same time, while the digital age has wrought profound shifts and reassessment of tradition and communication within the digital umma, longstanding historical themes associated with Islam and Muslim identity retain a common thread. This is no less true of the cyber world than the physical one, which reminds us of the continuities across those worlds that are felt and expressed by the umma at large.

Further Reading

Bunt, Gary R. *Islam in the Digital Age: E-jihad, Online Fatwas and Cyber Islamic Environments*. London, 2003.

Eickelman, Dale and Jon W. Anderson, ed. *New Media in the Muslim World: The Emerging Public Sphere*. 2nd ed. Bloomington, IN, 2000.

Ernst, Carl W., 'Ideological and Technological Transformations of Contemporary Sufism', in Miriam Cooke and Bruce B. Lawrence, ed. *Muslim Networks from Hajj to Hip Hop*, Chapel Hill, NC, 2005.

Karim, Karim H., ed. *The Media of Diaspora: Mapping the Globe.* London, 2003.

Mandaville, Peter G. *Transnational Muslim Politics: Reimagining the Umma.* London, 2001.

Poole, Elizabeth and John E. Richardson, ed. *Muslims and the News Media.* London, 2006.

Roy, Olivier. *Globalised Islam: The Search for a New Ummah.* London, 2004.

Sakr, Naomi, ed. *Arab Media and Political Renewal: Community, Legitimacy and Public Life.* London, 2007.

Index

Abbasids, 159, 214, 223
Abduh, Muhammad, 10, 67
Abou El Fadl, Khaled, 77, 81–82
Abrahamic tradition, 211, 221, 244, 245
Abyssinia, emigration to, 90
adl (social justice), 133
Adonis (Ali Ahmed Said Asbar),
    282–285, 286–287
al-Afghani, Jamal al-din, 10, 67, 246
Afghanistan, 19, 20, 27, 102–103, 125,
    127, 178, 256
Africanus, Leo (Hasan al-Wazzan), 10,
    110
Aga Khan
    Architecture Programme, 17, 178
ahd, see covenant
Ahl al-Kitab (People of the Book), 14,
    47, 158, 167, 173
Akbar (Mughal ruler), 232, 233, 272
Ali b. Abi Talib, 159, 168
Almohads, 218–221, 222, 224, 229, 235
Almoravids, 217–219, 220, 222
Aman (Fatimid), 19, 158–159, 161–163,
    164, 165, 166, 167, 168, 169–173
Amman Declaration, 2005, 7, 255
Andalusia (Muslim/Moorish Spain), 20,
    109, 157, 158
aql, see intellect
Aquinas, Thomas, 117
Arkoun, Mohammed, 80, 82
Arwa, Sulayhid queen, 174
al-Asam, al-Hasan, 164
Asbar, Ali Ahmed Said, 282
Asharis (medieval movement), 15, 63, 64

Attar, Farid al-din, 273
Ayman al-Zawahiri, 126, 308
Ayyubids, 224, 225
al-Azhar university, 17, 20, 134, 223, 243,
    293

Babylon, 20, 222
Badshahi Mosque, 185
Baghdad, 4, 6, 9, 13, 17, 95, 116, 129,
    183, 216, 228, 239, 240, 243
Bahrain, 22, 164, 295
baraka (blessings), 271
Barlas, Asma, 72–73, 77, 78
batin (esoteric meaning), 62, 203
Bayt al-Hikma, 95, 174, 239, 243
baya (allegiance), 33, 147
Bible, 5, 13
bin Laden, Osama, 8, 126, 308
BRAC (Bangladesh Rural Advancement
    Committee), 258
blogs, 292, 294, 302, 303, 309
Bucaille, Maurice, 69
Buddhist, 20
Byzantine empire, 14, 39, 41, 49, 60, 164,
    213, 222

Cairo, 16, 17, 209, 213, 222–227, see also
    al-Qahira
calligraphy, 181–182, 224
caravanserai, 110–111
Catholics, 6, 203, 210, 215
Charter of Medina (also Constitution
    of), 157–158, 168
China, 9, 111, 112, 185, 203, 204, 238

Chinese civilisation, 5
Chishti Nizami Habibi (Sufi order), 304
Christianity, Christians, 5, 18, 20, 39, 45,
    46, 47, 49, 50, 60, 88–89, 90, 92,
    94–95, 97, 98, 100, 101, 102, 110, 158,
    190, 192, 203, 211, 214, 215, 216, 221,
    228, 231, 241, 245
civil liberties, 8
civil society, 23, 102, 103, 258, 260
'clash of civilisations', 4
'clash of ignorance', 5, 104
colonialism, 126, 134, 135
complementary/non-formal education,
    256
Conference of the Birds, 23
Cordoba, 16, 95, 203, 213–217, 221, 235,
    240
cosmopolitanism, 20, 104, 110, 119
contextualist (see also textualist,
    exegesis), 73–74
covenant (*ahd*), 49, 167–168, 172
cyber-hajj, 123
cybernauts, 124, 125, 129, 130
cyberspace, 21, 108, 124, 129, 130, 293,
    307, 309
Cyrus II, of Persia, 20

Damascus, 13, 28, 60, 214
Daniel, Norman, 96
Danish cartoons episode, 303
Dar al-Hikma, 174
Dar al-Islam, 110, 115, 128, 129, 192,
    198, 210, 212, 213
Darwish, Mahmoud, 18, 282, 287–288
dawa, 160, 163, 174
Dawoodi Bohras, 306
Delhi, 16, 213, 231–235
Descartes, René, 246
dhimma, 167, 168, 221
digital divide, 294–299, 307, 308
Digital Opportunity Index (DOI), 295
Diwan al-Insha, 240
Djenne, Great Mosque of, 184

Eck, Diana, 87
Education, 6, 17, 120, 136, 222, 237–241,
    242–244, 246, 247–250, 252–254,
    255–258, 260, 261–262, 297, 301

and alternative education, 256, 257, 260,
    261
and formal schooling, 255, 256, 257,
    262
and learning ethos, 238, 248
tertiary, 252
Education For All (EFA), 238, 248, 250,
    258
Egypt, 7, 10, 72, 147, 157, 158, 159–161,
    162, 163, 164, 165, 166, 167, 169, 173,
    198, 223, 226, 227, 240, 252
Eliot, T.S., 265, 268–269
Enlightenment, 92, 117, 119, 179, 245
Esack, Farid, 74, 93
Esposito, John L., 5, 7
ethics, 17, 22, 23, 58, 75, 93, 102, 103,
    148, 255, 261
Europe, 5, 9, 22, 95, 96, 116, 117, 118,
    119–120, 121, 135, 190, 193, 206, 209,
    212, 235, 245–246, 258, 296, 309
exegesis, 15, 42, 58, 59, 60, 61, 62, 63–73,
    77, 82, 83, 84

Faiz, Ahmed Faiz, 276–277, 279
fatwa (legal opinion), 21, 78, 166, 172,
    293–294, 303
al-Farabi, 15, 66, 79, 245
Farrokhzad, Forough, 288
Faruqi, Ismail, 254
Fathy, Hassan, 198
Fatimids, 19, 157, 158, 159, 162, 164,
    166, 167, 168, 173, 174, 223–224,
    240
'five pillars' (of Islam), 11, 12, 114
France, 5, 8, 9, 10, 235, 246

geometry, 181, 229
Ghalib, Mirza, 263, 275–276
ghazal (poetic form), 263, 276, 277
al-Ghazali, 69, 117, 244
globalisation, 9, 23, 200, 202–203, 238,
    255, 260, 262, 281, 308
Guémar, Soleiman Adel, 285, 286,
    287

hadith, 11, 12, 18, 42, 44, 61, 62, 64–65,
    114, 136, 138–139, 180, 237, 240
Hafiz, 263, 273, 280

hajj (pilgrimage), 12, 96, 108–109, 123, 183, 185
Hassan II Mosque, 189, 201
Hindu, 20, 102, 192, 232, 233, 234
Hill, Geoffrey, 265, 269, 270
hijab, 40–41, 81, 96
Hizbullah, 305
Hodgson, Marshall, 4, 11, 33
Homer, 270, 274
Hulegu (Khan), 4
human rights, 15, 76, 134, 255, 286, 287
Huntington, Samuel, 4
hybrid schools, 17, 256
hypostyle, mosque architecture, 184

ibadat (worship), 139, 232
Ifriqiya (Tunisia and Eastern Algeria), 159, 168, 214
Ibn Arabi, 15, 66, 272, 283
Ibn Battuta, 10, 21, 109, 110, 111, 112, 114, 115, 116, 117, 121, 128, 129, 228, 244
Ibn Farid, 283
Ibn Ishaq, 90, 95
Ibn Khaldun, 3, 109, 110, 212, 242, 243
Ibn Rushd, 15, 66, 96, 245
Ibn Sina, 66, 75, 117, 245
identity, 11, 20, 97, 102, 136, 178, 192–193, 194, 196, 199, 200, 202, 203–205, 289, 309
Idris, Imad al-din, 162, 222
al-Idrisi, 9, 96
ijaza, 113
ijma (consensus), 138
ijtihad (independent interpretation), 19, 124, 137, 138, 154, 278
Ikhwan al-Safa (Brethren of Purity), 15
Imam-caliph, 158, 161, 166, 168
Imam Hatip schools, 256
iman (faith), 12
Indian domed mosque, 184
Indonesia, 72, 75, 185, 187, 203, 204, 252
Information Age, 122, 129, 130
intellect (*aql*), 237
interfaith dialogue, 7, 87, 88, 89, 90, 97, 98, 103

International Telecommunications Union (ITU), 295
internet, 9, 21, 22, 122–123, 124, 126, 127, 129, 130, 291, 292–294, 295–297, 298, 299, 300, 301, 302, 303–304, 307, 308–309
Iqbal, Muhammad, 67, 246, 277, 278
Iraq, 102, 118, 128, 197, 228, 296, 302
Iran, 4, 6, 27, 40, 94, 118, 184, 193, 201, 228, 231, 293
Isfahan, 16, 184, 213, 227–231, 234, 235
Islamic socialism, 195
Islamisation, 165, 254
islamophobia, 259
isnad (chain of transmission), 42
Ismaili, 104, 159, 160, 162, 164, 190, 231, 306, 307
Istanbul, 9, 188, 223, 227

jahiliyya (time of darkness), 15, 150, 211
al-Jahiz, 239, 247
jamatkhana, 190
Jami al-hikmatayn, 273
Jayyusi, Salma Khadra, 288
Jews, Jewish, 5, 14, 18, 19, 20, 27, 28–29, 30, 31, 45, 46, 47–48, 49, 50, 89, 90, 95, 96, 158, 167, 215, 218, 221, 227
jihad, 22, 96, 118, 126, 220, 224, 278, 288, 303, 307–308
Jinnah, Muhammad Ali, 194, 247–248
Jordan, 7, 153, 255
Judaism, 28, 49, 88, 89, 211, 215, 245
Jyllands-Posten (Danish newspaper), 8

Karamah, 154
Khadija (Muhammad's wife), 18, 36, 38, 142
Khan, Sayyid Ahmed, 10, 67
khanqah (Sufi lodge), 15, 226, 304, 305
Kharaji, 61, 62–63, 157, 159
Khusraw, Nasir-i, 273–274
Khutbat al-wadaa, 148, 152
al-Khwarazmi, 9
al-Kindi, 245
knowledge societies, 4, 17, 260
kuttab (religious school), 242

al-Labi, Kafur, 160
law, schools of, 12, 14, 19, 65, 84, 167
Leo X, Pope, 10
Lebanon, 192, 231, 305
literacy, 17, 129, 224, 238, 249, 250, 297, 307

madhhab, 65, 166, 172, 173
madrassa, 17, 114, 212, 230, 239, 240, 242, 243, 248, 252, 255, 256, 258, 261
al-Mahdi billah, 159
al-Malaika, Nazik, 288
Malik, Imam, 138
Maliki, school of law, 65, 114, 137
Mamluks, 212, 224, 225–227
al-Maqrizi, Taqi al-din Ahmad, 161, 162, 223, 226
Marrakesh, 213, 217–222, 229, 235
maslaha (public good), 12
masjid (house of prayer), 26, 94, 185, 186
Masjid al-Quba, 183
Masjid-i Jami, 184
Mathnavi, 266
maydan (public square), 228, 229, 231, 235
media, 3, 5, 22, 101, 122, 134, 292, 303, 307
Medina, 16, 19, 27–28, 30, 31, 32, 34, 47, 48, 90, 92, 167, 168, 211
City of the Prophet (*Madinat al-Nabi*), 27, 211
Menocal, Maria Rosa, 97
mihrab (niche for direction of prayer), 16, 179, 182, 187, 196, 204
Milani, Farzaneh, 288
Millennium Development Goals (MDGs), 296
minaret, 16, 185, 187–188, 201, 203, 204, 205, 220
Mir, Mustansir, 70
Mir, Mir Taqi, 276
mobile phones, 292, 294, 296
Modernity, 9, 10, 67, 120, 195, 245, 246
Modernism (in architecture), 177, 192, 193, 198, 201
Mongols, 3, 112, 228
Moses ben Maimonides, 96, 244, 245

mosque, 16, 40, 177, 178, 179, 180, 181, 182, 183–189, 194, 195, 196–198, 200, 201, 202–206, 207, 210, 214, 217, 218, 220, 223, 227, 229, 232, 234, 235
muamalat (social relations), 137, 139, 140
Mughals, 4, 95, 118, 190, 232–233, 234
Muhammad (the Prophet), 8, 12, 13, 14, 19, 26–27, 28, 29, 30–31, 32, 33–35, 36, 37, 38, 39–41, 42, 45, 46–53, 57, 62, 74, 75, 88–89, 90, 92–93, 98, 111, 147, 148, 157, 167, 173, 182, 184, 211, 216, 237, 241, 303, 305
al-Muizz li-din Allah, 158, 159, 160, 161, 164, 169, 172, 173
muqarnas, 181, 187, 188
Murids (Sufi order), 118, 119
mushairas (poetry gathering), 263, 274
Muslim Education Conferences, 253
Muslim-minority settings, 88, 92, 99, 102, 126, 157, 238
Muslim Personal Law (MPL), 121
Muslim Student Associations, 124
Mutazili, 63, 64

nafs (self, soul), 139, 143, 146
Naqshbandiya (Sufi order), 118
nationalism, 120, 192
networks, 21–23, 107–111, 112, 113, 115, 117, 118, 119, 120, 121, 123–124, 125–126, 127–131, 291, 292, 294, 304, 306, 307
Nizami, 273
Nizamiyya, 17, 240, 242, 243
Nimatullahi (Sufi order), 305
North America, 16, 17, 22, 87, 98, 99, 101, 117, 135, 178, 202, 206, 258, 309

Odyssey, 270
Organisation of Islamic Conference (OIC), 253, 254–255
Orientalist, 33, 209, 212, 227, 280
Ottomans, 4, 183, 224, 203, 227
Ottoman empire, 95, 157, 190, 192, 193, 224, 227, 245–246

Padel, Ruth, 266
Pakistan, 19, 100, 119, 123–124, 185, 192, 194, 195, 202, 247–248, 258

Palestine, 28, 287
Persian, 18, 82, 95, 112, 116, 120, 193, 230, 234, 245, 279, 301
pesantren, 252, 256
Piri Reis, 9
pluralism, 47, 87–88, 95, 101–102, 104, 255
poetry, 17–18, 23, 116, 263–268, 269–270, 272, 273–274, 275, 276–283, 284, 285, 286–287, 288, 289
polyandry, 37
polygamy, 19, 37, 68, 149–150
polygyny, 38, 39
post-colonialism, 4, 200, 253, 255
postmodernist, 15, 80, 82
pre-Islamic, 21, 33, 36, 37, 58, 59, 150, 211, 213, 227, 239
Protestants, 6, 98

qadi (judge), 115
al-Qaeda, 7, 126, 127, 307, 308
al-Qahira (Cairo), 158, 223, 224, 225
al-Qaim bi-Amr Allah, 159
Qairawan, Great Mosque of, 184
Qaramita, 164
qibla (wall marking prayer direction), 47, 48, 187, 189
qisas (retribution) (see also Retribution, law of), 150
Quran, 12, 13, 14, 15, 17, 18, 19, 32, 35, 38, 39, 41, 42, 43–44, 45–46, 47, 48–50, 55–58, 59, 60, 61, 62, 63–65, 66, 67, 68, 69, 70, 71–73, 74, 75–77, 78, 79, 80, 81, 82, 83–84, 89, 90, 91, 92, 93–94, 102, 104, 124, 130, 133, 135, 136, 137, 138, 139–140, 142, 143, 144, 145, 146, 147–154, 168, 179, 180, 182, 183, 184, 187, 188, 196, 201, 225, 237, 239–240, 241, 242, 243, 273, 274, 292, 293, 300, 305
Qutb, Sayyid, 10, 11, 70–71

rabha (plaza), 219, 229, 235
Rahman, Fazlur, 72, 74–77, 84
al-Razi, Fakhr al-din, 43
Renaissance, 4, 10, 96, 188, 190, 245
Retribution, law of, 29, 33, 34

Revolutionary Association of the Women of Afghanistan (RAWA), 127
rihla, 109
Rudaki, Abulhasan, 273
Rumi, Jalal al-din, 17, 266, 269–273, 277

sadaq (marriage gift), 133, 140–141
al-Sadiq, Jafar, 62, 65
Safavids, 4, 213, 229, 232
Said, Edward, 4, 190
  in *Covering Islam*, 4
  in *Orientalism*, 4, 190
Salafi (revivalist), 126, 127
salat (ritual prayer), 12, 56, 185
Sassanian empire, 14, 39, 41, 227
Saudi Arabia, 7, 19, 122, 128, 196, 197, 199, 204, 303
sawm (fast), 12
Seljuk empire, 240
September 11, 2001, 3, 7, 88, 100–101, 122, 125, 126, 127, 133, 255, 259, 262, 307
Scholastic philosophy, 245
Shafii, Imam, 226
shahada (attestation), 12, 33
Shahjahanabad (see also Delhi), 213, 229, 231–235
Shahrour, Mohamad, 79
sharia, 14, 19, 58, 68, 130, 133, 166, 171, 254
Shia, Shii, 6, 9, 12, 11, 19, 62, 63, 84, 103, 104, 118, 128, 157, 159, 163, 166, 167, 223, 224, 228, 229, 231, 293, 304, 306
shura (consultative body), 103, 148, 222
Silk Road, 9, 21, 107, 111
Singapore, 9
al-Siqilli, Jawhar, 158, 161, 162–163
Sitruk, Rabbi Joseph, 8
Smith, Wilfred Cantwell, 87, 99, 100
Somalia, 297
Somaliland, 297
Soroush, Abdolkarim, 23, 82–84, 103
Spain, 5, 9, 95, 97, 109, 110, 182, 203, 213, 220, 244

Steiner, George, 264
Sufi, 12, 65, 66, 84, 94, 111, 113, 118,
   283, 300, 304, 305, 306
al-Suri, Abu Musab, 307, 308
symbolic/symbolism, 102, 119, 141,
   178–179, 181, 183, 188, 192, 195, 203,
   204, 220

al-Tabari, Muhammad ibn Jahrir, 30,
   36–37, 62, 90
al-Tahtawi, Rifaa, 10
Taliban, 19, 127
tarab, 285
tariqa (esoteric order), 62, 305
taskhir (reciprocity), 112
tawhid (Oneness of God), 179
textualist (see also contextualist), 73, 74,
   82
theology, 12, 63, 64, 82, 88, 102
thawabit (fundamentals), 139
tolerance, 20, 72, 82, 87, 94, 102, 103
turath (legacy), 281
al-Tustari, Sahl, 15, 65

Ubuntu, 299–300, 301
ulama, 76, 112, 113, 114, 124, 130, 168,
   252
ulil amr, 168
Umar, caliph, 38, 45, 94–95
Umm al-Kitab (Quran as 'Mother of
   Books'), 14, 46, 47
Ummayads, 213–214, 215, 217, 220, 221,
   223
UNESCO, 256, 260
United Nations Development Program
   (UNDP), 295–296

United Arab Emirates, 22, 295
United Kingdom, 9, 75, 178, 258
United Nations, 294, 295
United States, 5–6, 7–8, 9, 10, 39, 97,
   124, 138, 206, 247, 288
Urdu, 120, 274–279, 285, 299, 301
USAID, 256

Wadud, Amina, 72, 75, 77–78, 206
Wahhabism, 81
waqf (pious endowment), 212, 248
Webb, Alexander Russell, 97
West Africa, 9, 16, 117, 118, 177, 184,
   198, 252
WLMUL (Women Living Under Muslim
   Laws), 121, 127
women reformer, 19, 72–73, 77–78
women's equity/equality, 7, 15, 18, 27,
   36, 45, 76, 139–140, 142, 206, 249
World Bank, 256, 258
World Federation of Khoja Shia
   Ithna-asharis, 306
wudu (ablutions), 189

Xian (China), 9
   Great Mosque of, 185, 187

zakat (alms giving), 12, 35, 61, 114, 248
zawiya (Sufi lodge, also *khanqah*), 111,
   113, 114
Zaynab (granddaughter of the Prophet),
   44, 128, 129
El-Zein, Amira, 288
Zheng He, 9, 112
Zoroastrian, 18, 39, 60, 88, 94, 210, 228,
   231